# The History of Discrimination in

# U.S. Education

## PREVIOUSLY PUBLISHED BY THE EDITOR

*Americanization, Acculturation, and Ethnic Identity: The Nisei Generation in Hawaii*

*Asian and Pacific Islander American Education: Social, Cultural, and Historical Contexts*
edited with Virgie Chattergy and Russell Endo

*A History of Hawaii*
with Linda Menton

*China: Understanding Its Past*
with Linda Menton, Noren Lush, and Francis Tsui

*The Rise of Modern Japan*
with Linda Menton, Noren Lush, and Chance Gusukuma

# THE HISTORY OF DISCRIMINATION IN

# U.S. EDUCATION

## MARGINALITY, AGENCY, AND POWER

Edited by Eileen H. Tamura

First published in 2008 by
PALGRAVE MACMILLAN™
175 Fifth Avenue, New York, N.Y. 10010 and
Houndmills, Basingstoke, Hampshire, England RG21 6XS.
Companies and representatives throughout the world.

PALGRAVE MACMILLAN is the global academic imprint of the Palgrave Macmillan division of St. Martin's Press, LLC and of Palgrave Macmillan Ltd. Macmillan® is a registered trademark in the United States, United Kingdom and other countries. Palgrave is a registered trademark in the European Union and other countries.

ISBN-13: 0-230-60043-3
ISBN-10: 978-0-230-60043-0

Library of Congress Cataloging-in-Publication Data

Tamura, Eileen H.
   The history of discrimination in U.S. education: marginality, agency, and power / by Eileen H. Tamura.
      p. cm.
   ISBN 0-230-60043-3 (alk. paper)
   1. Education—United States—History. 2. Marginality, Social—United States. 3. Discrimination in education—United States. I. Title.

LA205.T36 2008
371.829073–dc22                                                        2007029569

A catalogue record of the book is available from the British Library.

Design by Scribe Inc.

First edition: March 2008

10 9 8 7 6 5 4 3 2 1

Printed in the United States of America.

# CONTENTS

# ABOUT THE CONTRIBUTORS

**Anna Bailey** is a PhD candidate in the Department of History at the University of Washington. She is currently completing a dissertation on Lumbee Indian identity.

**Richard M. Breaux** is an assistant professor in the Center for the Applied Study for American Ethnicity and Department of History at Colorado State University. His work has appeared in the *Journal of African American History* and the *Great Plains Quarterly*.

**Steven E. Brown** is a historian and assistant professor of disability studies at the Center on Disability Studies, University of; Hawai'i and cofounder, Institute on Disability Culture. He is the author of numerous articles and monographs about disability rights and disability culture. Many of his essays have been collected in *Movie Stars and Sensuous Scars: Essays on the Journey from Disability Shame to Disability Pride*.

**Lynne Marie Getz** is associate professor of history at Appalachian State University. She is the author of *Schools of Their Own: The Education of Hispanos in New Mexico, 1850–1940*. She contributed a chapter on the effect of World War II on Hispanic education to *Mexican Americans & World War II*, edited by Maggie Rivas-Rodriguez, and recently published an article on gender, migration, and reform in *Frontiers: A Journal of Women's Studies*. Her current research project is a study of families, migration, and memory in the nineteenth and early twentieth century.

**Karen L. Graves** is a historian of education who teaches at Denison University in Granville, Ohio. Her publications include *Girl's Schooling during the Progressive Era: From Female Scholar to Domesticated Citizen*, and *Inexcusable Omissions*, edited with Timothy Glander and Christine Shea.

**Heidi L. Matiyow** is a doctoral candidate in educational foundations and policy at the University of Michigan's School of Education. Her research focuses on using archival records to craft histories of educational policy and program planning for high-risk student groups. Her current project involves an analysis of federal policy toward delinquent youths during the 1960s and '70s.

**Eileen H. Tamura** is a historian and professor of education at the College of Education, University of Hawai'i. Her publications have been on Asian Americans and minority issues and have appeared in journals such as *History of Education Quarterly, Journal of American Ethnic History, Amerasia Journal, Pacific Historical Review,* and *The Journal of Negro Education.*

**Hannah M. Tavares** is an assistant professor at the College of Education, University of Hawai'i. Her program of research, teaching, and scholarly activities have focused on the politics of education. Her publications have appeared in journals such as *Educational Studies, Educational Theory, The Review of Education/Pedagogy/Cultural Studies,* and *Theory & Event.*

# ACKNOWLEDGMENTS

I would like to thank the researcher-authors for their valuable contributions to this volume. They worked with enthusiasm to craft and recraft their essays, responding agreeably to requests for revisions. They also wrote constructive commentaries on the almost-final drafts of the essays of fellow contributors. I appreciate their fine scholarship and their patience as this book moved to its final form. Thank you, Anna Bailey, Richard Breaux, Steven Brown, Lynne Getz, Karen Graves, Heidi Matiyow, and Hannah Tavares.

Many thanks to the following people who consented to be interviewed: Mary Lou Breslin, Frederick Fay, Michael Frogley, Linda Haerens, Tim Nugent, and Shirley Wohlfield. Much gratitude also goes to the University of Illinois Division of Rehabilitation-Education Services for permission to quote from *The Banquet: A Final Look Back at 50 Years of Progress*.

We contributors owe considerable debt to the many archivists and librarians who helped us in our research: in particular, Miriam Gan-Spalding and Boyd Murphree of the State Archives of Florida; Father Michael Kotlanger, S. J. of the University of San Francisco Archives; William J. Maher of the University of Illinois Archives; and Dennis Northcott of the Missouri Historical Society.

Great appreciation goes to Amanda Johnson Moon, editor at Palgrave Macmillan, who first approached me with the idea of submitting a proposal that eventually developed into this book. And most important, to my husband, Dave Raney, who was, without fail, a source of constant encouragement and support.

# Introduction

## Eileen H. Tamura

> The soul is actively produced
> and positively shaped and consummated
> only in the category of the *other*.
>
> —Mikhail M. Bakhtin[1]

> Power—no matter how great—
> was never absolute, but always contingent.
>
> —Ira Berlin[2]

IN THE 1920S AND '30S, THE SOCIOLOGIST ROBERT PARK CONCEPTUALIZED the notion of marginality as a core experience of ethnic and racial minorities.[3] According to Park, the "marginal man" is caught between two societies that are "antagonistic."[4] As he navigates his way between these two societies, he experiences a "conflict of cultures," and with it, "inner turmoil and intense self-consciousness."[5] Park's notion of the "marginal man" had a strong influence on American social thought.

While Park focused on the inner conflicts of marginal people as they lived between two worlds, more recent scholars have tended to shift the emphasis away from the inner self and notions of individual ambivalence and uncertainty to the inequities and conflicts between those at the center and those on society's perimeter—dissidents, women, ethnic groups, radicals, and other minorities.[6] The essays in this volume on American education during the past century examine the disparities and conflicts between center and periphery and at the same time attend to individual self-consciousness.

Unlike many works on education, which are concerned solely with schools, this volume uses a broader definition of education—"the deliberate, systematic, and sustained effort to transmit, evoke, or acquire knowledge, attitudes, values, skills, or sensibilities, as well as any outcomes of that effort."[7] This definition includes schooling but also goes beyond it. Conversely, it is more limited than the larger processes of socialization and acculturation. The broader definition of education used here is important for those concerned with formal policies and actual practices as they affect minorities, because so much of education occurs outside the schools.[8]

As they delve into their historical subjects, the authors provide different "angles of vision"[9] on two major themes that form the conceptual core of this book. The themes are captured in the passages that lead off this introduction: the self-other relationship and the fluidity of power.

## BAKHTIN: THE SELF-OTHER RELATIONSHIP

The passage from Bakhtin underscores the dialogic nature of the relationship between those at the margins and those in the mainstream. According to Bakhtin, the self can only exist and have meaning in relationship to the other.[10] In this light, those on the periphery develop their sense of themselves and their aspirations in terms of those at the center.

Eileen H. Tamura's "Searching for America" examines the efforts of a Japanese American in the first three decades of the twentieth century as he sought to identify himself in terms of his notions of what "true" Americans were like. He was an American citizen by virtue of his birth; nevertheless, most European Americans refused to accept him and other Asian Americans as true Americans. He responded to this mind-set by enrolling in schools that he believed would model American values and behaviors and by embracing European American ideas of true Americanism. Lynn Getz's "Romance and Reality of Hispano Identity" shows that leading educators defined the Hispano community in terms of the Anglo majority.[11] They portrayed Hispanos as a nonthreatening people who sought to keep their cultural traditions while accommodating themselves to Anglo domination. This benign portrait, while mitigating antagonism between two groups, failed to challenge the status quo. Richard Breaux's "Using the Press to Fight Jim Crow" reveals the disparities black university students witnessed as they compared their position on the fringes of campus life and in the larger society with whites who had greater access to resources and privileges. They were like the aspiring students with physical disabilities in Steven Brown's "Breaking Barriers," who sought to reshape the mental and physical terrain at their university so that they could have the opportunity to participate fully in campus life.

While those on the periphery of society develop their selfhood and their aspirations in terms of those at the center, they also develop their identity in terms of others also on the margins. Anna Bailey's "'It Is the Center to Which We Should Cling'" illuminates the ways in which the Croatan Indians, in their push to gain acceptance and greater access to quality schooling, defined themselves as different from and superior to African Americans in the North Carolina community of Robeson County. Bailey examines the Indians' effort to define themselves in terms of both whites and blacks—positioning themselves midway between those most privileged and those least so.

But even those at the center, who have greater access to resources, define themselves in terms of those on the fringes of society. Hannah Tavares's "The Racial Subjection of Filipinos" discusses early twentieth-century texts, in which European Americans objectified Filipinos as primitive. This characterization provided an important image with which those in power used to contrast themselves. Karen Graves's "Containing the Perimeter" analyzes the efforts of the Florida Legislative Investigation Committee to vilify members of the National Association for the Advancement of Colored People (NAACP) and gay and lesbian schoolteachers. Politicians used racism and homophobia to target two outlier groups and, by doing so, distinguished themselves from the two groups.

When two groups embrace differing worldviews, each is able to define itself more clearly in opposition to what it sees before it. In Heidi Matiyow's "Mothers Battle Busing and Nontraditional Education," the mothers who took to the streets defined their perspective in relation to the ideas of those in positions of power. In this case the mothers rejected what they believed were unacceptable notions pressed onto their children by educational leaders. Taking matters into their own hands, they protested vigorously against both busing and the curriculum in their children's schools.

## BERLIN: THE FLUIDITY OF POWER

The second passage that leads this introduction comes from Ira Berlin's book on slavery, *Many Thousands Gone*. Berlin notes that even in the "most extreme form of domination," the relationship between master and slave was constantly negotiated and renegotiated, because power was "never absolute, but always contingent."[12]

Tamura's "Searching for America" sets forth the actions of a young man, stigmatized because of his ancestry, who did not hesitate to assert himself and even engage in fistfights when assaulted. His actions and reactions enabled him to navigate his way through the power shifts that occurred between him and those around him. Bailey's "'It Is the Center to Which We Should Cling'" shows how the Croatan Indians negotiated with state and local leaders to improve the educational opportunities and academic achievements of their children. Bailey further shows how the Croatans took advantage of national policy loopholes that allowed them to send their children to public schools in the state rather than to Indian boarding schools.

Like the Croatans, who acted to control the schooling of their youths, New Mexican educators found ways to support the learning needs of Hispano students. Getz's "Romance and Reality of Hispano Identity" shows how directives from above could be deflected by educators in the field. For example, New Mexico Department of Public Instruction officials attempted to enforce an English-only policy and to segregate Hispano students in order to teach them English, but teachers in rural schools far away from the reach of government officials continued to use Spanish as the language of instruction. In addition, educators who were sympathetic to Hispano interests implemented programs that countered the English-only policy and promoted cultural preservation.

Another illustration of the relativity of power can be seen in Brown's "Breaking Barriers." In the 1950s, when people with disabilities were largely invisible to the larger population, there were those who refused to accept this status and who understood the value of constant renegotiation as they took action to convince university officials to accommodate their educational aspirations and thus their subsequent desired entry into mainstream postuniversity life. Likewise, Breaux's "Using the Press to Fight Jim Crow" shows the ways in which a minority of black college students and their supporters used the press to help them push through the barriers of university policies that separated them from full participation in campus life.

Even when those directing the flow of events have the authority of government on their side, their power was contingent on the actions and reactions of those defamed. In "The Racial Subjection of Filipinos," Tavares shows that Filipino opposition to the U.S. takeover of the Philippines forced imperialists to expend extraordinary efforts to convince the public that their actions were justified. In "Containing the

Perimeter," Graves demonstrates how members of the NAACP were able to resist state power and compel legislators to end hearings aimed at discrediting black civil rights activists.

Finally, as Matiyow's "Mothers Battle Busing and Nontraditional Education" shows, the fluidity of power can mean that people once considered marginal may well, over time, become a dominant force in society.

## MARGINALITY, AGENCY, AND POWER

To further illuminate the two themes of this book—Bakhtin's notion of the self-other relationship and Berlin's idea of the contingency of power—the authors respond to a central question: How have power and agency been revealed in educational issues involving minorities? More specifically, how have politicians, policymakers, practitioners, and others in the mainstream used and misused their power in relation to those in the margins? How have those in the margins asserted their agency and negotiated their way within the larger society? What have been the relationships, not only between those more powerful and those less powerful, but also among those on the fringes of society? How have people sought to bridge the gap separating those in the margins and those in the mainstream?

Tavares's essay examines an instance of the abuse of power in the early twentieth century, when the U.S. government moved to conquer the Philippines in the aftermath of the Spanish-American war. In fierce opposition to this colonial agenda, Filipino resistance fighters battled U.S. troops in a three-year war. In the United States, anti-imperialists protested loudly. Given such strong opposition on two fronts, U.S. government officials and their supporters felt compelled to respond systematically to the challenge. They justified U.S. military aggression in the Philippines by issuing reports and studies and by creating elaborate Filipino exhibitions at world's fairs, all aimed at producing a racist stereotype of Filipinos as subaltern and lacking the ability to govern themselves. Tavares demonstrates the ways in which hegemonic discourse and representation can dominate what she refers to as an "image-repertoire" of a subordinated group. While the events she examines in her essay took place over a century ago, her analysis offers a rich source for present-day critical understanding of the power of dominant discourses and the need to listen to and heed "other circuits of thought" that widen perspectives and challenge assumptions.

Fast-forward sixty years later to Florida and its state legislators. Graves's essay analyzes another concerted effort to denigrate less-powerful groups. Politicians had first attempted to link the NAACP with Communism. The idea was to use people's fears in the 1950s to halt efforts at desegregation. "Containing the Perimeter" illustrates the sophistication and deft responses of NAACP activists to questions posed to them at the Florida legislative hearings. Despite their precarious position, black civil rights activists who were called to testify kept their composure while evading questions politely, stalling the process, and otherwise frustrating committee interrogators. When the NAACP demonstrated that they had the ability to resist state action against them, legislators targeted a more vulnerable group, gay and lesbian schoolteachers, who lacked legal protection and the organizational strength to push back and resist the assault. The invisibility of gays and lesbians during the mid-twentieth century made them easy targets for legislators in the smear campaign that would sustain a level of support for the investigation committee, floundering in its anti-civil rights agenda. As it was then, there are instances today in which those in positions of power use tactics of distraction and fear mongering to play on sentiments of unease in the country. As Graves so aptly states, "Holding this shell-game strategy up for examination is one way to disrupt" efforts to manipulate public thinking.

Bailey's essay provides yet another instance of the abuse of power. To further their political objectives, leaders of the Democratic Party in North Carolina tapped into the Croatan Indians' desire for better educational opportunities. They made a political bargain with the Indians: they agreed to support the Indians' efforts to gain increased funding for their public schools if the Indians agreed to support Democratic Party leaders' efforts to disenfranchise blacks. The Croatans agreed with this pact. For them, the school represented their ticket to the mainstream. Thus—at the expense of North Carolina's blacks—the Indians were able to gain much-needed funding to shore up their schools. Bailey's essay shows how a dominant group can misuse its power by exercising a strategy of divide and conquer.

Tamura's essay moves the reader's attention away from those at the center of power. It highlights the struggles of a Japanese American man who was marginalized by racial stereotypes. Japanese immigrants to the U.S. West Coast, like the Chinese before them, constituted a relatively small proportion of the population, and, like the Chinese, they encountered rabid hostility.[13] State and federal laws sought to cripple the economic gains made by Japanese immigrant farmers and denied them naturalization rights. Locally, the San Francisco school board attempted to force Japanese American children to attend a segregated public school for Chinese. To be sure, Joseph Kurihara, the young man in Tamura's essay, attended educational institutions—in this case private schools—that opened their doors to Japanese Americans and other minorities, despite intense racial animosity. Nonetheless, anti-Asian and antiminority sentiment prevailed during this period, and it was in this atmosphere that Kurihara was assaulted, spat at, and stoned in the streets. His story illustrates the tremendous energy that marginalized people often expend in their effort to gain acceptance. Just as he did, many on the margins tolerate an incredible amount of ill-treatment meted out to them. As Tamura states, the young man's story provides an account of "the often invisible emotional scars" that immigrant children "can carry as they struggle to adjust and gain full acceptance from the larger society."

Another group seeking acceptance in the decades before World War II were black college students attending predominantly white colleges and universities. Breaux's essay examines instances of campus racism at the University of Minnesota and the University of Kansas, where black students asserted their rights to equal opportunity. Using campus, local, and regional black newspapers, they publicized discriminatory actions by white students, professors, and university officials. Black students and their supporters further challenged the status quo by taking legal action and otherwise bringing discriminatory policies and practices to public view. Breaux's essay shows that decades before civil rights activists began prying open segregated public universities in the Deep South, black students had been studying at Midwestern public universities. As he demonstrates, however, matriculation at these institutions of higher learning was only the first step in the long road to full access and equal opportunity. Relegated to the fringes of campus life, black students undertook the slow and incremental process of transforming the status quo. They were successful in making inroads only after persistent struggle, use of the media and the courts, and intervention from supporters.

Also struggling to change the status quo in the decades before World War II were Hispano and Anglo educators who worked to advance Hispano students' self-esteem and promote their interest in school by implementing programs such as preschool classes and bilingual instruction. At the same time, while emphasizing folklore and crafts in the curriculum and romanticizing New Mexico's past, these well-meaning educators ignored the discrimination that contributed to the economic subordination of the Hispano community. An exception was the Nuevomexicano George I. Sánchez, who challenged discriminatory policies and the second-class citizenship status of Hispanos. Although his threat to the status quo cost him his job as division director in the New Mexico Department of Public Instruction, his efforts were not entirely in vain, for he has become a model for Hispanic advocates of equal opportunity. Other instances of activism are revealed in the next two essays. Brown's "Breaking Barriers" recounts the efforts that those with physical disabilities undertook in the 1950s, staging protests and otherwise calling attention to their appeal to be engaged fully as matriculating university students.

In the previous century, policymakers had ignored people with disabilities or placed them in asylums. It was not until disabled veterans of World War I returned home that federal and state officials—understanding the political power of veterans who had risked their lives for their country—initiated programs for individuals with disabilities. Federal assistance to disabled veterans increased even more dramatically after World War II. It was in this context that the University of Illinois began a program in 1948 for students with disabilities. Led by director Timothy Nugent, the program had a rocky start. Early on, when it was threatened with closure, Nugent and the program's students fought back. As Brown notes, this response "typified the attitude that Nugent inculcated in both his program and in his students." Throughout the 1950s, as the program slowly developed, students met with numerous hurdles—personal as well as institutional. The fighting spirit that Nugent promoted enabled students to face their challenges, gain greater confidence in themselves, and persist to ensure the program's survival. Nugent's desire for students to achieve "complete social integration" might be criticized today by advocates of minority rights. And it brings up the question that continues to confront minority groups: to what extent should a group strive for integration into mainstream society and to what extent should it attempt to maintain a distinctive ethnic/cultural identity?

The final essay in this book features a group of white working- and lower-middle-class housewives who galvanized themselves out of the home and into the political arena in the 1970s to protest busing and school-initiated threats to their ideas of family values. This was in response to actions taken by policymakers and practitioners who imposed busing and educational reforms on unwilling parents. While the school board members and judges who decided in favor of desegregation and the educators who offered new curricula for the schools hoped to promote greater equity and social justice, in the eyes of the mothers who protested, these decisions were inflicted on their children without parental approval. Matiyow shows us that what may seem like a clear-cut reason for resistance—in this case, racism—may actually have a complex set of motivations. In the case of the Mothers' Alert Detroit (MAD) members in Detroit, several top-down initiatives—forced busing, sex education, a curriculum that seemed to encourage moral relativism, and the effort to remove sexism in textbooks—dovetailed to ignite the protests of angry white lower-class parents, who saw federal and state authorities as "intruder and oppressor." Political leaders ignored and discounted these protestors at their own peril. As Matiyow demonstrates, the efforts of activists like MAD served as an early indication of things to come—the growth and activism of neoconservative forces that would take many by surprise. The failure of liberals to understand the concerns of working- and lower-middle-class Americans—and the power of words like morality and family values—would later haunt them, as a once-peripheral segment of society would later broaden its reach to become a dominant force in American society.

While all of the essays in this book discuss the relationship between those more powerful and those less so, three essays also illuminate the relationship between groups on the margins of society. One is the case of the Croatans in North Carolina. To gain increased funding for their public schools in the early 1900s, their leaders sought to differentiate and disassociate themselves from blacks in their community. And the Croatans went further: they prohibited students from enrolling in their schools if they suspected that the students had mixed black-Indian ancestry. Similarly, the Hispanos of New Mexico sought to avoid identification as "mixed-blood" people. In their case, leaders in their community denied any Native American ancestry, promoting instead the notion that Hispanos were whites—descendants solely of Spanish *conquistadores*. One can appreciate the irony of this position when it is placed in juxtaposition to the stance taken by the Croatans of North Carolina, who—in a similar effort to raise their status—denied any mixed black-Indian ancestry.

In the Detroit busing case, black residents were impatient with what they believed were protracted efforts to improve the school climate for the increasing number of black students in the city's schools. They called for the hiring of more black teachers and administrators, the offering of multicultural curricula, and the desegregation of the schools' student bodies. At the same time, white working- and lower-middle-class Detroiters were becoming increasingly concerned with the changes that were being made to satisfy blacks. When the NAACP filed a lawsuit that protested segregation, conflict surfaced between these two marginal groups, and race trumped class as a defining element in grassroots activism, despite the fact that both black and white parents, although in different degrees, opposed forced busing.

In these three instances, outlier groups refused to recognize common ground with each other. Civil rights advocates such as Lani Guinier and Gerald Torres have pointed to the need to avoid antagonistic, or at best, nonsupportive, relationships. Their analysis offers alternatives that seek interracial coalition building and power sharing. While difficult to achieve, such efforts can provide constructive outcomes that benefit minority groups, as long as they do not harm other marginal groups.[14]

The final question posed in this section of the introduction asks how people have sought to bridge the gap separating the worlds of those in the margins and those in the mainstream. Two concepts embody this effort. One is the bridge concept, which Tamura discusses in her essay. The idea was that immigrants' American-born children, having dual identities, would serve as intermediaries between two sociocultural worlds.[15] As Tamura notes, this idea became a central theme among Japanese immigrants during a time of intense anti-Japanese antagonism in the first three decades of the twentieth century. A similar concept, encapsulated in the phrase "cultural broker," can be seen in the literature on American Indians.[16] During the more than five-hundred-year relationship between native Americans and European Americans, thousands of natives and whites served as cultural brokers—"people between the borders," who were able to "juggle the ways of different societies."[17]

The young man portrayed in Tamura's essay was conversant in the world of Japanese America as well as the dominant European American society. He was able to do this by "keeping one foot inside and the other outside the Japanese community." He adopted what he believed to be European American behaviors and also integrated Japanese cultural ideas into the American context. As an accountant and small business manager, he served as an intermediary between Japanese America and

European America by helping Japanese immigrant farmers and distributors navigate their way within the larger California economy.

Tim Nugent, the central figure in Brown's essay, was part of both the disabled and mainstream sociocultural worlds in which he worked. As a faculty member of a university department, Nugent was able to move with ease within the university bureaucracy and negotiate with university officials and faculty in his advocacy for the students in his program. Physically disabled himself, he understood the social, physical, and personal barriers facing students with disabilities and was accepted as one of them. By maintaining his ties with the two sociocultural worlds, Nugent was able to serve as their broker.

Two figures in Getz's essay served as brokers between New Mexico's Hispano and Anglo communities. One was Nina Otero-Warren, a Hispano who served as Santa Fe school superintendent and who sought compatibility between Anglos and Hispanos. Attempting to improve conditions in the schooling of young Hispanos, she presented a nonthreatening portrait of Hispanos at the same time that she promoted school programs that highlighted Hispano cultural practices. In contrast to this strategy of accommodation, the second cultural broker, the Hispano George Sánchez, gave public voice to systemic inequities facing Hispanos and called for radical remedies. While both intermediaries were able to bridge two worlds in their own careers, their successes on behalf of the Hispanos of New Mexico were modest at best. Yet, their early efforts to improve the lives of Hispanos serve to inform later generations of activists who continue in the struggle to improve the socioeconomic status of marginalized peoples.

## DIALOGUE IN THE MARGINS

Gary Okihiro and other scholars argue that groups on the periphery have had an important role in opening up the system. According to Okihiro, challenges by minorities to the status quo have benefited the larger society by pushing it to become more inclusive and democratic, and thus closer to American ideals. Core American values and ideals, he states, come from marginal groups in their struggle to be included.[18] In a compatible yet different analysis, Guinier and Torres use the compelling metaphor—articulated earlier by Felix Cohen—of the canary in the coal mine to bring home the necessity of listening to the voices of marginalized people. In coal mining, the canary served a critical role. If it flopped over and died, miners knew that there was poison in the air. The canary saved the miners from breathing in more of the noxious gases. Likewise, Guinier and Torres, in a call to action, argue that society needs to listen to the canary—society's marginalized people. Guinier and Torres explain that by examining the social ills and discrimination experienced by minorities and women, people may be able to uncover systemic flaws that also affect adversely the larger society. Thus, a victory for a particular group in achieving greater equality and institutional change through collective action is also a victory for the whole.[19]

It is important to keep in mind, however, that those in positions of power have not always sought to deny greater access to more individuals. At different times in U.S. history, they have worked to increase social justice, as in the case of court actions to enforce desegregation. And Matiyow's "Mothers Battle Busing and Nontraditional Education" shows that challenges from the margins can be retrogressive.

Within the framework of education and history, the essays in this volume provide telling instances in which minorities challenged those at the seat of power. The essays give voice to the perspectives and actions of those on the periphery, highlighting what they did themselves: protest, reject, contest, agitate for changes, and work to craft their futures. At the same time, the essays recount and analyze what was done to those in the margins—the ways in which those in power perceived and acted upon those less powerful. The essays bring home the stark realities faced by those who were ignored, objectified, and stigmatized, who often pursued their goals to effect changes in their favor despite having minimal economic and social capital.

This collection highlights the importance for educational policymakers to listen to the dialogue in the margins, to direct their attention to those who are often unheard and unseen. As these essays show, the burden to change and adjust cannot be left on the shoulders of those who often struggle to fit within the dominant framework. Daryl Smith notes that the way in which a problem is perceived, defined, and framed "can dramatically affect the solutions sought." [20] Instead of perceiving the powerless as the root of the problem, Smith argues that the gaze of those in power should turn to institutional, structural, and organizational barriers that prevent accessibility and achievement. These essays give voice to those often discounted for being different, and by doing so, help to reframe the nature of the problem.

In offering historical instances of the multiple dimensions of marginality, the essays provide a window into the perspectives of those less powerful. Gaining greater understanding of these world views is crucial for members of societies that have struggled with diversity. By analyzing issues of race, ethnicity, class, culture, sexual orientation, and disability in the context of education, the essays demonstrate that the boundaries of the center as well as the periphery are ambiguous at best, altering over time and space in nonlinear ways. At the same time, tensions between, as well as within, margin and mainstream are dynamic and ever changing.[21]

The essays in this book demonstrate the contribution that educational history offers to issues of policy and practice. Digging into the past, the authors bring to life the conditions, struggles, frustrations, disappointments, triumphs, and successes of those marginalized. The value of history is in its use of the passage of time, which provides needed perspective in analyzing actions past and present. This book is intended to serve as a stimulus for reflection, further inquiry, and action.

## NOTES

1.  Mikhail M. Bakhtin, *Art and Answerability: Early Philosophical Essays*, eds. Michael Holquist and Vadim Liapunov, translated by Vadim Liapunov and Kenneth Brostrom (Austin: University of Texas Press, 1990), 132.

2.  Ira Berlin, *Many Thousands Gone: The First Two Centuries of Slavery in North America* (Cambridge, MA: Harvard University Press, 1998), 3. I would like to thank Barbara Finkelstein for bringing Berlin's book to my attention.

3.  This introduction includes the terms race and ethnicity with the full knowledge that decades ago scholars pointed to these terms as social constructs. See, for example, Stephen Jay Gould, *The Mismeasure of Man* (New York: W. W. Norton and Co., 1996 [1981]), 399–406. For more recent explanations, see *American Anthropological Association Statement on "Race"* (17 May 1998), *www.aaanet.org/stmts/racepp.htm* (accessed 4 November 2006); and *Race: The Power of an Illusion* (San Francisco: California Newsreel, 2003), 3 videocassettes. Nonetheless, I use the words because people continue to behave in ways that show that they believe that the terms signify reality. I use the word "racist" to refer to discriminatory actions against others based on races and ethnicity.

4.  Robert Park, "Cultural Conflict and the Marginal Man," in *The Collected Papers of Robert Ezra Park, vol. I, Race and Culture*, eds. E. C. Hughes, C. S. Johnson, J. Masuoka, R. Redfield, and L. Wirth (Glencoe, Illinois: Free Press, 1950), 373.

5.  Robert Park, "Human Migration and the Marginal Man," in *The Collected Papers of Robert Ezra Park, vol. I, Race and Culture*, eds. E. C. Hughes, C. S. Johnson, J. Masuoka, R. Redfield, and L. Wirth (Glencoe, IL: Free Press, 1950),

355. Henry Yu, *Thinking Orientals* (New York: Oxford University Press, 2001), 100–1, 108–9, 234 n. 21, discusses Park's role in formulating the marginal man concept. Everett V. Stonequist, who was Park's student, further elaborated on the concept of marginal man. See Stonequist, *The Marginal Man: A Study in Personality and Culture Conflict* (New York: Scribner's Sons, 1937).

6. See, for example, Robert Jensen, *Writing Dissent: Taking Radical Ideas from the Margins to the Mainstream* (New York: Peter Lang Publishing, 2001); Martin Duberman, *Left Out: The Politics of Exclusion* (New York: Basic Books, 1999); and Josefina Figueira-McDonough and Rosemary C. Sarri, eds. *Women at the Margins: Neglect, Punishment, and Resistance* (New York: Haworth, 2002).

7. Lawrence A. Cremin, *Public Education* (New York: Basic Books, 1976), 27.

8. David Tyack and Elizabeth Hansot, *Learning Together: A History of Coeducation in American Schools* (New Haven, CT: Yale University Press), 2, provides a useful distinction between policies and practices: Policies refer to "explicit rules," while practices refer to "customary arrangement, regularities of expected behavior crystallized into patterns that may or may not reflect official policies."

9. The quote comes from Cremin, *Public Education*, 28.

10. Katerina Clark and Michael Holquist, *Mikhail Bakhtin* (Cambridge, MA: Harvard University Press, 1984), 63–65.

11. Lynne Getz's essay in this volume defines Hispanos as New Mexicans of Spanish descent.

12. Berlin, *Many Thousands Gone*, 3.

13. Sucheng Chan, *Asian Americans: An Interpretive History* (Boston: Twayne, 1991), 45–61; Elmer C. Sandmeyer, *The Anti-Chinese Movement in California* (Urbana: University of Illinois Press, 1939); Roger Daniels, ed. *Anti-Chinese Violence in North America* (New York: Arno, 1978); Daniels, *The Politics of Prejudice: The Anti-Japanese Movement in California and the Struggle for Japanese Exclusion* (Berkeley: University of California Press, 1962); Yuji Ichioka, *The Issei: The World of the First Generation Japanese Immigrants, 1885–1924* (New York: Free Press, 1988), 176–254.

14. Lani Guinier and Gerald Torres, *The Miner's Canary: Enlisting Race, Resisting Power, Transforming Democracy* (Boston: Harvard University Press, 2002), 131–38. For example, in Greensboro, North Carolina, workers at the Kmart distribution center effected changes that ultimately benefited the larger community. Workers at the center—the only one with a predominantly black workforce—received less in wages and benefits than any other Kmart center in the country. What began as an analysis of black discrimination moved to a recognition that white workers at the center were also discriminated against, affecting all of the workers' families and the larger community. Through interracial coalition building, power sharing, and community involvement, the workers and their supporters challenged successfully the status quo.

15. Peter Jamero's memoir, *Growing Up Brown: Memoirs of a Filipino American* (Seattle: University of Washington Press, 2006), also calls the children of immigrants the "bridge generation."

16. I would like to thank Lourene Thaxton and T. Gregory Barrett for introducing me to the concept of cultural broker.

17. Margaret Connell Szasz, *Between Indian and White Worlds: The Cultural Broker* (Norman: University of Oklahoma Press, 1994), 3, 6, 17–18. Interpreters, traders, teachers, and diplomats, for example, served as cultural brokers. And previous to, as well as during the period of contact with whites, native intermediaries linked native peoples who had separate and distinct identities. See Daniel K. Richter, "Cultural Brokers and Intercultural Politics: New York Iroquois Relations, 1664–1701," *Journal of American History* 75, no. 1 (June 1988): 40–67; Nancy L. Hagedorn, "'A Friend to Go between Them': The Interpreter as Cultural Broker during Anglo-Iroquois Councils, 1740–1770," *Ethnohistory* 35 (Winter 1988): 60–80; James A. Clifton, ed., *Being and Becoming Indian: Biographical Studies of North American Frontiers* (Chicago: Dorsey, 1989).

18. Gary Okihiro, *Margins and Mainstreams: Asians in American History and Culture* (Seattle: University of Washington Press, 1994), 148–75.

19. Guinier and Torres, *The Miner's Canary*, 11, 15; Felix S. Cohen, "The Erosion of Indian Rights, 1950–1953: A Case Study in Bureaucracy," *Yale Law Journal* 62 (1953): 348, 390. Guinier and Torres, *The Miner's Canary*, 307, n. 1, acknowledge Cohen for this metaphor.

20. Daryl Smith, *The Challenge of Diversity: Involvement or Alienation in the Academy?* (Washington, DC: George Washington University, 1989), 7; Amy Agbayani, "The Education of Filipinos in Hawai'i" *Social Process in Hawaii* 37 (1996): 150.

21. Barbara Beatty offered these thoughts in her role as discussant on a panel on margins and mainstream that I organized for the April 2004 meeting of the American Educational Research Association.

# The Racial Subjection of Filipinos in the Early Twentieth Century

## Hannah M. Tavares

This essay grows out of an effort to uncover the discursive processes by which subordination is achieved. My concern here is with racial subjection. Subjection, as Judith Butler explains, "signifies the process of becoming subordinated by power as well as the process of becoming a subject."[1] Butler is drawing on Michel Foucault's insight that subjection involves the simultaneous *forming* and *regulating* of the subject. This theme of subjection is part of a broader inquiry concerning the interrelation between discourse, representational practices, and the constituting of human subjectivity as subaltern. Like my previous work that treats representations of the racialized Asian and Pacific Islander, I take a historical perspective to understand the conditions and specificity of these connections.

In this essay, I critically read "expert" accounts concerning Filipinos and their self-governing capabilities from a variety of English-language sources during the early twentieth century that construct the American colonial archive on Filipinos.[2] These accounts, namely the *Report of the Philippine Commission to the President* (1900–1901), *The "Bontoc Igorot" Department of the Interior Ethnological Survey* (1905), and *The Racial Anatomy of the Philippine Islanders* (1910), however exaggerated or distorted they may have been, entered into wider discursive networks and

consequently were repeatedly given voice. For the American reading public, these accounts, with their inclusion of photographs and their citation
in newspapers, scholarly studies, congressional testimonies, schoolbooks,
and travel narratives, gave shape to their understanding of "the Philippines" and "Filipinos." For the purpose of my inquiry, they serve to illustrate the textualization of Filipinos as subaltern and the discursive
production of the racialized other. Written for a metropolitan audience
in the United States, the representations that circulated were crucial to
formulating and naturalizing a particular kind of knowledge about Filipinos in the Philippines and elsewhere.

In addition to these materials, I examine the role of international
expositions, also known as world's fairs, in promoting and circulating
racialized stereotypes through their systems of scientific classification and
explanation. Often touted as the "university for the masses," world's fairs
were organized as dynamic educational experiences showcasing the
industrial and artistic achievements of nation-states. For many Americans, world's fairs in the United States were a primary means by which
information of the world outside their own borders was received. My
essay treats two fairs, the 1901 Pan-American Exposition at Buffalo, New
York, and the 1904 Louisiana Purchase International Exposition at Saint
Louis, Missouri, which had living exhibits of people from the Philippines. In this part of my essay, I draw on the official guides, bulletins, and
periodicals, which published accounts of the exhibits for prospective visitors. Taken together, these materials are important sources for identify-
ing the social location of a discourse's production and a reminder of who
had the means to make their "point-of-view" substantial through the
books, articles, photographs, and pictures they circulated. More important, they serve to illustrate how certain ways of seeing and thinking
about people from the Philippines worked in conjunction with particular fields of power/knowledge.[3]

I should emphasize that my primary concern here is disclosing the
ways in which social difference is discursively constructed. I aim to
divulge the complex of practices through which human beings identified
as "Filipinos" came to be known and seen in the United States during the
early twentieth century. Above all, I seek to reveal the exercise of power in
discourse and visual display. My essay draws on poststructural, postcolonial, and psychoanalytical frames of sociocultural inquiry. Poststructural-
ism underscores the relations between formations of power/knowledge
and the making of particular kinds of subjects. It is especially appropriate

here, because my concern is with the processes through which human beings have been constituted as racial types with differential status. The most influential strands of poststructural thought, which guide my inquiry, are those that are attentive to matters of language and representation. The implication of these strands is that the field of representations and language are no longer to be seen as simply "reflecting" or "communicating" the world; rather, they contribute to the making of this world.

In addition to this primary focus, my essay aims to illustrate the political significance of postcolonial problematizations. The merits of a problematizing approach when reading history, as Robert Castel so insightfully reminds, is the conviction that "the present bears a burden, a weight that comes from the past, and the task of the present is to bring this burden up to date in order to understand its current ramifications."[4] Tempered by postcolonial critique, my essay takes into account the specificity of colonial encounters, specifically the U.S.-Philippine imperial relationship, and the representation of the "other" in imperialist and patriarchal discourse. I am especially concerned with how the representations of Filipinos who emerged from that encounter shaped the *screen* through which Filipinos came to be seen and known.[5] In our century, that screen, which normalized specific images and knowledge of Filipinos, remains haunted by the exclusions of empire. By critically examining the textualization of that encounter, I hope my essay can contribute to new insights to our understanding of current Filipino and Filipino American critical cultural practices. Drawing on these theoretic lens provides a critical frame for analyzing the complex of power relations, representations, and practices and the constitutive role they play in the formation of subjects.

### THE PHILIPPINE-AMERICAN WAR: A NONEVENT?

The 1899 Philippine-American War is not the sort of topic the Filipino public likes to talk about. To imagine Filipinos warring with Americans simply contradicts the dominant trope of the Philippine-American relationship. In popular, and to some extent, official discourse as well, the Philippine-American relationship has been a special one, expressed in kinship terms, like "compadre colonialism" and "little brown brother."

—Reynaldo C. Ileto[6]

The Philippine-American War, a war that has been the subject of collective and individual forms of forgetting, ostensibly began when the U.S.

Army moved to take possession, in February 1899, of the colonial territories it had acquired from Spain in December 1898. Until its "official" end on July 4, 1902, the Filipino republican army fought a defensive war. The circumstances under which this largely forgotten war took place must be located within a broader context of American naval expansion, U.S. foreign policy, obtaining new outlets for surplus goods and capital investments, and the politics of memory.[7]

George Dewey, who was ordered by Assistant Secretary of the Navy Theodore Roosevelt to prepare to strike the Spanish fleet in Manila Bay, attacked and succeeded in destroying the fleet on May 1, 1898. What precipitated the assault was the alleged sinking of the U.S. battleship *Maine* in Havana harbor by Spain on February 15. At the time, Cuban revolutionaries were revolting against Spanish colonial power. Concerned that the conflict would jeopardize American interests in overseas markets, the administration of U.S president William McKinley took political interest in the Cuban revolt against Spanish colonial rule and sent the battleship *Maine* to circuit Havana harbor.

The Cuban revolt coincided with a growing rebellion in the Philippines against the government of imperial Spain. Philippine resistance to Spanish rule emerged in 1896, a year after the Cuban revolution began. By the summer of 1898, Philippine troops led by Emilio Aguinaldo had driven the Spanish colonialists out of the countryside on the main island of Luzon into the capital city of Manila, with U. S. assistance. Thus, when American troops arrived following Dewey's attack on Spain's fleet, they found themselves facing the armed forces of Philippine national resistance.

The extent of U.S. military involvement in the Philippines following the actions of Dewey at Manila Bay and subsequent refusal to recognize the republican government formed by Filipino nationalists was by no means apparent or uncontested. It fostered debates in the United States between those who saw U.S. involvement as necessary toward advancing progress and extending American civilized ideals and those who feared military force on another people as undermining the ideals of democratic republicanism. "In the midst of these debates," writes one historian, "a peace protocol was signed with Spain on August 12 calling for treaty negotiations in Paris."[8] Once in negotiation, the U.S. commission, advised by American generals and European diplomats, made the decision to take the entire archipelago. On December 10, 1898, Spain signed the treaty. Weeks before the Senate's vote on ratification, McKinley announced during a speaking tour that "it [was] the duty of the army of occupation to announce and proclaim in the most public manner that we have come, not as invaders or conquerors, but as friends to protect the natives in their homes, in their businesses, and in their personal or religious liberty."[9]

The "splendid little war," a customary representation of the U.S. war with Spain, erased the imperial origins of the U.S. and Philippine relationship. What is often removed from the popular and official recounting of the Spanish-American war and subsequent accord, which put Spain's colonies under the sovereignty of the United States, is the memory of the Philippine-American war and how Filipinos were reluctant to become the subjects of another colonial power.

In February 1899, when the U.S. military continued to occupy and eventually move beyond Manila, tensions increased between the U.S. and Filipino nationalist armies. In the early morning of February 5, the U.S. Navy opened fire on Filipino army positions followed by a land-based artillery barrage and eventually infantry fighting with murderous results. "The war," as one scholar on the topic put it, "destroyed a fledgling Philippine republic and turned that country into a U.S. colony bereft of the independence it had newly won from Spain."[10] Filipino nationalists had not been prepared for such devastating loses. Reporting to his parents, an American soldier assured them that, "I hardly think I was born to be killed by a nigger."[11] Other young soldiers reported back to their parents that "picking off niggers in the water" was "more fun than a turkey shoot."[12] Racial prejudice, displayed in American soldiers' correspondence back home, also shaped how the war was fought. The magnitude of death and destruction and the tactics ordered by those in command, such as torture, murdering prisoners and civilians, and burning villages and towns, became the subject of numerous investigations in 1902.[13] Americans in command rationalized their conduct by arguing that Filipinos not only were "cruel and barbarous savages," but also belonged to an "inferior race."[14]

In January 1899, in this context of overseas expansionism, capitalism, militarism, and effective Filipino resistance, President McKinley appointed a commission of seven men to investigate the conditions existing in the Philippine Islands.[15] The commission was to report on the social and political state of the various populations and recommend, without interfering with the military occupation, what improvements might be achievable.[16] The information collected as well as their observations and personal reflections were to be considered in guiding executive action toward the Philippines. In addition, the members of the commission had an advisory role concerning the preparation for the organization of a civil administration of government and providing an assessment of persons "fit" for appointment to office.

Shortly after the members assembled in Manila a proclamation to the people of the Philippines printed in English, Spanish, and Tagalog was distributed on April 4, 1899. The intent was to forestall any misunderstanding concerning the aims and purposes of the U.S. military in the Philippines. The members of the commission expressed the desire of the United States to establish in the Philippines an enlightened system of government, as well as the well-being, prosperity, happiness, elevation, and advancement of Filipinos. The proclamation also invited enlightened natives to confer with the commission on the form of government most conducive to the Philippine Islands and peoples.

## CONSTRUCTIONS OF THE RACIALIZED OTHER

The four-volume *Report of the Philippine Commission to the President* (1900–1901) is the official account of the commission's observations and recommendations to McKinley. While the contents of the four-volume report cover numerous topics, my interest here is the crafting of a racial typology that worked to bolster the appraisals given by members of the commission concerning aptitudes, needs, aspirations, and self-governing capabilities of human life in the archipelago.

Dean C. Worcester, professor of zoology at the University of Michigan and member of the commission, was largely responsible for writing and preparing the ethnologic and educational information contained in the first and third volumes of the report. The report provides a point of entry for elaborating on the discursive formation of racial identities. Worcester opened the first volume with a section titled "The Native Peoples of the Philippines" by introducing readers to two contradictory views concerning the degree and number of civilized inhabitants, collectively known as Filipinos, of the Philippine Islands. One view credited Filipinos with a "high degree of civilization," comparable to the "Pilgrim Fathers" of America, while the other view regarded even the "more highly civilized tribes" as "little better than barbarians."[17] Worcester set out to resolve this contradiction by appealing to the foundational claims on which they purportedly rested. He asserted, "the inhabitants of the Philippines belong to three sharply distinct races—the Negrito race, Indonesian race, and the Malayan race."[18] Worcester then claimed, "It is *universally conceded* [italics mine] that the Negritos of to-day are the disappearing remnants of a people which once populated the entire archipelago. They are physically weaklings of low stature, with black skin, closely-curling hair, flat noses, thick lips, and large, clumsy feet. In the matter of intelligence they stand at or near the bottom of the human series, and they are believed to be incapable of any considerable degree of civilization or advancement."[19] These purported universal truths were followed by assertions about their movement from the coastal regions to the interior sections of the islands, resulting from Malay invaders. Worcester warned that their nomadic life, wandering half naked through the forests, living on fruits and game, which they bring down with their poisoned arrows would, in a short time, disappear.

Apart from the racial typology that separated the human life in the Philippines into three sharply distinct racial groups, there was also the ordering of that life. The language of extinction, heard in the voices that made up nineteenth-century colonialist empiricism, might under different circumstances elicit a compassionate response on behalf of the plight of this purportedly disappearing people. The text, however, placed the reader in a nonidentification relation to Negritos. This relation was achieved largely through Worcester's densely coded narrative and the mobilizing of culturally specific codes.[20] Situated within a socially established meaning system, as a result of America's racial tradition, his narrative inscribed differences as absolute and consigned Negritos to an inferior status.[21]

The active production of a racial hierarchy is most vivid when Worcester turned the discussion to the other "races" that populated the Philippines. He claimed that the representatives of the Indonesian race were "physically superior" to the Negritos and the Malayans. But, what exactly made Indonesians "superior" to the other "races"? He noted, "they are tall and well developed, with high foreheads, aquiline noses, wavy hair, and often abundant beards. The color of their skin is quite light."[22] For Worcester the superiority of the Indonesian race was based on their somatic differences. Worcester presumed the correlation of lightness and superiority *as if* it were self-evident rather than historically conditioned. He seemed to have forgotten that such correlations were a matter of institutionalized practices. Clearly, he was not the first to conflate skin color with superiority, moral or otherwise. Such a perspective has a cultural history. One of the earliest European philosophers to conflate color with character and intellectual capacity was David Hume. In an oft-repeated passage, Hume asserted that Negroes were naturally inferior to whites: "I am apt to suspect the negroes and in general all other species . . . to be naturally inferior to whites."[23] Although Worcester's remarks operated as if they were unmediated observations, it is clear that they relied on historically conditioned cultural assumptions about human beings.

The third volume of the report is another site where looking was removed from its historically and culturally specific institutionalized practices. The focus of my efforts are on two sections pertaining to the characteristics of the races and their customs. These topics are treated in volume three under "*Paper No. VII Ethnography.*" Although Worcester is acknowledged for compiling the information for the ethnologic sections, it is significant to note that much of the "data" in these sections were taken from other sources. In "Characteristics of the Races Inhabiting the Philippines," thirteen plates representing "types" were distributed throughout the narrative. The "general" characteristics identified by Worcester were again organized around somatic differences, such as physical stature, size and shape of head, color of skin, texture of hair, size of feet, length and width of nose and forehead, shape of lips and eyes, and, finally, capacities such as intelligence. These general characteristics were then made to constitute the representation of the variety of "types" of human life in the Philippine islands. To account for "modified" or "uncommon" or "mixed" races, new categories were formulated. For example, the category of "peculiarities" was introduced to capture and contain all that exceeded the category of "general."

The proliferation of categories operate as formidable tools of control and power. They produce new objects of knowledge and study that bear directly on human bodies. What is apparent from examining the plates and accompanying narrative is the constituting activity of discourse. That is to say, racial identities with differential status are not naturally there—data waiting to be discovered; rather, they had to be actively made.

There are several recurring motifs in the ethnographic papers that require critical attention. The first is the "nature" of Filipinos as "naturally indolent," "apathetic," "docile," "simple," and when "under the direction of others, excellent."[24] The idea of natural essence, signified by the term "nature," does its ideological work by attributing intrinsic essences to Filipinos. Scholars of the cultural politics of race argue that when "nature" assumes "an ontological foundation," it "appears to precede history," ultimately erasing the historical traces of its own making.[25] Moreover, when "nature" is conjoined to "race," as it is in the ethnographic papers, it legitimizes social hierarchies and authorizes exclusions. Another recurring motif in the papers concerned Filipino ability. Purportedly Filipinos were "endowed" with "great talent for imitation."[26] This particular character trait implied that Filipinos were incapable of initiating their own ideas. "He imitates everything and adapts himself to everything, but seldom ever applies himself to anything."[27] The observation that Filipinos lacked the ability to reflect on their circumstances and environment suggested that without the direction and guidance of others they would "naturally" succumb to their passions. Their supposed penchant for mimicry worked with assertions about their capacity (or lack thereof) to exercise reason. "Ordinarily they act without forethought, intent only on satisfying their momentary passions, be these what they may, without thinking of results."[28] To be construed in this manner was, in effect, to be rendered inferior. *Logos*, or reason, in the history of Western intellectual thought, is what characterizes the human species as rational beings; it is what distinguishes humans from animals. Reason is what anchors *human* identity. While this account did not characterize Filipinos as completely devoid of intellectual capacities, it put their capacity for reason into question.

The specific constructs that were produced in the account of human life by the commission was not confined to the publication and circulation of the *Report*. In fact, they were reiterated in other expert accounts. The ethnologic investigations carried out by Albert Jenks on the Igorot of Bontoc Province is a case in point. The aim of his survey was to identify the typical Igorot. Jenks took up residence in Bontoc for five months. During his residence, he observed, classified, and recorded every detail of the social, economic, political, esthetic, religious, and mental life of humans living in Bontoc. The survey, *"The Bontoc Igorot": Department of the Interior Ethnological Survey Publications*, included more than one hundred illustrations, mainly from photographs taken by Worcester and government photographer Charles Martin, which were used as visible evidence for Jenks's assertions. Jenks used the same racial typology that was published in Worcester's *Report*, which separated and ranked human life in the Philippines into three sharply distinct racial groups. He identified the Igorot as belonging to the Malay race. In the introduction to his survey Jenks reported, "Physically he is clean-limbed, well-built, dark-brown man of medium stature, with no evidence of degeneracy. He belongs to that extensive stock of primitive people of which the Malay is the most commonly named."[29] Jenks also placed the Igorot of Bontoc above the Negrito, whom he deemed as being the "lowest" type of savage man the historic world had seen.[30] Jenks's survey included nearly seven pages of detailed somatic measurements of men, women, and children from the province. The corporeal differences that were made visible for readers—"brown," "saffron undertone," or "very dark brown"; and the women's breasts as "large," their hips "broad," their thighs "sturdy," with "prominent buttocks,"—mobilized an array of associations that were derived from a broader cultural context beyond the immediate environment of Bontoc. Moreover, the imagery encouraged an understanding of human life in terms of binary oppositions, such as primitive/civilized, and anchored the view that what was most significant about human life in Bontoc was its complete otherness.

Another study published some years later by Robert Bennett Bean, professor of anatomy at Tulane University, introduced new methods of anthropology and their application to Filipinos. His book *The Racial Anatomy of the Philippine Islanders* (1910) was the result of a three-year study of Filipinos that aimed to establish definite "types of man." Similar to Jenks, he used Worcester's collection of photographs as visible proof for his assertions. The aim of Bean's book was to establish "definite types of man" by way of "ear form, cephalic index, nasal index, and other factors."[31] It should be noted here that the subject matter of Bean's book had been published in other scholarly journals, including the *Philippine Journal of Science*.

The view that it was possible and indeed desirable to explain and master the nature of human life in the Philippines so that judgments about human capacities could be made is best understood within the horizon of nineteenth-century raciocultural thought. George Stocking asserts that by 1858 many of the major themes of raciocultural thought were well established and commonplace.[32] Robert Young makes a similar point, arguing how "racialized thinking" in the nineteenth century permeated the entire academic establishment. He is worth quoting at length: "Racial theory, substantiated and 'proved' by various forms of science such as comparative and historical philology, anatomy, anthropometry (including osteometry, craniology, craniometry, and pelvimetry), physiology, physiognomy and phrenology, became in turn endemic not just to other forms of science, such as biology and natural history . . . but was also used as a general category of understanding that extended to theories of anthropology, archaeology, classics, ethnology, geography, geology, folklore, history, language, law, literature, and theology."[33]

Thus, it is possible to identify discursive threads of polygenist thinking and sociocultural developmentalism woven together with Anglo American physical anthropology (sometimes designated somatology) in the representational practices of Worcester, Jenks, and Bean. Without a doubt these are complex formations of "scientific" knowledge; I underscore them to indicate the constitutive role that configurations of power/knowledge hold, how racial categories work in relation to specific events and contexts, and how discursive processes inscribe human life in particular ways.

While one effect of the *Report* was the discursive production of racialized others—which in time would produce definite social relations—another effect was that it worked to substantiate empirically that Filipinos were not a unified people.[34] The absence of national unity in the Philippines and therefore their failure to become "a people," bolstered the commissioner's assessment that Filipinos were lacking in self-governing capacities. The heterogeneity of tribes, languages, and characteristics became the empirical evidence that Filipinos did not have a common culture or a sovereign republic. This "fact" worked to enhance the argument that the U.S. presence in the Philippines was not a conquest, and therefore, not an attempt to take over another people's sovereignty.[35]

The presumption that pluralism in terms of linguistic and cultural practices indicated a fractured multitude that warranted U.S. colonial rule permitted the demeaning assertions circulating about the aptitudes of Filipinos to seem *natural* rather than humanly constructed. Wedded to the official discourse of the commissioners' report and subsequent colonial accounts is the image of the errant child in need of discipline. At the same time, even though most of the members of the commission viewed Filipinos as inferior, they also believed that some were capable of enlightenment. So, while Filipinos were unfit at the present moment for self-government, they did, according to the report, have the capability for future development. Thus, we see how the construct of essential differences in "character," "race," and "culture" all came together to authorize and legitimate the subordination of Filipinos.

Stereotypes of the racialized other and the construction of Filipinos lacking self-governing capacities was a salient feature in scholarly studies, surveys, reports, travel narratives, newspapers and periodicals written on the Philippines during the early twentieth century. For many Americans these constructs would be given concrete existence via public exhibitions. For many Filipinos, the constructs would become part of their everyday life and existence—conditions under which they would have to navigate, marks that they would have to erase, and knowledge about their being that they would have to unlearn. In the next section, I shift my analysis to world's fairs where racial stereotyping was on public display. I raise questions about *how* the 1901 Pan-American Exposition in Buffalo, New York, and the 1904 Louisiana Purchase Exposition in St. Louis, Missouri, attempted to regulate the look of fair goers, restricting how they were to see and think about the people from the Philippines who were put on display.

### LEARNING TO LOOK

Education was the fetish of exhibitions, especially the kind which sought to edify the masses.[36]

Education was an increasingly important theme in world's fairs as they evolved.[37]

If official publications and academic studies written on Filipinos during the late nineteenth and early twentieth century were addressed to elites, world fairs were designed to reach the average folk. National expositions had developed in the eighteenth century, although most who have written on world's fairs assert that the Crystal Palace Exposition held in London in 1851 marks the first modern world's fair. Soon afterward the international exposition was replicated in many countries, including fairs in Paris, Vienna, Brussels, Dublin, Florence, Amsterdam, Sydney, and Melbourne. The 1901 Pan-American Exposition and the 1904 Louisiana Purchase Exposition are two fairs that were ideologically consistent with the Chicago World's Columbian Exposition of 1893 and subsequent world's fairs, where the major purpose was providing visitors with "visible examples of the actual and potential morality, progress, and culture of the nation."[38] In line with that project, the stated aim of the organizers for the Pan-American Exposition was "promoting and conducting an exposition to illustrate the material progress of the New World during the nineteenth century."[39]

The decision to include an exhibit of the Philippines at the Pan-American Exposition was precipitated by the events culminating from the Spanish-American War and the consequent territorial acquisitions. From the start, organizers of the fair selected the Philippines to be a major focus of the exhibits that were to feature the newly acquired "possessions." The U.S. government embraced the idea, expecting that such an exhibit would help counter a growing anti-imperialist movement threatening America's involvement in the Philippines.[40] Frank Hilder, a government ethnologist, was sent to the Philippines by the federal government's exposition board to acquire materials for an anthropological exhibit. Hilder was in the Philippines for a month collecting cultural artifacts, taking photographs, and developing statistical tables on the Philippine economy. It was his collection that formed the center of the Philippine exhibit in the government building. The cultural artifacts and photographs that he assembled became one of the most popular aspects of the exhibit.

In addition to the federal exhibit, there was a Filipino village placed on the fair's Midway. The Midway was an area extending about a mile that accommodated restaurants, amusements, attractions, and ethnological villages. It held exhibits that were often promoted as "educational" and private enterprises in the manner of concessions. In one periodical, the writer encouraged visitors to see the exhibits from distant and interesting lands, arguing that "travel is a tremendous factor in education."[41] On the Midway, visitors encountered "popular" ethnologies of culture that contrasted with the "scientific" perspectives found in the exposition buildings. Cultural theorist Andrew Ross says that our contemporary "ethnic theme parks" are the "historical lineage" of the exhibits found on the Midway.[42]

The Filipino Village was situated on an eleven-acre enclosure. It was populated with Filipinos who were there as ethnographic subjects exhibiting their daily life. In a magazine article describing the worthwhile shows to see, Mary Bronson Hartt enthusiastically related the following: "Of these the most novel is certainly the Filipino Village, one of the most thoroughly native things on the street of streets. The performance in the pretty little theater is charmingly varied and daintily amusing, and between-times the inhabitants go about their business, wash their clothes tropical fashion by slapping them on stones, hold cock-fights, ride about after awkward water buffalo, and give you every opportunity to see them live."[43]

In a discussion concerning technologies of display, Gillian Rose offers important distinctions regarding techniques of display and their effects.[44] The Filipino Village display, staged from photographs of villages in the Philippines and populated with live human specimens, prompted a different effect from a display case of artifacts. The Filipino Village display was a *reconstruction* that relied on the presence of "real" cultural artifacts in an "accurate" combination that worked to make the representational display seem truthful. The truth-effect of the display also depended on the visitors' trust or faith in the authority of scientific knowledge. In the case of the Filipino Village, the authority of ethnological knowledge was key. There was then a certain amount of representational accuracy that was needed in this particular technique; hence the indispensable "real" Filipinos and "real" water buffalo, among other things. The glass case display of objects, in contrast, depends on a classificatory schema for its truth-effect. Whether that schema is provided by the ethnologist or the museum curator, the effect on the visitor, says Rose, is an analytic one rather than a representational one.

While the ethnologic exhibits of the Philippines and Filipinos were deliberately crafted as spaces of structured experience, the artistic treatment of the grounds and buildings within the fair had additional significance. They too were designed and organized to regulate the look of visitors and enable the overall message of the fair planners. John M. Carrère, chairman of the board of architects, was responsible for constructing the general plan of the Pan-American exposition. He recognized that in order to put into effect the narrative of civilizational stages, it was essential to bring together as "allied arts" architecture, sculpture, and color.[45] Accordingly, Karl Bitter, director of sculpture, carefully selected and strategically placed sculptural pieces that would impart "a clear, distinct, well-defined meaning."[46] Color was considered in a similar generative fashion by Charles Turner, who served as director of color for the fair. The following passage illustrates the central role of color: "The color treatment of the Pan-American Exposition does not mean only the paint which is applied to the surfaces of the buildings . . . it means what the artist calls color, the play of light and shade, form, outline, proportion, as well as actual color, all blending or contrasting with each other, as the case may require, and producing an artistic effect from whatever point one may look at the exposition, like a well-composed landscape, of which, in this case, architecture, sculpture, and painting, as well as nature, are component parts."[47]
In one promotional pamphlet for the fair, the author proclaimed that "an ethical significance is aimed in the chromatic arrangement as in the architectural plan; the whole symbolizing progression from a less civilized stage to a higher. Thus the strongest, crudest colors are nearest the

entrances."[48] These remarks reveal the extraordinary interdependence of the arts with the organization and maintenance of the cultural order. Visitors and those on display were, therefore, more apt to see themselves in binary and racialized terms, as subject or object, as modern or primitive, as superior or inferior.

## THE 1904 PHILIPPINE EXHIBIT: A FAIR WITHIN A FAIR

Education is the grand purpose of the whole enterprise.[49]

The 1904 Louisiana Purchase International Exposition in St. Louis had a more elaborate display of human life from the Philippines. It was organized to commemorate the centennial of the 1803 land purchase of the Louisiana territory and was at its time the largest and most dramatic exposition seen by the country, with over twelve million visitors.[50] The St. Louis fair covered 1,272 acres (almost twice as large as the 1893 World's Columbian Exposition and five times larger than the 1876 Centennial Exposition in Philadelphia), and like previous fairs, it included the main buildings, commercial and technological exhibits, foreign pavilions, and a midway. It also featured the most extensive anthropological exhibit of any world's fair.

The exhibits, the displays, and the regulated space in which the fair was configured were devised to convey the theme of American expansion and progress. The organization logic of the exhibits instituted by Frederick Skiff, director of exhibits, encouraged this view. Skiff felt that visitors would derive full value from the exposition if they had "the objects of [their] study so grouped and presented that [they] may apply [themselves] directly to the examination of them without having to mentally assemble them, [themselves], from different parts of the exposition."[51] By placing objects in relation to one another, visitors could draw comparisons and analytically comprehend the progressive march of civilization. So, for example, the exhibit of historical locomotives was arranged to illustrate their development from the first steam engine through the most modern and technologically advanced engine to date.[52] This organizational schema was evident in the other exhibits at the fair.

W. J. McGee, a distinguished government anthropologist for the Bureau of American Ethnology from 1893 to 1903 and director of the exposition's Department of Anthropology, announced in an article published in the *World's Fair Bulletin* that the motive of his department was to bring together "the world's races and peoples in a harmonious assemblage," so that "all the world may profit by mutual and sympathetic study of Man and Man's achievements."[53] Further along the article, in his description of the arrangement of the living displays, a clearer picture of what that assemblage would look like began to take shape beginning with the least advanced humans to the most advanced.

The department of anthropology's exhibits offered archaeological displays, a section of history, and sections of anthropometry and psychometry whose primary motive was "determining and recording the physical and intellectual characteristics of the race-types and culture-types assembled on the Exposition grounds."[54] The anthropometry and psychometry sections were housed in the anthropology building, each having its own exhibit hall with adjacent laboratory. The exhibits were provided by different American universities and museums, including Columbia, Yale, Harvard, and the American Museum of Natural History. There were also exhibits from different countries; for example, Switzerland, France, Germany, and Belgium had exhibits on loan.

In these sections, visitors could view different anthropometric instruments used to compare and record the "physical and intellectual characteristics of the race-types and culture-types assembled on the Exposition grounds."[55] Among the various instruments on display were: metallic cranium supporter with measuring attachment, compass, measuring tape, calipers, and arm-spread measuring rod. These anthropometric instruments were used for measuring head and facial parts (e.g., nose, mouth, ears) as well as stature and the skull. A central purpose for which somatic measurements were made is traceable to the mid-nineteenth-century belief that the surface of the body, and especially the face and head, bore the outward signs of an individual's inner character. In addition to these different measuring instruments there were life casts of various "aliens and other primitives," photographs illustrating ethnic-types and native-types, and a map showing distributions of fair-haired and dark-haired ethnic-types, and photographs of natives.

In his studies on modern articulations of power, Foucault unveils the individualizing and totalizing technologies concealed in a scientific discourse of norms. These technologies, exercised in the anthropometry and psychometry sections, connect at the level of knowledge through the construction of "types," such as the *primitive-type*, which allows for an increasing refinement of these technologies through the proliferation of types of types.[56] The central point here is that such anthropometric instruments are not innocent of power/knowledge relations. What these methods of scientific practice strongly suggest is that the "truth" of human "types" was not self-evident data; rather it had to be actively made.

Opposite the anthropological exhibit across Arrowhead Lake lay the U.S. Philippine exhibit. Accessible only by bridges, the exhibit occupied 47 acres of exposition ground, nearly 100 buildings, 75,000 artifacts, and 1,100 representatives of "types" of the islands, "a virtual fair within a fair" as one scholar put it. It was the largest single exhibit of the Louisiana Purchase Exposition and described repeatedly as the most remarkable. As reported in a reference guidebook to the fair, "In scope, thoroughness and general interest, it far exceeds any other display on the grounds."[57]

The Philippine exhibit was supported by the American administration in the Philippines and funded by Congress in response to domestic disputes over the appropriation of the islands. William Howard Taft was instrumental in arranging the exhibit. An Exposition Board was appointed by the Philippine Commission, which was responsible for collecting suitable articles to show the people of the United States what their new possessions were capable of producing. The Philippine exhibit included a reproduction of the Walled City of Manila; this was where visitors met the U.S. War Department's fort and viewed photographs of recent American military victories. Housed in this area was an extensive display of "war relics." This weapons exhibit comprised "specimens of all the different lethal weapons" used since the time of Magellan. Observing the organizational logic favored by Skiff, the display of weapons were arranged beginning with the most primitive Negrito blowguns to the most advanced American Mausers.[58]

The exhibit of Philippine ethnology showcased articles made and used by the different peoples of the archipelago that purported to tell their stories. But it is clear from the narrative in the *World's Fair Bulletin* that the story that would be told was already fueled by previously encountered images and words: "The Ethnological Museum . . . has brought together from various characteristic peoples of the Islands the articles which tell the story of the culture of each group. . . . All [the articles] truly show that in spite of the uniform shallowness of the Philippine culture, here and there something has impelled a group of savages to develop to a high degree an industrial activity which elsewhere in the archipelago may yet be in its crudest development."[59]

The forty-seven-acre Philippine exhibit, conveying the planners' themes of progress and advancement, was arranged into three areas. Fair goers could select one of the areas to visit: Spanish period, native tribes and their cultures, or the American presence.[60] It was in the area display-ing native tribes that visitors could learn about, as noted by the *World's Fair Bulletin*, "all the gradations of the civilization of the islands."[61]

The native tribes were housed in six encampments collectively called "The Reservation." Here visitors would find an exhibit of types arranged in an evolutionary scheme, beginning with the "lowly" and "wild" Negri-tos, followed by the advanced but still "primitive" Igorot, and finally the Visayans who were repeatedly represented as the "highest type" of tribe.[62] Elaborating on the novelty of the encampments, a reference guide to the fair stated: "The native Filipinos are gathered in villages, in houses built by their own hands. Here they live, abiding by the customs of their vari-ous tribes."[63]

The other groups on display were the more than five hundred Philip-pine Constabulary and Scouts. The Scouts collaborated with the Ameri-can military establishment in the Philippines in suppressing the nationalist rebellion against American military occupation. The Philip-pine Constabulary was a paramilitary police force controlled by the Philippine government. What stands out in the photographs circulated of this group is their elevated position in relation to the other Filipinos. Images of their disciplined bodies and orderly performances seemed to furnish a needed contrast to the other Filipino groups on display. Observers also appeared to identify with these bodies and repeatedly complimented these Filipinos on their conduct, fitness, cleanliness, and intelligence.[64] At the same time, such comments were nearly always coun-tered by the colonial trope "little brown brother." In one illustrated pub-lication of the fair, for example, that dedicated fourteen pages to images of Filipinos, a caption below a full-page image of the Philippine Con-stabulary read, "No one who has listened to one of the two daily concerts in the Philippine band pavilion will question the statement that the little brown men are natural musicians and capable of the highest training."[65] Certainly not out of keeping with the essentialist discourse circulated in government reports and academic studies, or the point of view crafted by fair planners of the 1901 Pan-American Exposition, the encampments were crafted spaces where meanings of race and culture were learned via the visible. This visual register, as this analysis has shown, is nearly always correlated with other forms of cultural assumptions concerning the pres-ence or absence of rational capacity, moral condition, and aesthetic status of racialized Others.[66]

## CONCLUSION: REFLECTIONS ON THE PRESENT

The screen that emerged from the accounts of the world's fairs was not confined to the there and then. The words and associations that circulated to name and know Filipinos did not end there; they would travel and filter into wider discursive networks, be given expression in academic journals, newspapers and magazines, travel narratives, schoolbooks, and Hollywood films. This screen would also become the condition of the racialized others' existence, structure their social relations and material situations, enlace their psyches, conjoin with panoptic and confessional technologies, and take the form of social pathologies.

The present inquiry, strangely enough, is part of that circuit, that relay, an attempt to work upon those words and images, turn them against the colonial image-repertoire, give them an existence they did not anticipate, and weave them into other constellations of words and images that might put them to critical use in the present. It is meant to disclose the historically conditioned discursive processes through which racial subjection proceeds. While it has underscored a horizon of thought exercised by Anglo American elite men in the late nineteenth and early twentieth centuries, it would be wrong headed to assume that this thought was all-encompassing, a *closed* horizon, and that these men were all-powerful in their ability to textualize Filipinos within a racial paradigm with differential status. To be sure, what I aimed to show is *how* diverse practices in disparate sites become organized into coherent patterns of racial subjection. At the same time, within the United States there were other circuits of thought that, while not completely foreign to one another, were to some extent independent of one another. The cultural criticism produced by turn-of-the-century black women intellectuals provide a counterpoint to the raciocultural thought so prevalent during this time. Hazel Carby's important work has shown that the cultural analyses found in the work of Anna Julia Cooper, Ida B. Williams, and Pauline Hopkins were instrumental in expanding the limits of conventional cultural practices.[67] These works and others by, for example, W. E. B. Du Bois, might have provided a politicized alternative to the scientific discourses of "types" and offered a discursive space for actuating human life not based on racial typologies. But, as pointed out by many of our contemporaries, the major consumers of black scholarship during the first decade of the twentieth century was African American schools and colleges.[68] The resolution against President McKinley's Philippine policies circulated by black anti-imperialists in *The Boston Post* (1899) is another example of a discursive space that offered a politicized view of thinking and seeing which did not instantiate the racist screen. In contrast with the Anti-imperialist League, black anti-imperialists framed the administration's unjustified invasion of the Philippines against the unrelenting racist practices in the republic.[69] Witnessing the denial of civil rights for black citizens in the South, the frequent lynchings of blacks, and the general failure by the administration to live by its proclaimed institutions and principles, black anti-imperialists provided a sober reminder of the domestic wrongs that still needed remedying.[70] Finally, what seems most important is resisting the attempt to formulate the "correct," or "authentic," representation of Filipino identity. My recourse to history is not to uncover the undistorted truth of Filipino cultures and identities, an impossible task; rather, it is to illustrate how particular discourses produce truth-effects and how the racial ordering of human life in the Philippine Islands had concrete and far-reaching implications. This is most evident in the anti-Filipino race riots that took place on the West Coast in the late 1920s and early 1930s and the 1934 Tydings-McDuffie Act, which restricted Filipino immigration to the United States to fifty persons a year. And while the scientific status of race has, in the present time, lost much of its scientific credibility, there is much work to do on the psychic effects of the interplay of racial designations and abject subjectivity. Such an endeavor might proceed, as this essay did, with a critical investigation of the discursive and visual field in producing racialized subjects with distinct status differences.

### NOTES

1. Judith Butler, *The Psychic Life of Power: Theories in Subjection* (Stanford, CA: Stanford University Press, 1997), 2.
2. I take the term "colonial archive" from Vicente Rafael. Rafael points out that the colonial archive inaugurates with Spanish rule and the textualization of the archipelago and human life existing there. While much of what Anglo Americans have said about the Philippines and Filipinos during the late nineteenth century and early twentieth century draws from the Spanish colonial archive, my essay will focus on the American colonial only. See Rafael's discussion in *White Love and Other Events in Filipino History* (Durham and London: Duke University Press, 2000), 3–18.
3. The expression power/knowledge, which designates a *relation*, is taken from the scholarly studies of Michel Foucault.

4. Robert Castel, "'Problematization' as a Mode of Reading History," in *Foucault and the Writing of History*, ed. Jan Goldstein (Cambridge, MA: Blackwell, 1994), 238.

5. Following Kaja Silverman, I use screen to convey the repertoire of representations through which the subject is apprehended. See *The Threshold of the Visible World* (New York and London: Routledge, 1996), 19.

6. Reynaldo C. Ileto, "The Philippine-American War: Friendship and Forgetting," in *Vestiges of War: The Philippine-American War and the Aftermath of an Imperial Dream 1899–1999*, ed. A. Velasco Shaw and Luis H. Francia (New York: New York University Press, 2002), 3.

7. Reynaldo C. Ileto, "Philippine Wars and the Politics of Memory," *Positions: East Asia Cultures Critique* 13 (2005): 216.

8. Stuart Creighton Miller, *"Benevolent Assimilation": The American Conquest of the Philippines, 1899–1903* (New Haven, CT, and London: Yale University Press, 1982), 11.

9. Ibid., 25.

10. Daniel B. Schirmer and Stephen R. Shalom, *The Philippines Reader: A History of Colonialism, Neocolonialism, Dictatorship, and Resistance* (Cambridge, MA: South End, 1987), 7.

11. Miller, *"Benevolent Assimilation,"* 67.

12. Ibid.

13. American atrocities are documented in ibid.

14. These were common expressions that were used by American military elites and many American soldiers writing home. See ibid., especially chapters 5 and 6.

15. The Commission was composed of Jacob Gould Shurman, Major General Elwell S. Otis, Rear Admiral George Dewey, Charles Denby, Dean C. Worcester, John R. MacArthur, and Rutherford Corbin.

16. *Report of the Philippine Commission to the President Volumes I–IV* (Washington, DC: Government Printing Office, 1900–1901), 186. Hereafter cited as *Report*.

17. *Report, vol. 1*, 11.

18. Ibid.

19. Ibid.

20. To paraphrase Silverman, a code in general represents a kind of bridge between texts. Its presence within one text involves a simultaneous reference to other texts in which it appears, and to the cultural reality which it helps to define. Kaja Silverman, *The Subject of Semiotics* (New York and Oxford: Oxford University Press, 1983), 239.

21. The various inclusion/exclusion federal laws and public policies, such as the legal status of slavery, the Naturalization Act of 1790 that reserved citizenship for whites only, Chinese Exclusion Act of 1882, the Geary Act of 1892, the 1904 Deficiency Act, as well, antimiscegenation state laws, are some examples of that tradition. For more specific examples of racist legislation and practices, see Hazel M. McFerson, *The Racial Dimension of American Overseas Colonial Policy* (Westport, CT: Greenwood, 1997).

22. *Report, vol. 1*, 12.

23. David Hume, "Of National Characters" (1748), in *The Philosophical Works*, ed. Thomas Hill Green and Thomas Hodge Grose (London, 1882; reprint Aalen: Scientia Verlag, 1964).
24. Ibid., 378, 380.
25. Donald S. Moore, Jake Kosek, and Anand Pandian, eds., *Race, Nature, and the Politics of Difference* (Durham, NC, and London: Duke University Press, 2003), 3.
26. *Report, vol. III*, 380.
27. Ibid.
28. Ibid., 380.
29. Albert E. Jenks, *"The Bontoc Igorot": Department of the Interior Ethnological Survey Publications, vol. 1* (Manila: Bureau of Public Printing, 1905), 14.
30. Ibid., 19.
31. Robert Bennett Bean, *The Racial Anatomy of the Philippine Islanders* (Philadelphia and London: J. B. Lippincott, 1910), 15.
32. George Stocking Jr., *Bones, Bodies, Behavior Essays on Biological Anthropology* (Madison, WI: University of Wisconsin Press, 1988), 7.
33. Robert J. C. Young, *Colonial Desire Hybridity in Theory, Culture, and Race* (London and New York: Routledge, 1995), 93.
34. *Report, vol. 1*, 12.
35. Rafael, *White Love and Other Events in Filipino History*, 20–23.
36. Paul Greenhalgh, *Ephemeral Vistas: The Expositions Universelles, Great Exhibitions, and World's Fairs, 1851–1939* (Manchester, England: Manchester University Press, 1988), 18.
37. Martha R. Clevenger, *Indescribably Grand: Diaries and Letters from the 1904 World's Fair* (St. Louis, MO: Missouri Historical Society, 1996), 9.
38. Robert W. Rydell, "The World's Columbian Exposition of 1893: Racist Underpinnings of a Utopian Artifact," *Journal of American Culture* 1, no.2 (Summer 1978): 254.
39. Lewis L. Gould, "Buffalo 1901 Pan-American Exposition," in *Historical Dictionary of World's Fairs and Expositions, 1851–1988*, ed. J. E. Findling (New York: Greenwood, 1990), 165.
40. Robert W. Rydell, John E. Findling, and Kimberly D. Pelle, *Fair America: World's Fairs in the United States* (Washington and London: Smithsonian Institution, 2000), 49.
41. Charles Edward Lloyd, "The Pan-American Exposition as an Educational Force," *The Chautauquan* 33 (July 1901): 336.
42. Andrew Ross, *The Chicago Gangster Theory of Life* (London and New York: Verso, 1994), 43.
43. Mary Bronson Hartt, "How to See the Pan-American Exposition," *Everybody's Magazine* 5 (October 1901): 489.
44. Gillian Rose, *Visual Methodologies* (London and Thousand Oaks, CA: Sage Publications, 2001), 176.
45. John M. Carrère, "The Architectural Scheme" (1901), 1. http://panam1901.bfn.org/documents/archscheme.html (retrieved February 19, 2005).
46. In Gould, "Buffalo 1901 Pan-American Exposition," 167.

47. Carrère, "The Architectural Scheme," 5.

48. In Gould, "Buffalo 1901 Pan-American Exposition," 167–68.

49. *The World's Fair: Comprising the Official Photographic Views of the Universal Exposition*, (St. Louis: Louisiana Purchase Exposition, 1903), 3.

50. The visitor count has varied in 1904 periodicals from 12 million to 20 million. Contemporary scholars put the number of visitors around 12.8 million. See Clevenger, *Indescribably Grand*, 32.

51. Ibid., 8.

52. Ibid.

53. W. J. McGee, "Anthropology," *World's Fair Bulletin* (February 1904): 4.

54. Louisiana Purchase Exposition Company Collection, Box 8/Folder 1, Sections of Anthropometry and Psychometry, 329. Missouri Historical Society Library.

55. Louisiana Purchase Exposition Company Collection, Box 8/Folder 1, Sections of Anthropometry and Psychometry, nd, 329. Missouri Historical Society Library.

56. David Owen, "Genealogy as exemplary critique: Reflections on Foucault and the Imagination of the Political," *Economy and Society* 24, no. 4 (November 1995): 493.

57. *World's Fair Authentic Guide Complete Reference Book to St. Louis and the Louisiana Purchase Exposition, 1904* (St. Louis: Official Guide Company of St. Louis, 1904), 17. Hereafter cited as *World's Fair Authentic Guide*.

58. Nancy J. Parezo, "The Exhibition within the Exhibition: The Philippine Reservation," *Gateway Heritage* 24, no. 4 (Spring 2004): 32.

59. William N. Swarthout, "A Descriptive Story of the Philippine Exhibit," *World's Fair Bulletin* (June 1904): 52.

60. Parezo, "The Exposition within the Exposition the Philippine Reservation," 32.

61. Swarthout, "A Descriptive Story of the Philippine Exhibit," 49.

62. Among the human life on display were "Christian Visayans, Islamic Lanao and Samal Moros, 'pagan' Tinguian, Manguin, Bontoc and Suyoc Igorot, Bagobo Moros, and Negritos."

63. *World's Fair Authentic Guide*, 117.

64. Clayton D. Laurie, "An Oddity of Empire," *Gateway Heritage Quarterly Journal of the Missouri Historical Society* 15, no 3 (Winter 1995): 52.

65. *Official Guide to the Louisiana Purchase Exposition* (St. Louis: Louisiana Purchase Exposition, 1904), 226.

66. Linda Martin Alcoff, "Philosophy and Racial Identity," in *Philosophies of Race and Ethnicity*, ed. P. Osborne and Stella Sandford (London and New York: Continuum, 2002), 16.

67. Hazel V. Carby, "'On the Threshold of Woman's Era': Lynching, Empire, and Sexuality in Black Feminist Theory," in *'Race,' Writing, and Difference*, ed. Henry Louis Gates, Jr.(Chicago and London: University of Chicago Press, 1985).

68. James Banks, "Multicultural Education Historical Development, Dimensions, and Practice," in *Handbook of Research on Multicultural Education*, ed. J. Banks and Cherry A. McGee Banks (San Francisco: Jossey-Bass, 2003), 7. I want to acknowledge Grace Livingston for introducing me to this scholarship.

69. Social criticism issued from the Anti-imperialist League offered an earnest alternative to the McKinley administration's policy of imperialism in the Philippines. Their platform condemned the administration's involvement, arguing that the subjugation of Filipinos betrayed American institutions and undermined the distinctive principles of the republic. Public support, however, eventually lapsed once the Philippine nationalist movement was defeated.

70. In *The Philippines Reader: A History of Colonialism, Neocolonialism, Dictatorship, and Resistance*, ed. D. B. Schirmer and Stephen R. Shalom (Cambridge, MA: South End, 1987), 32.

# CHAPTER 2

# CONTAINING THE PERIMETER: DYNAMICS OF RACE, SEXUAL ORIENTATION, AND THE STATE IN THE 1950S AND '60S

KAREN L. GRAVES

PERHAPS NO PERIOD IN RECENT U.S. HISTORY OFFERS MORE FERTILE ground for study of "insiders" and "outsiders" than the cold war. Scholars such as Mary Dudziak, Elaine May, and Stephen Preskill have noted that "containment" characterized domestic as well as foreign policy in the 1950s.[1] A society obsessed with containment is a society conscious of boundaries, and one likely to keep a vigilant eye on those who transgress or contest them.

The history of the Florida Legislative Investigation Committee (FLIC) is emerging from the broad field of cold war narratives as an important site of inquiry into domestic containment as it applied to education. Early scholarship on the FLIC, also known as the Johns Committee—so named for its most zealous member, Charley Johns—gives evidence of a complex history that invites sustained dialogue on a number of topics;[2] in this essay I draw attention to the dynamic between an established, privileged center and groups on the periphery of a society troubled by challenges to its status quo.

The state legislators who sat on the FLIC, along with the investigators they hired and the dominant ideology they represented, occupy the powerful center in this analysis. For much of its nine-year existence (1956–65), the FLIC targeted two marginal groups in its investigations: civil rights activists, especially members of the National Association for the Advancement of Colored People (NAACP), and gay and lesbian schoolteachers. American racism affixed marginal status to African American civil rights activists. Cultural invisibility defined the general status of lesbian and gay schoolteachers before the Committee's investigation; upon exposure, an utter sense of powerlessness reinforced their minority status. One way to understand the dynamic at the core of this essay is to think of energy, or motion, in relation to force. In 1956 the Florida legislature established the FLIC to suppress the NAACP's efforts toward desegregation. The organizational structure of the NAACP, however, proved a strong defense against the raw force of the state embodied by the committee. The combined counterforce of the civil rights movement and federal pressure in the form of a Supreme Court decision deflected the FLIC attack, and the committee took aim at a more vulnerable target in the context of the cold war: gay and lesbian schoolteachers. Standing beyond the bounds of any legal protection, seemingly alone and without allies, the schoolteachers caught in the FLIC dragnet were outsiders in every sense of the word. Unable to deflect the force coming from the center, they simply absorbed the attack.

Observations regarding the dynamic between margins and the mainstream that emanate from the FLIC history support claims put forward by Gary Okihiro and Lani Guinier and Gerald Torres as illustrated in the introduction to this volume. This scholarship suggests that the democratic advances made by some groups on the margin affect the entire society. Timing was a significant factor in how each group on the periphery was able to respond to the FLIC assault. The committee confronted the NAACP as the civil rights movement was beginning to crest; activists claimed the power born of resistance and organized protest. The defining event of the gay rights movement was still on the horizon, however, when the FLIC expired in July 1965. Without any sense of group solidarity, individual teachers quietly fell victim to the FLIC during its heyday. Ultimately those in the vanguard of the gay rights movement would benefit from the African American civil rights movement, in terms of learning effective strategies and simply believing in the feasibility of social transformation; yet, while the teacher purge was raging, political mechanisms to leverage social change were beyond the reach of gay and lesbian teachers.

The intellectual benefit of analyzing the FLIC history extends beyond the value such a study adds to educational history, gay and lesbian history, or queer theory. When the FLIC shifted its investigation from the NAACP to lesbian and gay schoolteachers, the maneuver allowed the committee to maintain political power and justify its existence long enough to keep its racist, anti-intellectual, and homophobic beliefs in the public consciousness. Stacy Lorraine Braukman concludes that although the public stopped listening to the Johns Committee in 1964, "the message itself survived, was driven underground periodically, and would reappear during the next thirty years."[3] A survey of anti-gay campaign rhetoric suggests that Braukman's observation was still very much on point during the 2004 national elections. But there is yet one more critical aspect to this analysis, regarding the committee's tactical shift from one marginal target to another: A dominant force in command of broad powers can employ a strategy of distraction to powerful effect. Neoconservative politicians, in particular, plied this tactic during the George W. Bush presidency. Consider the design and passage of the ill-named Patriot Act, for example. The law that suspended a number of constitutional rights (including the need for the state to show probable cause prior to engaging in investigations) was printed for congressional perusal just hours before House members voted 337 to 79 to approve the act in October 2001. Representative David R. Obey (D-WI) correctly described the bill as a "back-room quick fix," given that few, if any, House members had had time to read the bill.[4] Holding this shell game strategy up for examination is one way to disrupt the force in the insider-outsider dynamic. The story of the FLIC is a fascinating place to begin such an investigation.

## DOING THE UNIMAGINED: NAACP REBUFFS FLIC

The Florida legislature met in special session in summer 1956 to discuss ways to maintain school segregation in the wake of *Brown v. Board of Education* and *Brown II*.[5] In the midst of heated discussion between moderate and conservative segregationists, State Senators Charley Johns, Dewey Johnson, and John Rawls introduced a bill to establish a special legislative investigation committee. Earlier in the decade, cold war opportunists usurped legislative investigative power on the national stage to suppress any activity they deemed "un-American." State investigations of suspected Communists and other citizens who transgressed political and cultural norms followed in the wake. Johns had tried to establish a committee to investigate criminal and political activity in the two previous sessions of the Florida legislature; these attempts failed. The interests of the Florida tourism industry did not coincide with increased public attention to crime in the sunshine state that a special legislative committee might stir up, and some politicians were wary of the broad powers Johns's committee would wield.[6] In the face of desegregation, however, legislators' concerns for potential abuse of the investigative power of the state evaporated; the bill passed and became law in August without the governor's signature. It was widely accepted that the Florida Legislative Investigation Committee was established to interrogate, harass, and intimidate members of the NAACP and other civil rights activists pushing for desegregation.[7] From the time the cold war began, Americans were taught to link any destabilization of the dominant culture with communism, whether or not the link, in fact, could be established. The civil rights challenge to American apartheid, however, was very real. It was the catalyst that pushed Florida lawmakers to adopt Johns's bill in 1956. Instituting the Johns Committee was one more example of how fear of the enemy—within society as well as without—led to a loss of liberty for citizens in the United States during the cold war.[8]

With decades of political and legal experience behind them, members of the NAACP mobilized against the Johns Committee before it held its first organizational meeting. Before the FLIC issued sixty-some subpoenas in fall 1956 to members of the NAACP, the Inter-Civic Council, the Negro's Teacher's Association, students, and Tallahassee bus boycotters, Thurgood Marshall and Roy Wilkins contacted the Florida branches of the NAACP, requesting all membership records be sent to the national office. The organization knew all too well the type of retaliation that could erupt once the Johns Committee had its hands on these files.[9]

Once the public hearings began, civil rights activists employed a number of strategies to resist the FLIC's attack. During the 1957 hearings in Tallahassee, witnesses found ways to evade interrogators' questions, hinder and stall the process, and frustrate the Johns Committee. The first witness to be called was a black applicant pressing for admittance to the University of Florida Law School. The student and his attorney stonewalled the FLIC with deliberate, precise answers, punctuated from time to time with lengthy ramblings. Chief Council to FLIC Mark Hawes, Senator Johns, and other FLIC members would explode with frustration, but the witness's polite responses left little room for the investigators to maneuver, as illustrated in this exchange between Hawes and the civil rights attorney.

> Q: You see, we are going to be here all night if you keep answering questions like that. I just asked you how long you had been on that committee or whether you hadn't been on it for six or seven years, and I got a three-minute dissertation which means nothing.
> A: Well, I am sorry, sir. I feel that I have been on that committee since about 1950.
> Q: You could have answered that question simply, 'Yes,' I think?
> A: I'm sorry that I did not answer it specifically as you desired, sir.[10]

The witness followed up by turning Hawes off track with a request (and subsequent discussion) for an increase in the per diem allowance for witnesses. The witness was dismissed and his client recalled. He was able to stall from the beginning.

> Q: Do you have or desire your counsel here?
> A: Well, I certainly would like to have him, but I think he is, possibly, tired. I hate to put anything more on his shoulders now—hate to do that; but I'll tell you what, I'll just go on without him.
> Q: Do you want him here?
> A: I would like to have him.
> Mr. Hawes: Well, step out there and ask him if he will come in here with you, then.
> THE WITNESS: Well, he might possibly be gone.
> [Another official]: He is just leaving here. I saw him leaving.
> THE WITNESS: All right. Well, it'll be too late.
> Q: Do you want to proceed without him?
> A: Yes. We will have to, sir.[11]

It took a series of six questions and answers for Hawes to elicit the first bit of testimony from the witness. Evidently, Hawes could sense the tenor of the testimony that would follow and requested clarification regarding his options in dealing with recalcitrant witnesses. The next day Attorney General Richard Ervin signed a memorandum informing Hawes that the FLIC could not cite witnesses for contempt directly. Citations could issue from the senate or house once they had convened, but imprisonment of those cited could not extend beyond the adjournment of the legislative session.[12]

When the president of Florida Agricultural and Mechanical University (FAMU) testified on 18 February 1957, the FLIC posed questions regarding faculty and student participation in the Tallahassee bus boycott. His responses were indicative of one trying to protect his institution from possible political retaliation; he noted that he had advised faculty and staff not to take an active part in the bus boycott "lest such participation . . . embarrass them and the university."[13] Yet, he did not forbid the activism outright and he did not, apparently, take action against those who did participate. He merely reminded them that he wouldn't be able to defend or protect them. For instance, when questioned about the university rule prohibiting coeds from riding in automobiles, the president admitted that the regulation had not been enforced since the boycott. He claimed not to know how many professors belonged to the NAACP, and he explained that he did not now belong to the American Association of University Professors, as administrators were not eligible for membership.[14] In his brief testimony, the president responded directly to the questions put before him, but he actually provided the Johns Committee very little information.

FLIC members W. C. Herrell and J. B. Hopkins joined Hawes in a lengthy interrogation of the head of the Department of Art at FAMU regarding her work with the Inter-Civic Council and subjected her to harassment because she failed to respond promptly to their subpoena. Apparently, she had been able to put off the committee's investigation for a time by citing illness and having been out of the state. The professor employed the tactics of denying involvement and "not remembering" when questioned about her participation in the bus boycott.

> Q: You never hauled any colored people from A. and M. over to Princetown and back, in order to keep them from riding the bus during this boycott movement?
> A: No, not for that particular purpose. I might have had a friend to take to a doctor, or something. I don't know about that.[15]

The chair of the Political Science Department (who was also the faculty adviser to the student branch of the NAACP at FAMU) employed the tactics of evasion and eloquence in his testimony before the Johns Committee. The professor had explained that he did not interpret the FAMU president's speech to the faculty as a warning to avoid the boycott. This prompted the interrogator to ask what the professor would do in the event that the president, or the Board of Control, did prohibit such activity.

> A: Well, when that happens I will make my decision at that time. . . . You are asking me a question requiring me to speculate.
> Q: You do not know whether or not you would respect the wishes of your employer in that regard at this time?
> A: I didn't say that.[16]

As this line of inquiry continued, the professor refused to allow the FLIC to steer the course of the interrogation away from the basic issue.

> A: I certainly am conscious of the responsibilities which I have both to Florida A. and M. University and to the State of Florida. I am conscious of that, but I am also conscious of the fact that, over and above the fact that the state pays my salary—and I am working for every penny that they pay me—they are not giving me anything—but there is a responsibility which the State of Florida and which Florida A. and M. have to me. After all, I am a human being in this community and a citizen, and I am teaching students to be citizens and to take part in the activities of their government. After all, I am a political scientist. I tell students to take part in the government, that this is a democracy; then to be told that I can't take part in a movement with which I might identify my interests—you see, to me that is a violation of my constitutional rights.[17]

By the time the committee got to its interrogation of FAMU students who had been arrested for integrating a city bus, it had had enough of the evasive, delaying tactics. At one point the chair of the FLIC burst out, "Witness, if you will answer these questions, now, we will get through with this. Quit quibbling about words, because you know these questions are plain, simple questions, so answer up instead of just quibbling around and pretending that you don't understand the questions. We want to get through with this."[18]

A week later the Johns Committee was holding hearings in Miami, where the focus was trained on school desegregation and the witnesses were just as skilled at resisting (and frustrating) the committee. The transcript of a witness from 25 February 1957 is a good example of the ways in which civil rights activists could take command of these public hearings. In eliciting testimony from parents who were suing for access to desegregated schools for their children, Hawes, Herrell, and other FLIC members would try to get the witnesses to agree that education in the segregated schools was adequate. Witnesses would interrupt the interrogator to make a point about the inadequacy of segregated facilities and to take every opportunity to speak against the principle of segregation.

> Q: That's not a—
> A: I know. I am glad you asked the question because I want everybody present today to know why I went into the school suit. I entered the school suit because I knew that there could never be equality in separation,. . . .
> Q: Are [the segregated schools] adequate?
> A: No, sir. I do not think so along with the fact that I wanted my boy to get the very best, and I knew he would never get the best in a separate set-up.
> Q: Are the facilities, as far as teaching and education are concerned—do you feel that they are inadequate and that your boy, in the school that he is now in, cannot receive proper and good education?
> A: I say that we have good facilities but I say, with all the power of emphasis at my command, my boy will never, never get the necessary education that he ought to have as long as he is segregated as he is. There is something that happens to his personality because at the very outset it stamps him as being inferior.[19]

Herrell continued to try to get the witness to agree that the state was providing the best possible facilities for children in segregated schools. The witness was adamant. He answered, "No, I don't think so. For instance, let me give you an example . . . We did not have running water in our science laboratory. We did not have a gym . . . and until the citizenry, the [N]egro citizenry raised a howl it was a long time before they got water in the science laboratory. More than that, the high schools, the white high schools here, had much better equipment in their schools than we could ever hope to have in the [N]egro schools."[20]

Herrell followed with a series of one-sentence questions; the witness responded to each with a longer statement, drawing on evidence regarding differences in the quality of schools for black and white students. Then, Senator Johns turned to the question with which he ended most interviews: "Did you ever belong to the Communist Party?" The witness said he did not. Then Johns asked if any members of the Miami branch of the NAACP belonged to the Communist Party. To this, the witness responded in a manner that must have brought a wry smile to at least some in the audience. He said, "Sir, we do not ask that as prerequisites for membership. Anybody may join. Until lately, even a member of the White Citizens Council could join, but we have passed a law now that no member of the White Citizens Council, no member of the Ku Klux Klan, no member of the Communist Party, can be a member of the NAACP, and I was at the National Convention when such a law was passed. I helped to pass it."[21]

With that, the witness denied the connection between the NAACP and the Communist Party that the Johns Committee was trying to establish. Toward the end of the next day's proceedings a minister interrupted the hearings from his seat on the floor. He charged the FLIC to identify just exactly what it was expecting to learn from the witnesses.

> I have been here for two days, and I am wondering if you would tell me and those who have been here just exactly the truths that you are trying to find out from the NAACP members? I am in a little bit of a fog, myself, as to just what truths the Committee is trying to find out.
>
> THE CHAIRMAN: I don't think at this time the Chair would be in a position to do that. In other words, the evidence would have to be surveyed a little more carefully. . . .
>
> REV——: But you were trying to find out some truths from the witnesses about the NAACP, what they have done and why they were interested, and I just wanted to know what truths you were looking for.[22]

At that point the chair retreated, citing FLIC policy of not allowing discussion between the floor and the committee. Overall, the Johns Committee's first foray into its investigation of the NAACP had not gone well. A letter to the editor of the *Orlando Sentinel* ridiculed "the farce of the year. A Florida legislative committee down in Miami investigating the NAACP for 'barratry,' 'attempting to incite violence,' etc., while members of white Citizens Councils and the KKK attempt to drive a Negro citizen out of his own home. It will be interesting to see how many other foolish ways the next session of the state legislature will think of to waste taxpayers' money."[23]

When the recharted FLIC opened proceedings in the state capitol building on 10 February 1958, Chair Charley Johns announced the objectives of its coming hearings. Now granted the authority to investigate subversive organizations, the Johns Committee was intent on finding evidence that would link the NAACP to the Communist Party. "Subsequent hearings . . . will deal specifically with the activities of people and organizations in this state . . . designed to carry out the purposes of the Communist Party. We shall attempt to determine the degree of influence that the Communist Party has succeeded in exerting on the actions of individuals and organizations presently active in Florida in the field of racial relations."[24] Perhaps the Johns Committee was surprised to learn that the NAACP, too, had stepped up its preparation. Witnesses called before the FLIC in February 1958 intensified their resistance. The response of many was to offer no response at all; they refused to testify. Others offered direct criticism to the FLIC or read prepared statements in defense of the principle of freedom of association or the First and Fourteenth Amendments. Surely, one of the most powerful moments came when a prominent reverend delivered an extemporaneous retort, "a personal expression of raw anger and indignance."[25] He refused to cooperate further with the Johns Committee and walked out of the courtroom to applause. The reverend was not alone in his explicit defiance of the FLIC. In a prepared statement, a witness charged that the committee was not empowered to conduct the hearings, therefore, she would not answer its questions. Another woman, a Miami Beach librarian and head of the Florida Conference of the NAACP, did not answer questions. Yet another witness went further, attacking Herrell's "intimidating remarks" and the "star chamber" proceedings.[26] A reporter for *The Worker* acknowledged that the strong resistance of the witnesses was anchored in community support, citing, in particular, substantial reinforcement from the South Florida Council of the American Jewish Congress and the American Civil Liberties Union (ACLU) of Greater Miami. While recognizing the critical importance of desegregation, the ACLU released a statement that called on citizens to cross borders in the defense of civil liberties.

> The intent of this investigation is [to] strike at the very heart of the people's civil liberties by striking at the right of free assembly and freedom of expression.
>     The ACLU therefore calls upon all citizens of this community, regardless of racial, religious and political differences, to recognize the hearings for the cynical political opportunism that they are and to reject such an investigation as a solution to the multiple and complex social problems of desegregation.[27]

While the ACLU stressed First Amendment principles rather than argued explicitly for desegregation, it was, nevertheless, a welcomed ally of the people who lived daily with the harsh realities of segregation.

The Johns Committee was aware, of course, of the NAACP's network of support in the wider community. One newsclipping in the FLIC's files reported on a garden party in Miami to raise funds to support litigation expenses for witnesses. Several letters in the files, however, praised Senator Johns and his committee's investigation of "the Communist N.A.A.C.P.," but even those writers could see that the NAACP was holding off the FLIC's attack. One writer wrote, "Dear Charlie . . . as one white citizen I appreciate what you are doing at the investigations. I know you haven't had a lot of luck with the N.A.A.C.P. but, I'm hoping that you can really make known to the people what they are really up to . . . we're with you all the way."[28] Everyone involved in this battle valued community support. As Johns acknowledged in his response to the letter writer, "It is through the support of such citizens as yourself and the help that you can give us, although it may seem to you very small, that this committee and its work will be successful."[29]

While it was important and proper for the NAACP and the ACLU to frame their resistance to the Johns Committee within the context of the principle of free association, both Johns and the witnesses knew that "white supremacy" lay at the core of the investigations. In a letter to a supporter in Eustis, Florida Johns admitted, "I thoroughly agree with you that the negro [sic] will not be satisfied with a little white association but will want to go all the way. I can assure you that this Committee's work will do everything in its power to expose to the people and the citizens of the State of Florida what has been going on behind their backs. It is very encouraging to learn that there are still some citizens in this State who are willing to stand up and be counted."[30] Some members of the FLIC were astute enough to realize that their bald attack against the NAACP, exclusively, was a detriment to their cause. Therefore, at the conclusion of the Miami hearings, Representative Herrell proposed that the Johns Committee demonstrate its "impartiality" by investigating certain members of the Ku Klux Klan, the Florida State's Rights Party, and other similar groups. The ploy was rather transparent. The *Miami Herald* reported public skepticism regarding the "committee's unanimously-passed resolution to investigate the Ku Klux Klan . . . [reminding readers that] a similar legislative committee created by the 1955 Florida Legislature also embarked on a series of probes which were to include the KKK. Nothing ever came of the Klan investigation—if there ever was one."[31] The skepticism was well founded. Although the Johns Committee made numerous recommendations regarding the NAACP to the 1959 legislature, it made no such recommendations regarding the KKK.

The outcome of the NAACP's resistance to the FLIC was most succinctly stated by the committee itself, in its report to the 1959 legislature. The Johns Committee was only able to hold three of its planned public meetings because of litigation launched by the NAACP. Sustained litigation prevented the FLIC from completing its investigations "in the fields of race relations, the coercive reform of educational and social practices . . . and of labor and education." That is, the legal organization of the NAACP deterred the Johns Committee from its attacks on citizens working to desegregate schools. The language in this document is telling of the effectiveness of the NAACP's strategy. "Since February 1958, the Committee has been subjected to numerous sustained legal assaults designed to destroy the Committee or to obstruct and frustrate the Committee's investigations until it expired."[32] The committee responded by citing witnesses for contempt, but that had the ultimate effect of moving the civil rights battle from Miami schoolyards and Tallahassee streets into the federal courts, an arena that in the days of the Johns Committee was beginning to acknowledge worldwide support for the American civil rights movement. Mary Dudziak has detailed how cold war politics pressured presidents and the High Court to dismantle racism in the law, at least at the federal level. An amicus curiae brief filed by the United States in the *Brown* case put the matter plainly: "It is in the context of the present world struggle between freedom and tyranny that the problem of race discrimination must be viewed."[33] It is clear that the federal commitment to civil rights in the United States was fueled by "national interest" in foreign policy, and therefore limited the scope of the government's response to the movement. The image of the United States as a democracy in which all citizens enjoyed social and political equality was at stake. As tepid as this support was, the higher courts, nonetheless, were more inclined to rule against civil rights abuses by 1963, the year in which the U.S. Supreme Court ruled against the FLIC in *Gibson v. Florida Legislative Investigation Committee*. In a 5 to 4 decision, the Court determined that NAACP membership records were off limits to state investigators. This was the final blow to the Johns Committee's case against the NAACP; even the FLIC knew, however, that—for all practical purposes—its efforts to stall the civil rights movement through state intimidation and harassment had begun to disintegrate in 1958 once the NAACP moved the battle to the courts.

## ABSOLUTELY APPALLING: FLIC AND THE "HOMOSEXUAL PERIL"

By 1959 the legal maneuvers of the NAACP had blocked the FLIC's advance. Or, as the committee put it in its report to the 1959 legislature, "being otherwise stayed from pursuing its other investigations," the Johns Committee directed its attention to rooting out homosexuality from Florida schools.[34] Taking care not to offend University of Florida alumni in the legislative chamber, the committee wrote, while it was not attacking the "good name of the University," it found the extent of "homosexual practices" at the university and in the public school system "absolutely appalling" and began to lay out its case for expanding its work to include an in-depth investigation of homosexuality in the state. They claimed faculty at the university level were "recruiting" college students into "homosexual practices," many of these becoming teachers who then went after children and adolescents in Florida's elementary and secondary schools. The situation was dire but, the committee members hastened to add, no worse in Florida than in other states of comparable size. In addition to playing heavily on the recruitment myth, the FLIC alleged, "homosexuals are made by training," not born; that homosexuality is more prevalent among those with advanced education—teachers and other professionals; and that the "problem of homosexuality in educational institutions, while not new, [was definitely] on the increase."[35] The report went on to describe an ineffectual personnel system that led to few prosecutions and allowed homosexual teachers to resign, maintain their credentials, and quietly move on to another school district.[36] Evidently, enough legislators found this description of the "homosexual peril" convincing; the body voted to extend the FLIC's charter and passed a law that required the state to revoke teaching certificates of gay and lesbian teachers on moral conduct charges. The Johns Committee went to work immediately, passing a motion to make its files on an individual's homosexual conduct available to that person's superior (if a public employee) and to require that the superior report action taken on the matter to the FLIC within thirty days. In its effort to "weed out known homosexuals" from Florida schools, the committee sent a memorandum to all county superintendents of public instruction, requesting names of all teachers dismissed on moral conduct charges within the past five years.[37]

Having given considerable public notice to the "homosexual problem," the Johns Committee then shifted to a stealth investigation. They had learned from their battles with the NAACP to keep operations hidden from public view, to interrogate witnesses in closed-door sessions, to release very little information to the media, and to let Chief Investigator R. J. Strickland take the lead in gathering information from subpoenaed witnesses. Strickland explained this strategy in a letter to FLIC member Cliff Herrell dated 15 December 1959. Strickland and Chief Counsel Hawes had decided that "as long as this investigation is producing in the manner that it is," FLIC members and Hawes should not yet step in with public hearings. Experience has shown that "when a member of the Committee appeared, then these people began to bring in their attorneys and upon advice therefrom, ceased to give information. . . . They don't seem to think it necessary to seek legal counsel as long as the investigation is being processed by others than the Committee members themselves."[38] Further, Strickland and state school officials had decided not to "expose or revoke the certificates of [teachers] until the investigation is completed . . . as it might have a tendency to completely stop this investigation or to run them underground."[39]

Strickland and the FLIC had one overriding objective regarding the interrogation of schoolteachers: "Our sole purpose is not . . . prosecution but for the purpose of having [gay men and lesbians] removed from the public and private schools."[40] Indeed, the methods they used to extract information from witnesses would not hold up in court, but that didn't keep interrogators from reminding witnesses that the penalty for "crimes against nature" was twenty years in state prison. Strickland raised this threat during interrogations to pry information from witnesses. Usually, officials had no evidence to support their suspicions, so, as one county superintendent noted, "We use every bit of influence we can to secure an immediate resignation."[41] L. J. Jenkins, superintendent of public instruction in Lake County, was more direct: "As you know, proof is next to impossible to get unless someone testifies or unless the person involved can be bluffed into admission."[42]

In testimony taken in January 1959, an art consultant asked if he were required to answer questions that might be self-incriminating. Hawes responded that he was not required to answer such questions, but added, "I want you, however, to realize that . . . we didn't just pick your name out of a hat . . . We have certain testimony concerning you, or we never would have called you over here." Hawes continued to define the situation in a way that, he hoped, would elicit cooperation. He finished, "You may decline to answer any question I ask you . . . but I want you to realize that you're doing that at your own peril . . . that this Committee may turn that testimony over . . . to a prosecutor.[43] The witness refused to answer some questions, answered in the negative to some, and when asked if he had "homosexual contact with more than two University of Florida faculty members," responded rather boldly, "Well, I have not said that I had relations with one yet."[44] Although Hawes applied the intimidating power of the state forcibly in this interview, he wasn't able to control the flow of the interrogation entirely. The witness had already raised the issue of Fifth Amendment protection, and when asked if he were homosexual responded, "Yes. Would you like some sort of proof of that?"[45] The interview continued, and then the witness was excused to consider whether he wished to obtain counsel before continuing answering questions. When he was recalled later in the day, the witness seemed to bring Hawes to a point of frustration.

> Q: I've told you that we cannot wait indefinitely for witnesses to make up their minds whether they want to testify or not.
> A: Well, I will make the testimony, but I make it under very strong emotional pressure—I don't know if you want that on this record—
> Q: What sort of emotional pressure are you talking about? You're not going to sit here and give me any testimony, Mr.——, prefacing, in the record, with a statement that you are being pressured, that you are being compelled to give any statement here. Do you understand that, sir?
> A: I realize that, Mr. Hawes. You don't have to raise your voice.[46]

As the interview wore on, however, it was quite clear that Hawes held the upper hand. The witness could not control the terms of his cooperation.

> A: Mr. Hawes, it was our understanding that I would not have to name other persons other than those with whom I had had direct homosexual contact.
> Q: Well, I don't know where you got that understanding——. I haven't told you that.[47]

The witness named some teachers, but Hawes did not relent.

> Q: Now, you have given us the names in the Duval county school system up there that you can presently remember. If we call you in a few days, two or three, if you think of others, will you give us those names, or will it be necessary that we ask you to come back down here, or issue a subpoena?
> A: Would you call me at my residence?

Confronted with Hawes's threats and kept off balance by not knowing exactly when or how the FLIC would act next, the witness consented. He must have been drained.

> Q: Will you do that, sir?
> A: Yes.
> Q: Will you do it?
> A: (No answer)
> Q: Will you do it, Mr.———.
> A: Yes, Mr. Hawes, I will do it.
> Q: Now, I'm trying to accommodate you by not calling you back down here—
> A: Yes, sir.
> Q: —after you've had a chance to refresh your memory. Will you do that?
> A: Yes.[48]

Most interrogations of teachers took place beyond the reach of public accountability, in county superintendent or sheriff offices, in the presence of very few people other than the witness, the interrogator, and perhaps a law enforcement officer or the county superintendent of public instruction. Public hearings, in point of fact, became a form of blackmail, the alternative to answering questions to the satisfaction of the interrogator.

> You realize this Committee has Supboena [sic] powers but in order to invoke the power to subpoena [sic here], we have to call a public hearing, which of course we can do and if necessary have such people face you that have already given us such testimony as we now have in hand but in order to do that you have all of your news-media press . . . so I want to warn you that if this Committee should so deem it necessary, after having been presented with the materials and the evidence in your case, decide to call you into such a hearing, then you will be required to be here by subpoena [sic, and] to face such witnesses and to put yourself in a position of publicity as it might be necessary. So I'd like for you to think about this for a moment.[49]

It was common practice to begin interviews with a series of questions regarding perjury, raising the threat of imprisonment for refusing to cooperate with the committee. In an interview at the Broward County School Administration Building, investigator James Barker turned to the Florida statute on perjury immediately after swearing in a teacher who had been a Fulbright scholar. Barker informed the teacher that "in this state [perjury] is a felony and it's punishable by a good number of years. So the only reason I bring this out is because you are under oath, it is not in the form of a threat, we don't mean it that way, but we want a person to have every advantage knowing fully what they're doing, see what I mean?"[50] If a witness had enough acuity to discern when a line of questioning was relying on hearsay, investigators simply dismissed the concern. Their objective was to collect information to use against schoolteachers; they brushed legalities aside unabashedly.

Investigators pressured some witnesses to take a polygraph examination. When one teacher refused, Strickland reminded him he was under subpoena and then launched into a series of questions regarding the man's medical history. Then came the question again.

> Q: Will you take the polygraph examination regarding the questions of your having sex with men, other males?
>
> A: Not this time, I'd like to see my lawyer first.
>
> Q: Who is your lawyer? [The witness answered.] And why did you want to see your lawyer?
>
> A: Because I, I, I don't think you have me, Why do you want me to take the test? I'm not . . .
>
> Q: Haven't I told you that it was to see whether or not the polygraph machine would reflect whether you were lying regarding questions of sex with other males?
>
> A: You said that, but I don't understand why you pick, I mean why I'm being questioned about these kind of things?
>
> Q: Because you have been accused by others of having had and participating in such acts and it's now up to you to refuse or refute or admit such acts and that's the reason I'm asking you these questions at this time. Now do you freely and voluntarily take the test or don't you?
>
> A: No.
>
> Q: You're not going to take it?
>
> A: Not, not at this time. That's not . . . [transcript ends][51]

The witness did not consent to Strickland's demands, but others were not able to withstand the relentless assault. Statements of educators who cooperated with the Johns Committee must be understood in this context. It's not entirely clear what one should make of a teacher's statement, for instance, who wished "that something could get straightened out and that we could up-rate the profession somehow." Yet when asked if she would assist in a "clean-up campaign" by turning in gay men and lesbian teachers, the witness refused, explaining "I like to let people be, you know."[52] It was not unusual for teachers to deny engaging in homosexual behavior or knowing gay or lesbian teachers early in an interview, but change testimony by the end of a grueling period of examination, or in a subsequent interrogation. Some teachers refused to give any information; others spoke at length, providing names and descriptions of meeting places and social activities. Cooperating with the Johns Committee, however, did not protect a person from attack. One witness apparently made a report on another teacher and found herself in the office of the superintendent of public instruction in Kissimmee being interrogated by investigator Strickland in the presence of three other men. She had made the initial report because "sometime you get into a spot where you look out and you see somebody doing something that you don't quite approve of and you feel that they—that maybe you have a certain duty to the majority of people and you wonder what is your duty sometimes and so you go ahead and you stick your neck out."[53] After nine pages of testimony regarding others, Strickland turned on the witness, asking if she had ever been involved in homosexuality. The teacher repeatedly denied engaging in any same sex activity, and by page 13 was asking for a lawyer.

> Q: This Committee does hold in file accusations made against you pertaining to your participation in homosexual activity. I wanted to give you the opportunity to answer questions. . . . You choose to either answer them or not answer them, whichever one you see fit.
> A: I choose to get a lawyer.
> Q: Then you do not want to answer any further questions?
> A: No. . . . I could mix myself up and tell you something that I wouldn't be able to explain . . . and if you wanted to use it you could make me into a beautiful liar . . . so I frankly would like a lawyer.
> Q: I'm not interested in making anyone into a liar, Miss——, we're interested in only the facts pertaining to these situations.
> A: I'll answer the questions on my own. You can dig up anything—you can make anybody look guilty at any time. I am not a homosexual. I am not practicing at all. I am not and I don't think there's any need for me to go on.[54]

But Strickland and the witness did go on. When the investigator asked if the teacher had ever spent the night with "any individual girl," she responded, "Sure wasn't a man I was with but I guess I'd better start saying how many men I've been out with, right? I haven't got affidavits on that."[55] Then Strickland attempted to clarify a definition of homosexuality for the record, asking the witness, "Are you also aware that there are several degrees of that, are you not?" The witness was evasive.

> Q: Have you ever caressed the private parts of any girl or adult person?
> A: No.
> Q: Have you ever kissed?
> A: No.
> Q: Any adult female?
> A No.
> Q: You realize of course certain degrees of that is [sic] classified as homosexuality, do you not?
> A: I would say so. Anything that would . . . an interest of the same sex, I would consider that.
> Q: Then you deny having ever participated in any of these types of homosexuality whatsoever?
> A: Yes. I deny it.[56]

Once a person was hauled in for questioning, the outcome was predictable, whether the teacher admitted being a homosexual, or not. One teacher denied all charges throughout the course of her interrogation.

> Q: If this Committee holds in file sworn affidavits to the effect that persons have had such acts with you would that be true or false?
> A: I'd take it to court.
> Q: I'm asking you would it be true or false?
> A: It would be false.[57]

When Strickland asked the witness to submit to a polygraph examination, she responded that she would consult her lawyer. The interview continued, but the witness did not crack. After thirteen pages of testimony Strickland tried again.

> Q: You still stand by the fact that you will take a polygraph examination after having consulted your attorney?
> A: No, I think I want to just go ahead and resign my position and let it go at that.
> Q: You refuse then to take the polygraph examination?
> A: Well on those grounds, yes I guess so, call it a refusal.[58]

Strickland hadn't been able to shake an admission from the teacher, but he got the resignation anyway. In another case a teacher did submit to the polygraph examination, and then acknowledged his sexual orientation. Then the investigator outlined the process that would follow.

> Q: In view of the different admissions that you have made today, both in this office and in the polygraph room, do you realize that you are in a position now where you are going to have to turn in your resignation. . . . and I, in the capacity as an investigator for the Florida Legislative Investigation Committee, will ask you to surrender your certificate. . . . The only alternative we have is to exercise . . . powers of this Committee and bring it out in it's [sic] entirety, a public hearing in Tallahassee. At this public hearing, we have no control of the news media or anything else, this is our only weapon.
> A: If I don't resign.
> Q: If you do not comply.
> A: I'll resign sir.[59]

The investigator continued, as was often the case, by getting the witness to admit, for the record, that he had not been coerced or intimidated during the interrogation.

> Q: Do you feel you've been treated fairly and squarely about this?
> A: I do sir, I do.[60]

And with that, another teacher's career came to an end.

In October 1962 the Supreme Court of Florida vacated the action of the State Board of Education in revoking the teaching certificates of three teachers in *Neal v. Bryant*. Although the case turned on technicalities and the State Board of Education, it appears, did eventually follow due process procedures to deprive the teachers of their certificates, the court's decision did dispossess the FLIC of its power to hunt down gay and lesbian teachers on behalf of the \Board of Education.[61] On 27 February 1963, the court refused to rehear the case, signaling the beginning of the end of the Johns Committee's outright pursuit of gay and lesbian teachers. By then, however, seventy-one educators across the state had lost their teaching certificates, and the right of the state to revoke credentials of gay and lesbians teachers was solidified in state law.[62] In response to the 1959 FLIC report, the legislature amended Section 229 of the Florida statutes, allowing the state to revoke the teaching credentials of lesbian and gay educators.

## CONCLUSION

A parallel examination of FLIC transcripts reveals that civil rights activists and lesbian and gay schoolteachers used a number of similar tactics during their testimonies: evasion, denials, stalling, obfuscation, and answering curtly so to provide only minimal information. More often, civil rights activists were able to frustrate the Johns Committee with these tactics while investigators generally prevailed in their attacks on schoolteachers. One reason for this is that, while the witnesses' strategies were similar, the terrain of confrontation was different. Context and timing are critical factors. Bruised by its battle with the NAACP, the FLIC determined to keep its interrogations of schoolteachers hidden from public accountability. The gay and lesbian teachers had no viable alternative; to claim their sexual identities in an open forum in the 1950s and 1960s was tantamount to resignation of their teaching position. It exposed them to public harassment, physical attack, and perhaps, prosecution. The Johns Committee knew what kind of latitude closed-door hearings allowed, and they violated the teachers' civil rights with reckless abandon. Although some teachers asked for an attorney at some point in their interviews, access to legal counsel was rare. Strickland would usually get the resignation he was seeking before the session ended, making the request for an attorney a moot point. Without the check against unlawful proceedings that counsel or a public hearing might provide, the FLIC violated Fifth Amendment protections against self-incrimination, pressured witnesses into admissions without evidence, and used hearsay information and polygraph examination reports (neither of which were admissible in a court of law). Most effectively, Johns Committee interrogators caught the witnesses in a Catch-22 vise. One could answer the questions honestly or risk a perjury conviction; however, if a witness admitted having engaged in same-sex behavior, he or she could be prosecuted for "crimes against nature." As Strickland was apt to point out, the maximum prison term for either conviction was twenty years.

The FLIC violated schoolteachers' civil rights in its proceedings whether or not these witnesses had transgressed the "crimes against nature" statute. But the lack of a shared consciousness of a healthy gay or lesbian identity in the late 1950s prevented teachers from challenging the violations of their rights. This points to an essential difference in the two sets of testimonies. Buoyed by a strong network of support, civil rights activists claimed their constitutional right to freedom of association. Judgments against the Johns Committee attack on the NAACP appeared in the press. The ACLU encouraged citizens to put aside racial, religious, and political differences and join forces to protect the First Amendment rights of freedom of assembly and expression. In contrast, according to its national policy the ACLU refused to argue for civil rights protections on behalf of gay and lesbian citizens until 1964.

Secure in the knowledge that right was on their side, NAACP members resisted the FLIC assault in full force, demonstrating democratic ideals to the entire nation and for citizens in generations to come. African American witnesses offered eloquent defense of civil rights in their testimonies. They interrupted the interrogators to keep the focus of the hearings on the evils of segregation. And when the strategy was right, they refused to testify. This prompted FLIC officials to cite noncooperative witnesses for contempt of court, but that action exposed the Achilles heel of the Johns Committee. Mired in court proceedings from 1958 to 1963, the FLIC found itself immobilized against the NAACP. The committee could only watch as the sit-ins, marches, and direct action against Jim Crow mounted. The convergence of grassroots protest and federal intervention in the form of the 1963 *Gibson v. Florida Legislative Investigation Committee* decision disarmed the FLIC threat to desegregation and thereby gutted the initial rationale for the very existence of the committee.

The history of the FLIC confirms some salient theoretical points regarding the dynamic between marginal and mainstream interests. Critical theorists have long commented on the absolute necessity of group solidarity in securing human and civil rights for marginal groups.[63] During the Florida investigations, civil rights activists benefited from both intragroup and intergroup support as they contested the dominant ideology. Gay and lesbian teachers, however, suffered the consequences of facing the state inquisition alone. Derrick Bell's interest-convergence theory is also relevant to the FLIC analysis. Challenges to the center are successful, Bell argues, only when the peripheral perspectives fall into alignment with dominant interests. An active federal interest in abolishing de jure segregation paralleled the entire run of the Johns Committee.[64] Although not apparent to many at the time, the Florida investigative force was bounded in its ability to preserve segregation where this interest contradicted federal aims. In contrast, no counterpart interest emerged from the center to deflect the attack on gay and lesbian teachers.

The FLIC legacy stands as an example for what can happen when dominant forces violate civil rights, or human rights, of marginalized groups. Repelled at one point in its attack, the center may locate a weaker point on the perimeter. If the integrity of a democratic system is to be preserved, let alone the human dignity of the most vulnerable, all members of the system must maintain vigilant watch. As the story of the Johns Committee makes clear, it is abuse from the center that must be contained.

## NOTES

1. See Mary L. Dudziak, *Cold War Civil Rights: Race and the Image of American Democracy* (Princeton, NJ: Princeton University Press, 2000); Elaine Tyler May, *Homeward Bound: American Families in the Cold War* (New York: Basic Books, 1988); and Stephen Preskill, "Contradictions of Domestic Containment: Forestalling Human Development during the Cold War," in *Inexcusable Omissions: Clarence Karier and the Critical Tradition in History of Education Scholarship*, ed. Karen Graves, Timothy Glander, and Christine Shea (New York: Peter Lang Publishing, 2001), 181-94.

2. See Allyson A. Beutke and Scott Litvack, *Behind Closed Doors: The Dark Legacy of the Johns Committee* (Documentary Institute in the College of Journalism and Communications, University of Florida, 2000); Stacy Lorraine Braukman, "Anticommunism and the Politics of Sex and Race in Florida, 1954–1965," (PhD. diss., University of North Carolina at Chapel Hill, 1999); Braukman, "'Nothing Else Matters But Sex': Cold War Narratives of Deviance and the Search for Lesbian Teachers in Florida, 1959–1963," *Feminist Studies* 27, no. 3 (Fall 2001): 553–75; John Loughery, "Hunting Gays in Gainesville," *The Harvard Gay and Lesbian Review* 18 (Winter 1996): 17–19; James A. Schnur, "Closet Crusaders: The Johns Committee and Homophobia, 1956–1965," in *Carryin' On in the Lesbian and Gay South*, ed. John Howard (New York: New York University Press, 1997), 132-63; Schnur, "Cold Warriors in the Hot Sunshine: USF and the Johns Committee," *The Sunland Tribune* 18 (November 1992): 9–15; James T. Sears, *Lonely Hunters: An Oral History of Lesbian and Gay Southern Life* (Boulder, CO: Westview, 1997); and Bonnie Stark, "McCarthyism in Florida: Charley Johns and the Florida Legislative Investigation Committee," Master's thesis, University of South Florida, 1985.

3. Braukman, "Anticommunism and the Politics of Sex and Race in Florida," 295.

4. See John Kaminski, "Are You a Patriot?" *Z Magazine* 14, no. 12 (December 2001): 9–12; Robin Toner and Neil A. Lewis, "A Nation Challenged: Congress;

House Passes Terrorism Bill Much Like Senate's, but with 5-Year Limit," *New York Times* 13 October, 2001.

5. In 1983, Grattan E. Graves remembered, "In the Miami hearings, witnesses from the NAACP did the unimagined. They rebelled at the unconstitutional inquiry, refused to submit unlawfully demanded records and displayed utter disregard by walking out on the committee." Quoted in Stark, "McCarthyism in Florida," 38. In its 1954 *Brown* decision, the U.S. Supreme Court did not offer a remedy for desegregation. The 1955 *Brown II* ruling kept all school desegregation cases under jurisdiction of the federal courts and required school districts to proceed toward desegregation "with all deliberate speed." See Clarence J. Karier, *The Individual, Society, and Education: A History of American Educational Ideas*, 2d ed. (Urbana: University of Illinois Press, 1986), 390–91; Gloria Ladson-Billings, "Landing on the Wrong Note: The Price We Paid for *Brown*," *Educational Researcher* 33, no. 7 (October 2004): 3–13.

6. Stark, "McCarthyism in Florida," 6–9.

7. See, for example, "NAACP Probing Law Is Indicated," Associated Press news report, 5 August, 1956, Florida State Archives, S1486, Box 16, File 2; "NAACP Probing Bill Becomes Law," Associated Press news report, 21 August, 1956, Florida State Archives, S1486, Box 16, File 2; Stark, "McCarthyism in Florida," 10–16.

8. See Karier, *The Individual, Society, and Education*, 358–59.

9. Stark, "McCarthyism in Florida," 21–23; Braukman, "Anticommunism and the Politics of Sex and Race in Florida," 50–51.

10. Testimony, 7 February 1957, Florida State Archives, S1486, Box 4, File 1, 660. The identities of some witnesses were released in media coverage, court proceedings, or other documents and are noted in secondary sources. However, references to S1486 records contained in the Florida State Archives comport with state law requiring that identities of witnesses not be disclosed, with the exception of members of FLIC, its staff, or public officials. See also Stark, "McCarthyism in Florida," chapter 2, 21–87, and Braukman, "Anticommunism and the Politics of Sex and Race in Florida," chapter 2, 47–111.

11. Testimony, 7 February 1957, Florida State Archives, S1486, Box 4, File 1, 670–71.

12. #11-1660, 8 February, 1957, Florida State Archives, S1486, Box 3.

13. Testimony, 18 February 1957, Florida State Archives, S1486, Box 4, File 2, 715–16.

14. Ibid.

15. Testimony, 18 February 1957, Florida State Archives, S1486, Box 4, File 2, 732.

16. Testimony, 18 February 1957, Florida State Archives, S1486, Box 4, File 2, 770.

17. Ibid., 779.

18. Testimony, 18 February 1957, Florida State Archives, S1486, Box 4, File 3, 914–15.

19. Testimony, 25 February 1957, Florida State Archives, S1486, Box 4, File 6, 124–25.

20. Ibid., 125.

21. Ibid., 127.
22. Testimony, 26 February 1957, Florida State Archives, S1486, Box 4, File 7, 1361–62.
23. Letter to the Editor, *Orlando Sentinel*, 1 March 1957, Florida State Archives, S1486, Box 16, File 3. FLIC's charter expired at the end of each legislative session. The legislature reauthorized the Johns Committee in 1957, 1959, 1961, and 1963.
24. "Before the Florida Legislative Investigation Committee, Transcript of Testimony," #7-62, 10 February 1958, Florida State Archives, S1486, Box 4, File 13, 3.
25. Braukman, "Anticommunism and the Politics of Sex and Race in Florida," 94–99.
26. "Resistance in Miami Stymies Witchhunt," *The Worker*, 16 March 1958, Florida State Archives, S1486, Box 16, File 4.
27. Ibid.
28. #11-1050, correspondence, 3 April 1958; #11-1108, correspondence, 19 April 1958, Florida State Archives, S1486, Box 3, File 9; "Garden Party's For Members," *Miami Daily News*, 27 April 1958, Florida State Archives, S1486, Box 16, File 2.
29. #11-1051, correspondence, 8 May 1958, Florida State Archives, S1486, Box 3, File 9.
30. #11-1049, correspondence, 8 May 1958, Florida State Archives, S1486, Box 3, File 9.
31. "Probes Are the Thing," *Miami Herald*, 16 March 1958, Florida State Archives, S1486, Box 16, File 2; "Resistance in Miami."
32. "Report of Florida Legislative Investigation Committee to 1959 Session of the Legislature," 13 April 1959, #10-19, Florida State Archives, S1486, Box 1, File 21, 1–2. The FLIC listed approximately thirty separate actions in the Circuit Courts of Florida, one case in the District Court of Appeal of Florida, two combined appeals in the Supreme Court of Florida, one case in the District Court of the United States, and one case in the U.S. Supreme Court.
33. Quoted in Dudziak, *Cold War Civil Rights*, 79.
34. "Report of Florida Legislative Investigation Committee To 1959 Session of the Legislature," 3.
35. Ibid., 3–5, 8.
36. Ibid., 5–7.
37. FLIC memorandum, n.d., #11-1491, Florida State Archives, S1486, Box 3, File 9; FLIC minutes, 14 April 1959, Florida State Archives, S1486, Box 1 File 16.
38. Strickland to Herrell, 15 December 1959, #11-1674, Florida State Archives, S1486, Box 3, File 9, 2.
39. Ibid.
40. Testimony, 17 February 1961, #1-49, Florida State Archives, S1486, Box 8, File 81, 2.
41. Testimony, 16 April 1962, #4-42, Florida State Archives, S1486, Box 9, File 102, 136.

42. Jenkins to Johns, 16 November 1961, #11-1577, Florida State Archives, S1486, Box 2, File 17, 1.

43. Testimony, 19 January 1957, #2-76, Florida State Archives, S1486, Box 7, File 10, 1147–49.

44. Ibid., 1151–52.

45. Ibid., 1153.

46. Ibid., 1192–94.

47. Ibid., 1199–1200.

48. Ibid., 1225–26.

49. Testimony, Florida State Archives, S1486, Box 8, File 36, 7.

50. Testimony, 22 October 1962, #4-34, Florida State Archives, S1486, Box 11, File 9, 1–2.

51. Testimony, 11 October 1962, #1-147, Florida State Archives, S1486, Box 10, File 147, 5–7.

52. Testimony, 11 January 1961, Florida State Archives, S1486, Box 8, File 73, 10.

53. Testimony, 7 March 1961, #3-118, Florida State Archives, S1486, Box 8, File 100, 2.

54. Ibid., 14.

55. Ibid., 15.

56. Ibid., 16.

57. Testimony, 10 October 1962, #2-31, Florida State Archives, S1486, Box 10, File 151, 3.

58. Ibid., 13.

59. Testimony, 11 October 1962, #1-54, Florida State Archives, S1486, Box 10, File 148, 7–8.

60. Ibid., 8.

61. *Neal v. Bryant*, 149 So. 2d 529, (1962 Fla. LEXIS 3332; 97 A.L.R. 2d 819); Karen M. Harbeck, *Gay and Lesbian Educators: Personal Freedoms, Public Constraints* (Malden, MA: Amethyst Press and Productions, 1997), 179–86; Braukman, "Anticommunism and the Politics of Sex and Race in Florida," 279–80.

62. Braukman, "Anticommunism and the Politics of Sex and Race," 180.

63. See, for example, Henry A. Giroux, *Teachers as Intellectuals: Toward a Critical Pedagogy of Learning* (New York: Bergin & Garvey, 1988); Beverly M. Gordon, "Knowledge Construction, Competing Critical Theories, and Education," in *Handbook of Research on Multicultural Education*, eds. James A. Banks and Cherry A. McGee Banks (New York: Macmillan Publishing, 1995), 189-190; Barry Kanpol, "Critical Pedagogy and Liberation Theology: Borders for a Transformative Agenda," *Educational Theory* 46 (Winter 1996): 106–15; and, Steven E. Tozer, Paul C. Violas, and Guy Senese, *School and Society: Historical and Contemporary Perspectives*, 4th ed. (Boston: McGraw-Hill, 2002), 258–82.

64. See Derrick Bell's discussion of his interest-convergence theory in Derrick Bell, "*Brown v. Board of Education and the Interest-Convergence Dilemma,*" 93 Harvard Law Review (1980): 518; and Derrick Bell, *Silent Covenants: Brown v. Board of Education and the Unfulfilled Hopes for Racial Reform* (Oxford, UK: Oxford University Press, 2004), 9, 49–58. On the Federal interest in the civil rights movement, see Dudziak, *Cold War Civil Rights*.

# "IT IS THE CENTER TO WHICH WE SHOULD CLING": INDIAN SCHOOLS IN ROBESON COUNTY, NORTH CAROLINA, 1900–1920

## ANNA BAILEY

IN 1897, WHEN OSCAR SAMPSON SAT DOWN TO WRITE HIS REPORT ON education for the Burnt Swamp Baptist Association of the Croatan Indians, he was understandably proud of the progress that his community had made in recent years.[1] "The time has been when there could hardly be found ten men of our race who could read and write, that time is no longer," wrote Sampson. "We now have twenty-two district schools filled with teachers of our own race, and one normal school." An act of the North Carolina General Assembly created these district primary schools for the Croatan Indians of Robeson County in 1885. The same act also granted the Croatans state recognition as Indians, thus forging an early connection between Croatan Indian identity and education. The Normal School, an institute that trained Croatan teachers, was established two years later, in 1887. While this network of Indian schools was a source of pride for the Croatans, leaders such as Sampson recognized that their success depended on sustained community support. "We would urge our young people to stir up renewed energy in the cause of education and clothe themselves in the chaste and elegant dress of the man of culture and education," Sampson wrote, looking ahead to the next century. "We would urge, therefore, that no means be spared in the effort to educate our children."[2]

Croatan Indian schools were not only symbols of community uplift and progress, they were also a site from which the Croatans distinguished themselves from the black community in Robeson County. Prior to their recognition as Indians in 1885, the Croatans, known today as the Lumbee Indians, shared the racial category of "free colored" and "mulatto" with a portion of the black population; Croatan schools were among the first institutions that created and reflected a division between the Croatans and the black community.[3] To maintain and improve their network of schools, the Croatans turned to the political party responsible for securing their identification as Indians: the Democrats.

As the twentieth century began, Democrats in North Carolina were actively campaigning for an amendment to disenfranchise black men. The Croatans had supported the Democratic Party in the state election of 1898, which broke a coalition of Populists and Republicans and returned the Democrats to power. And so, in 1900 Democrats once again turned to the Croatans for political support of the amendment that would definitively establish a regime of white supremacy in North Carolina by disenfranchising black men. In exchange for their votes, Democrats promised to continue to act as advocates for the Croatans' education.[4] This essay traces the evolution of the relationship of political reciprocity between the Croatans and the Democrats, arguing that this alliance, coupled with the activism of Indian leaders, yielded increased state funding for Croatan education and created a path to federal funding for their school system.

By 1913 the Croatans' Democratic congressional representatives had secured an opportunity for the Croatans to appear before the House Committee on Indian Affairs to explain why their community deserved a portion of the federal funding for Indian education. The dialogues in this hearing illuminate a juxtaposition between national conceptions of Indian identity that the House Committee members held and the localized, regionally inflected versions of Indianess that the Croatans articulated. When this testimony before the House Committee is situated next to the dialogues presented in a court case regarding the expulsion of an allegedly black student from a Croatan school in Robeson County, the localized aspects of Croatan Indian identity are further clarified. In the North Carolina courtroom, the issues of tribal descent and exact measurements of Indian blood, themes emphasized in the Croatans' congressional testimony, fell away and the focus shifted to phenotype, the concepts of reputation and association, and where one attended church and school. These ideas worked to delineate the boundary between Indians and blacks in Robeson County and defined the regional aspects of Croatan identity.

While legislation created the initial link between Indian schools and Croatan identity, the Croatans transformed their network of schools into symbolic sites where their Indian identity was defined. In efforts to increase school funding, in struggles to secure a portion of the federal funding for Indian education, and in a fight to control admission to their schools, the Croatans refined the nature of their Indian identity. Three dimensions of Croatan identity were sharpened in the midst of these struggles: the political link between the Croatans and the Democratic Party, the tension between local conceptions of Croatan identity and national definitions of Indianess, and finally, the boundary between the Croatans and the black community of Robeson County. This essay charts the trajectory of Croatan Indian schools in the decades after Sampson called on the Croatans to "renew their energy for the cause of education" and reveals the process by which Indian schools became the cornerstone of Croatan Indian identity, or in the words of one Indian leader, "the center to which we should cling."[5]

## CROATAN DEMOCRATS, 1900–1910

"Public education . . . reached its nadir in North Carolina by the end of the 1890s," writes H. Leon Prather in *Resurgent Politics and Educational Progressivism in the New South*, "at which time the state maintained perhaps the poorest public educational system in the South."[6] Just as North Carolina earned a reputation for having one of the worst school systems in the South, the county of Robeson distinguished itself as having one of the poorest school systems in the state. In 1899 the statewide average school term was thirteen and a half weeks. Public schools in Robeson for Indians, blacks, and whites were open just seven weeks a year. Only one county of the state's ninety-seven had a shorter school term for whites, and only four other counties matched Robeson's seven-week term for black schoolchildren. The value of Robeson's schoolhouses was also well below the state average.[7] These buildings fit the description of poor schoolhouses offered by Prather: "log houses, shanties, or tenant houses . . . symbolic of the very mudsill of the educational plight."[8] White schools were the most valuable and least crowded, but the percentage of Indian and black children enrolled in school surpassed the average for all races in the state and the average for Robeson's white population.[9] However, the higher rate of enrollment for Robeson's black and Indian population may be explained by the access of white children to private schools. In 1900 there were nine private institutes available to whites throughout Robeson County, but their doors were closed to black and Indian students, who were left to struggle through one of the nation's worst public school systems.[10]

In an effort to improve the disastrous condition of their schools, Croatan Indian leaders turned to state and local Democrats. In 1898 Democrats in North Carolina were engaged in a vicious campaign to break the coalition of poor white Populists and black Republicans who captured the state government between 1894 and 1896. The victories of this interracial "Fusion" coalition were significant because it was the first time since Radical Reconstruction that black North Carolinians and a sizable portion of the white population had united for a political purpose. For Democrats, the 1898 election became a battle to restore white supremacy to the state—a goal they set out to accomplish through electoral fraud and threats of violence.[11]

While the statewide Democratic campaign of 1898 was marked by vitriolic racist appeals against "Negro rule" and the white men who aligned themselves with it, Democrats in Robeson County took a more nuanced approach when it came time to sway the Croatans toward their cause. "It became necessary to win back into the Democratic fold the Croatans Indians of Robeson County, who were chiefly Republican at the time," recalled the Croatans' congressional representative, John D. Bellamy, in his *Memoirs of an Octogenarian*.[12] To this end, Bellamy and his fellow Democrats from the area "devised a scheme," where, with Bellamy bearing the expenses, they would have a series of educational meetings at Croatan population centers. Bellamy would then visit Robeson, where, "I should speak to them about the necessity of education and pride in their ancestry."[13] According to Bellamy, these meetings were a tremendous success: "We had numerous picnics and some educational and political meetings, and when the election came on, ninety percent of the Croatans voted for me for Congress!"[14] After his election, Bellamy, true to his campaign promise, introduced a bill "providing for the education and support of the children of the Croatan Indians of North Carolina."[15] Although his speech in support of the bill before the House of Representatives was met with great applause, the bill died quietly on the House floor.[16] Five months later, Bellamy returned to Robeson County. He kept his word to act as an advocate for the Croatans in Congress, and now it was time for the Croatans to repay him by supporting an amendment to disenfranchise black male voters once and for all.

During his brief trip to Robeson, Bellamy addressed audiences at the White Supremacy Club in Lumberton and the Croatan Normal School with what was most likely different versions of the same message: shore up support in your community for the amendment to disenfranchise black men.[17] The amendment stated that anyone whose ancestors did not vote before 1 January 1867 would be disenfranchised. The Croatans had voted until 1835, so they would still be eligible to vote. To reassure the Croatans that they would retain their voting rights, local white Democrats ran editorials in the *Robesonian*, the county's Democratic newspaper. T. C. Henderson, the head of the Normal School, implored every Croatan to "carefully consider his interest and the interest of his race, and by doing so be convinced that the proposed amendment . . . will promote the general welfare of his race and protect him from the dominion of the ignorant Negro."[18] Henderson also explained that the Croatans would not be disenfranchised by the amendment. With a similar message, fellow Democrat W. H. Humphrey wrote into the *Robesonian* to "say to my Croatan friends all over the country that you are duty bound to support the amendment. It will not disfranchise a one of you." Humphrey also bluntly laid out the political pact that the Croatans made with the Democrats, claiming, "you are bound to support it as evidence of your appreciation for what has been done for your race." He then listed several concrete examples of Democratic patronage, all of which institutionalized separations between Croatans and the black community: "Your insane don't any longer go to the Negro asylum, but to the white asylum in Raleigh . . . you don't have to list your taxes or vote as colored . . . and your marriage licenses are issued to you as Croatans." Finally, Humphrey included a reference to Bellamy's recent legislation to improve Croatan educational opportunities. "Our Congressman, Mr. Bellamy, is trying to get $50,000 for you . . . more legislation for you as a race than for any other race."[19]

Croatan community leaders responded to these proclamations with their own editorials expressing support for the amendment. Because of a clause in the legislation that established a literacy test for all voters after 1908, they could support the amendment with the argument that it would necessitate an improvement in educational conditions throughout the state, although most editorials mixed this theme with an endorsement of white supremacy. "I am in favor of the amendment for many reasons," wrote O. R. Sampson, an Indian teacher and minister, to the *Robesonian*. "First, it will stimulate education to a higher degree in North Carolina. It will give us an intelligent ballot, and establish White Supremacy in North Carolina."[20] Writing for his Indian community in the settlement of Pates, A. N. Locklear echoed Sampson by emphasizing the effect the amendment would have on education, calling it "a greater incentive to the cause of education than anything that was ever submitted to the citizens of North Carolina." But Locklear also reminded his "Indian fellow citizens" of the benefits of Democratic patronage, asking the Croatans, "Don't you want a share in the pie; if so, come and go with us on the amendment and we will do thee good."[21]

The Croatans did more than write editorials in support of the amendment; they demonstrated their allegiance to the Democratic Party by participating in a rally for the amendment that invited "the noble champions of the white manhood and womanhood of North Carolina" to show their support for a regime of white supremacy.[22] Croatans boarded trains heading for this rally, joining members of the Democratic clubs who showed up in their "red shirts," an emblem to denote membership in the white supremacy wing of the Democratic party.[23] On 1 July 1902, the amendment to disenfranchise black men took effect. The Croatans' public support of white supremacy worked to strengthen their relationship of political reciprocity with the Democratic Party and, in the years ahead, Croatans would use this relationship to gain measurable improvements to their school system.

With the question of black political participation resolved, state leaders focused their attention on the abysmal state of their public education system. "The country at large is spending $2.83 for the education of its children," declared the newly elected Governor Charles Aycock in his public address entitled "Declaration against Illiteracy," "North Carolina is spending barely .67 cents." These statistics, combined with Aycock's rhetoric that "every child, regardless of condition in life, or circumstances of fortunes, may receive that opportunity for training," were meant to inspire a spirit of revival for the cause of education.[24] It worked. In the next decade, the public school movement would dramatically change the course of education in North Carolina, improving school buildings, raising teacher's salaries, lengthening the school term, and consolidating districts. Yet, this movement to improve the educational conditions for "every child" fractured along racial lines. Despite legislation that prohibited racial discrimination in the allocation of school funds, it was well known throughout the state that white children received the greatest portion of school funding. "The negroes . . . constitute about one-third of the school population," noted the *Biennial Report from the Department of Public Instruction for 1904–1906*, "and receive in the apportionment for the same purposes less than one-fifth of the school money."[25] Would Indian schools rank above or below black schools in distribution of the school fund and the resulting overall school conditions? This question would be answered definitively in the next five years.

By 1906, schools for all students in Robeson County demonstrated improvement—brought by an influx of funds from the statewide education revival—with an increase in the value of schoolhouses and the length of the school term. School facilities for white children were the most improved, and their classrooms remained the least crowded. Black schools surpassed those for Indians in length of the school term, percentage of population enrolled, and value of school property.[26] Indian community leaders recognized that, while their district schools were a source of pride, they remained at the bottom rung in the county's three-tiered public school system. "We have a good public school system of which we are justly proud . . . and we should do all we can in making these schools all that could be desired by anyone," wrote church leader A. S. Locklear in his 1906 report on education for the Indian Burnt Swamp Baptist Association. "We should wake up to the fact that we are far behind in general education, and we should never cease until all the schools are properly patronized."[27] Even though community leaders recognized that their school system needed improvement, the district schools remained a source of pride for the community, because they were institutions that reflected separate spaces for Indians in the segregated landscape of Robeson County.

While the Croatan district schools represented different communities throughout Robeson, it was the community's Normal school or teacher training institute that was, in the words of Locklear, "the center to which we should cling." "Now, let the small hearted and prejudicial fellow say what he may of this Indian Normal School at Pembroke, N.C., it's our hope for the present," wrote Locklear in his 1910 report on education. "It is one of the causes of the prosperity of the Indian people of Robeson County. We know this is why our public school rooms are mastered by teachers of our own race, of which we should be proud."[28] While the network of Indian primary schools represented various Indian communities throughout Robeson County, the Normal served as a mechanism that literally drew members of these communities together. The Normal not only trained Indian teachers for the Indian primary schools throughout Robeson, it also promoted progressive values; the code of conduct for students forbade swearing and drinking and encouraged students to live according to a Christian code of ethics. The "college," as it came to be known, also hosted political rallies, fundraisers, and community celebrations. A village eventually developed around the school, which was populated by the faculty and staff from the Normal and home to businesses that catered to the Indian community. The Normal would become, as Locklear had hoped, the center of Indian life in Robeson County and a symbol of the community's commitment to education.

To increase the funding for the Normal, Indian leaders once again relied on their Democratic advocates, this time enlisting Col. N. A. McLean, a former Confederate officer and local Democrat who "wore the highest cap" in the rally to support the amendment to disenfranchise black men. "Col. N. A. McLean . . . has carried our cry to the Legislature of North Carolina and it was heard," wrote A. N. Locklear in an editorial to the *Robesonian*, "and raised our normal school appropriation from $500 to $1250."[29] It was not just the Indian leaders who were focused on improving the conditions of their school system—this network of schools also inspired widespread support among the entire Indian community. When a two-year effort to raise money for a new Normal school building fell $600 short, both Oscar Sampson and Doctor Fuller Lowry, Croatan community leaders from different settlements, made personal canvasses throughout the county, fund-raising from door to door. "Many of the old Croatans, gray headed, stooped and tottering with age, who have never had the opportunity of spending a day in school," read an article in the *Robesonian* about one of these rallies to raise funds, "could be seen pushing through the crowd to hand over their hard-earned money in order that their children may have the advantage of an education."[30]

By 1910, the Croatan school districts had established their position as the middle rung of the county's public school system. While the percentage of students enrolled and the length of the school term remained roughly equivalent to those for the black population of Robeson, the Croatan schools now surpassed black ones in the value of school property. Croatan schools were also much less crowded than black schools.[31] Perhaps most important, the Croatans now ranked below the whites and above the blacks in the amount of school funds spent per student: the average amount for a white student was $2.75, $1.76 for Croatans, and $1.21 for Blacks.[32] Were these disparities in funding another result of Democratic patronage? Democrats dominated the county board of education, and the distribution of the school fund was entirely within their control, but there is no explicit acknowledgement in the minutes of the board of education that the Croatans were favored because of their relationship to the Democratic Party. However, because local Democrats sponsored legislation initially to create Indian schools and later increased funding for the Normal, and in light of the fact that the Croatans actively supported the Democratic Party, it is likely that the Democrats would intentionally favor the Croatans over the black population when it came time to distribute school funding. Now that the Croatans had secured the middle position in the county's three-tiered school system, they would focus on obtaining federal funding, an accomplishment that could release the Croatans from their obligations to the Democratic Party and its regime of white supremacy.

## Name Changes and National Investigations, 1910–1915

"The most unique committee hearing of any Legislature in recent years was that of the Senate judiciary committee this evening to consider the Cobb bill," reported the *Robesonian* on February 6, 1911, "to change the name of the Croatan Indians in Robeson County to Cherokee Indians of Robeson."[33] This proposed legislation, so named for W. S. Cobb, a senator in the state assembly who promised during his election campaign to "do all in his power to increase [the Croatan] appropriation for their school and help them in any other way possible," was another tangible result of the relationship of political reciprocity between the Democratic Party and the Croatan Indians.[34] In the previous decade, Croatan community leaders had focused exclusively on securing additional funds for their school system. Now, they added a twin goal: changing their name to the Cherokee Indians of Robeson County. According to A. S. Locklear, a Croatan who wrote to the *Robesonian* to explain the community's desire for a name change, the designation of Cherokee would "fix our presence among the Indian tribes of the United States" and was chosen after "we have gotten together all the data and early history of North Carolina, coupled with tradition, and by careful study we are sure that we are a branch of the Cherokees."[35] If the Indians of Robeson received a nationally recognized tribal designation—in other words, if their localized Indian identity was nationalized—then the Croatans would have access to an alternative source of funding for their school system and perhaps even surpass the local white schools in terms of the quality of educational opportunities in Robeson County.

Opposing this name change was none other than the Cherokee Tribe in North Carolina, whose representatives traveled from the western mountains of the state to attend the senate hearing. Cherokee chiefs Welsh and Sounock appeared with the superintendent of the Indian school at Cherokee. Indian community leaders, along with local Democratic advocates and the state superintendent of public instruction, represented the Croatans. Chief Welsh, speaking through an interpreter, said that his tribe had nothing against the Croatans but simply did not believe that they had any claim to the name Cherokee. After hearing the testimony that the Croatans presented about the links between the tribes, committee members conducted their own research. They asked the two tribal chiefs and three Croatans to stand in line to see if there was any resemblance. Then the chairman of the committee asked Chief Walsh of the Cherokees to look at a Croatan to determine if he bore any resemblance to the tribe. Chief Walsh, responding in Cherokee, said that he did not see the resemblance. The committee deferred action on the bill, and the two delegations returned to their corners of the state.[36]

One month later, in March, the state assembly changed the name of the Croatans to the "Indians of Robeson County." Croatan community leaders were far from satisfied with this new designation. But good news was close at hand. North Carolina's U.S. senator, Furnifold Simmons, introduced legislation in August to establish an industrial school for the Indians of Robeson County, with $50,000 for construction and $10,000 annually for maintenance.[37] In response to this proposed legislation, Charles F. Pierce, federal supervisor of Indian schools, was dispatched to Robeson.

The goal of Pierce's trip to Robeson was to determine whether the Croatans warranted a portion of the federal funding for Indian education. This would require, among other things, that the Croatans meet national criteria of Indianess, which included both measurements of Indian blood and a recognizable line of tribal descent. To this end, Pierce described the community as having "few full bloods . . . although one would readily class a large majority as being at least 3/4ths Indian."[38] As for their line of tribal descent, Pierce reviewed the theory that the Croatans were descendents of John White's Lost Colony of Roanoke, an argument introduced in the 1880s by a local Democrat. Pierce also acknowledged "there has been considerable doubt in the past as to the ancestry of these people" but "historians . . . now practically agreed they are a mixture of white and Indian."[39] Pierce went on to emphasize the localized inflections of Croatan identity, explaining that "they do not associate with the Negro race, looking upon them in about the same way as do the whites of their community" and, above all else, "they are crazy on the subject of education."[40] Would the Croatans' mix of local and national Indian characteristics be enough to convince Pierce to recommend that they receive funding for a government Indian school?

Rather than making a judgment about whether or not the Croatans were "Indian enough" to receive federal funds, Pierce simply concluded that the state of North Carolina "has a well organized plan for the education of Indians within her borders, and there does not appear to be any justification for any interference or aid on the part of the government."[41] In other words, the Croatans were "Indian enough" to receive support from the state of North Carolina but not from the federal government. Pierce's recommendations matched the undercurrent of national Indian policies—the federal government was attempting to reduce rather than increase their involvement with Indian communities—but contradicted local assessments, by the principal of the Normal among others, that funding from the state alone was insufficient. Yet, even without the endorsement of Pierce, the bill passed in the U.S. Senate and went to the U.S. House of Representatives for consideration. Croatan leaders, joined by their local Democratic advocate and future governor, Angus McLean, boarded trains to Washington, D.C., to offer their testimony to the House Committee on Indian Affairs about why the government should establish a federally funded industrial school for Indians in Robeson County.

Like Charles Pierce before them, the House Committee attempted to determine if the Croatans held national markers of Indian identity. Questions focused on how the Croatans divided their land, whether they had a language of "their own," if the government had ever "exercised any supervision over them in any way, shape, or form" and their degree of blood quantum.[42] The committee seemed more interested in ascertaining the qualities the community *lacked*—a reservation, language, and treaty history—than understanding that the Croatans defined their Indianess through their network of schools, along with Indian-only churches and kinship networks. The committee was especially preoccupied with whether community members paid taxes on their real estate, and whether this money was used to finance district public schools. A focus on landownership and tax-supported schools was understandable, as the government was in the midst of dealing with the failures of the allotment of Indian lands and also trying to move Indians into public schools. Beyond these issues, committee members seemed confounded by the fact that the Croatans lived and farmed "just like white men."[43] On behalf of the Indians, North Carolina senator Simmons, Congressman Hannibal Godwin, and Robeson County Democrat Angus McLean tried to make the committee understand the ways this community forged its identity in the crucible of the segregated South.

When committee members asked why the Indians of Robeson County did not attend white schools, Senator Simmons reminded the committee that, in the state of North Carolina, "we made it a crime to intermix the races in schools."[44] The legislation that initially established segregated schools did not explicitly mention Indians, but according to Simmons, the Indians of Robeson County "utterly refused to attend the colored schools" and held out for a network of their own schools.[45] While segregation was institutionalized by the school system, it went beyond the schools and influenced residential patterns, a theme Simmons also addressed. "This band of Indians," Simmons argued, "is probably more segregated from the white people and the colored people of the section in which they live than the Cherokee band across the mountains." Simmons continued, "[T]hey constitute largely one compact community where they have lived as far back as our history goes. They have not allowed the whites or the blacks to come in. In that sense they have maintained their tribal characteristics of seclusion and sequestration to a very remarkable extent."[46]

In his testimony, Congressman Godwin reminded the committee that the Croatans had no opportunities for higher education beyond their Normal school, unlike the whites and blacks of Robeson who could attended a network of state-funded institutions. The Indians, Godwin argued, could not be blamed for refusing to attend black institutes for higher learning, because in the South education and racial identification were bound together. The purpose of the hearing, in Godwin's estimation, was to determine whether or not the federal government would intervene to equalize educational opportunities for Indians in this section of North Carolina. Finally, Angus McLean, a local Democrat and advocate for the Croatans who followed in the footsteps of his father, Col. N. A. McLean, in supporting the Croatan community, submitted a written statement that outlined the Croatans' claimed descent from the Cherokee and included descriptions of individual Croatans and their "Indian characteristics," such as the ability to recall remnants of an Indian language. Taken as a whole, the testimony before the House committee conceptualized Croatan Indian identity as constituted by both local components and nationally recognized ones—an identity expressed through local structures of segregation but also included national markers, such as a recognizable line of tribal descent.

Halfway through the hearing, committee member Charles Burke, the future head of the Office of Indian Affairs, rendered his opinion about the status of the Indians of Robeson County: "It is my belief that these Indians have no right to enter any Indian school because they are not full-blooded Indians."[47] Even though Simmons assured Burke that members of the community were "full bloods"—Simmons even pointed to a member of the community attending the hearing as an example of a "full blood Indian"—Burke remained unconvinced. He combined all of the Indian characteristics that the committee inquired about—a treaty history with the U.S. government, an Indian language, and property rights—into the singular concept of Indian blood. Other committee members followed suit. When Congressman Godwin asked the committee if they would like to question the Indian representatives who attended the hearing, the committee chair pointed to D. F. Lowry and asked if he was a "full blood."[48] Measuring Indian identity in terms of blood quantum sent a clear message to the Indians of Robeson County: the federal government chose the indices of Indianess and was not interested in an alternative, locally inflected version of Indian identity, especially at a time when Indian policies were directed at assimilating, rather than recognizing, Indian tribes.

Community leaders returned to Robeson County to await the official word on their pending legislation. In the meantime, on 11 March 1913, the General Assembly of North Carolina passed an act "to restore the Indians residing in Robeson and adjoining counties to their rightful and

ancient name . . . the Cherokee Indians of Robeson County." Perhaps
inspired by this local victory, a delegation from the community returned
to Washington, D.C., to inquire about the fate of their school legislation.
The Office of Indians Affairs finally decided that another investigation
into the "status and conditions of the Indians of Robeson and adjoining
counties" was necessary to determine "whether the Government would
be warranted in making suitable provisions for their support and education."[49] A new federal official, O. M. McPherson, arrived in Robeson
and, after the most extensive investigation to date, he reached two conclusions: the Indians of Robeson desperately needed additional funds for
their education; nevertheless, they should not receive federal funds
because they did not have a history of treaty relations with the United
States. By invoking a history of treaty making over blood quantum in his
evaluation of Croatan identity, McPherson reminded the Croatans that
the federal government could select from several parameters of Indianess
to suit their purposes. The legislation to establish an industrial school
finally died, leaving the community's Normal school as the only institute
of higher learning for the Cherokee Indians of Robeson County.

In the midst of these national setbacks, the Croatan (now Cherokee)
district primary schools continued to improve, maintaining their position below white schools and above black schools in terms of value of
school property and funding per student. In 1915 the county spent
$3.06 per white student, $2.03 per Indian student, and $1.09 per black
student.[50] The average value of white rural school property in Robeson
was $2,303, $352 for Indians, and $287 for blacks. Length of school
term and enrollment percentage remained roughly equivalent for all
three groups, while black schools were once again the most crowded, far
surpassing those for whites and Indians in terms of students per school.[51]
Because of the Croatans' failure to obtain federal funds for their education, community leaders surely realized the importance of maintaining
their Indian identity on the state level, and in 1915 a key aspect of
Croatan identity—the boundary between themselves and the black community—was threatened by the issue of school admissions.

SCHOOL ADMISSIONS AND RACIAL PEDIGREE: *Goins vs. Board of
Trustees of the Indian Normal Training School*, **1915**

On 16 April 1914, the principal of the Normal, H. L. Edens, published
an editorial in the *Robesonian* to explain the "true cause of frequent

contentions among the Indians of Robeson over school matters."[52] In the preceding few years, the issue of admission to Indian schools had frequently tied up meetings of the county board of education, the governing body that ultimately decided which schools the county's children attended. On several different occasions, the board ordered local Indian school committee members to accept children they had rejected or to offer their resignations and grew increasingly frustrated by the time spent on this issue. Public sentiment seemed to mirror the frustrations of the board, and so Preston Locklear, an Indian leader and minister, asked Edens to clarify for the public what was at stake in the issue of school admissions.

"For a number of years," wrote Edens, "mixed blooded people, with little or no Indian blood, living in other counties . . . and being anxious to improve themselves . . . move into Robeson with their families, with the purpose of forcing themselves into the schools for the Indians." Their ultimate goal, argued Edens, was amalgamation by marriage, and these schools were a means to this end. When members of the Indian school committees rejected those with "African origin," they were "fighting not only for their schools . . . but [also] for their churches, their homes, their children, and the perpetuation of their race." Because of the importance of these Indian schools to community identity, Edens argued, the ultimate authority in school admissions should rest with the all-Indian Board of Trustees at the Normal, who were chosen for this position by the county board of education in recognition of their "good judgment and fairness."[53] This suggestion would later be reconsidered by the board of education, but at the time of Edens's editorial, issues of school admissions could go all the way to the North Carolina Supreme Court—and that was what happened in October 1915 in the case of *Goins vs. the Board of Trustees of the Indian Normal Training School.*

Fannie Goins, the woman whose nephews were denied admission to the primary department at the Normal School, moved to Robeson County in 1905. She married Eli Chavis, a Croatan from Robeson County who testified that, before marrying Goins, he "investigated" her "race and nationality" and "learned that she belonged to the Indian race."[54] Although Fannie's new husband was satisfied that she was an Indian, members of the community had questions. When Fannie Chavis attempted to enroll in the Indian Normal School, the board of trustees asked for proof of her Indian "pedigree." Her brother, Walter Goins, traveled back to Sumter County, South Carolina, where the Goins siblings were born and raised, and received papers from L. I. Parott, the clerk of the court for Sumter County. The certificate said, "The families of the Smilings and Goinses of this county have been known as 'Red Bones' [a term used to indicate Indian ancestry] ever since I have been acquainted with the people."[55] Furthermore, like the Croatans, a local white had taken the trouble to "trace up" their origins in order to establish the fact that they were descendents of Indians.[56] Based on this evidence, Fannie Goins was admitted to the Normal, and it was understood that her siblings and her siblings' children would be able to attend the public schools for Indians in the county. Yet, in the eyes of the trustees of the Normal, the acceptance of the Goins family was probationary. As James Dial, a trustee of the Normal later recalled, "we admitted them with the understanding if we got up any more proof . . . we would exclude them."[57] This happened eight years later.

By 1913 Fannie Chavis had graduated from the Normal and was teaching at the Indian public school in the community of Magnolia. Her younger brother, Arthur Goins, was attending the Normal and her two other brothers, Walter and William Goins, had children of school age who were supposedly eligible for local public Indian schools or the primary department at the Normal. All of this changed when Ralph Lowrie, a member of the board of trustees at the Indian Normal, encountered L. I. Parrot at the train station in Pembroke. According to Lowrie, the clerk "stated that during the time he was clerk at Sumpter, South Carolina, he signed a paper for some Goinses to come over here to a school . . . he didn't know very much about the Goinses. He said one thing he did know was that Walter Goins' uncle was a Negro preacher."[58] Apparently, Lowrie made an effort to investigate this claim and met Walter Goins, the father of the Goins siblings. "From his physical appearance and my knowledge of these Indian people," Lowrie recalled, "in my opinion from his looks and appearance he is of the Negro race."[59] This was considered sufficient evidence to dismiss the Goinses and their children from the Indian school system.

The Goinses fought back and took their case to the North Carolina Superior Court. The defendants, the board of trustees of the Normal, contended that the plaintiffs' children were "of Negro blood within the prohibited degree" and that they did not belong to the "that class of persons designated as Croatan Indians . . . under acts establishing said school."[60] On the first issue—who were the intended beneficiaries of "separate schools for the Croatan Indians of Robeson County" provided by the act of 1885—the judge charged the jury that the Normal School did not "embrace alone the Croatan Indians of Robeson County but Croatan Indians who put themselves within the limits of the school in good faith and became residents within the limits that would embrace them though they came from other territory, adjacent territory, or neighboring territory."[61] With this statement, the judge dismissed the idea that one had to be from Robeson County to be a Croatan. Instead, the judge decided that the case hinged on one issue: degree of "Negro" blood. "You start with the child and then its parents and then its grand-parents," explained the judge in his explicit instructions to the jury on how to calculate degree of blood, "and if, after that far back there is no Negro blood . . . then they are entitled to admission into the school."[62]

The jury found in favor of the plaintiffs and ordered them admitted to the Indian schools of Robeson. The board of trustees at the Normal appealed this decision to the Supreme Court of North Carolina. Upon reviewing the testimony from the plaintiffs and defendants, the supreme court reached the conclusion that both parties had agreed on the basic parameters of Indianess in Robeson County. Rather than emphasizing line of tribal descent or specific measurements of Indian blood, the plaintiffs and defendants used a mixture of physical traits and reputation or associations, coupled with enrollment in churches and schools recognized as Indian, to determine who was an Indian.[63] With the burden of proof on the defendants, it was for the court to decide who had the more persuasive testimony.

"We have never associated with the Negroes in our immediate family; never have in my remembrance," testified Willie Goins. "We always stood aloof from them. There are them that do such but we pulled out from that class of people that associated with darkies. There is no Negro blood in me nor my family that I have ever read of or heard of."[64] Despite Goins's contention that his family "always stood aloof" from the black community, by arguing that his family "pulled out" from those who associated with "the darkies," he implicitly admitted that his family did have ties to the black community at one time. Goins's brother went on to describe the particular moment when his family chose to separate themselves from their extended community: it was when their church hired a "Negro preacher" that they "pulled out and built a church separately."[65] In fact, that church joined the Burnt Swamp Baptist Association of Robeson County, and before they were admitted, a church committee "made an investigation" and were satisfied with the background of the church members. Willie Goins also testified that "we had a separate school for our people," but "there was such a few of us" that maintaining the school and church became impossible, and so the Goins family moved to Robeson County.[66]

While the Goins family members adamantly denied that they had associated with the black population of Sumpter County, the details of their Indian ancestry were vague. Even Willie Goins admitted, "We belong to the Indian race of people *if any* to my knowledge."[67] Their mother, Emma Goins, sought to explain the Indian ancestry of their family by testifying that her mother was "reputed to have Indian blood in her veins" and "coal black" hair, while her grandmother's "hair was coal black and long; she could sit on it," her skin was "bright brown," and she had a reputation that she belonged to the "Indian race."[68] Finally, Goins offered that none of "the ancestors of my children on either side were ever slaves."[69] Pauline Goins, the wife of Walter Goins, also testified "the reputation is that my mother belonged to the Indian people."[70] Several of the Goinses' white neighbors furthered the plaintiffs' claim of having a "reputation" of being Indian or "Red Bones."[71] But again, none of their white neighbors testified as to the tribal descent of the Goins family. As opposed to national ideas that linked the category of Indian to specific tribes and measurements of blood quantum, local conversations about Indianess in this section of North Carolina revolved around the concepts of reputation and associations.

Witnesses for the defendants told a different story. The strategy of the defendants was to establish definitively that the father of the Goins siblings, William Goins Sr., was black. This would prevent his grandchildren from attending Indian schools, as they would have one quarter "Negro blood." Gaston Locklear met William Goins Sr. and concluded, "he is according to the way I look at it . . . of the Negro blood."[72] James Dial, a trustee at the Normal, also met William Goins Sr. and argued, "from the physical appearance of William Goins, in my opinion he does not belong to our race."[73] Finally, H. L. Locklear testified "from my knowledge of the Indian people and appearance of the Negro and appearance of William Goins, I believe he belongs to the colored race."[74] After the "Negro blood" of William Goins Sr. was established, the defendants also called the white neighbors of the Goinses in South Carolina, who testified that they had never heard the Goinses classified as Indians, or, for that matter, that there were any Indians at all in Sumpter County.

To be Indian, the defendants suggested, was to be recognized as such by your white neighbors.

Finally, witnesses for the defense described why the Goinses should be considered black. Gaston Locklear had conducted his own investigation in Sumter County and found that "the general reputation was that they were colored people."[75] Locklear's brother-in-law, Chesley Jones, lived in Georgia for three years, worked at turpentine mills with the two Goins brothers, and said that the reputation of Willie Goins was that "he went with the darkies" and "lived with a colored woman."[76] Here were the three aspects of their refusal to acknowledge the Goinses as Indians: definitive statements that a family member was black, no recognition by local whites of their Indianess, and finally, "associations" with the black community.

When the decision was rendered in fall of 1915, the supreme court supported the previous decision, and the appeal was denied. The Goins family was allowed access to the Indian schools of Robeson County. And yet, although the Goinses had fought for this victory, they did not enroll in Croatan schools, choosing instead to form their own church and school. While the Goinses' church and school were categorized as Indian, the Cherokees of Robeson remained aloof from them, and this community eventually took their own name: the Smilings or Independent Indians. Segregation in Robeson County now had a fourth tier.

## CONCLUSION

In the first two decades of the twentieth century, the Indian schools of Robeson County, North Carolina, became active sites of identity formation for the Croatan Indians. This school system was the particular location from which community leaders linked the Croatans to the Democratic Party, launched their campaign for federal education funding and recognition, and drew the racial boundary between the Croatans and the black community. While these schools played an important role in refining Croatan identity, they also can be understood and related to the experiences of other marginalized communities because they represent what scholar Evelyn Nakano Glenn calls "points of slippage between national and local and within the local" that create "opportunities for maneuvering and negotiation, and thus for significant agency on the part of both dominant and subordinate groups."[77]

As a state-recognized tribe, the Croatan Indians were not subject to the regime of assimilation that characterized federal Indian education policies in this era.[78] While children from federally recognized tribes were being sent off to boarding schools to be taught a set of skills that would ostensibly further their integration into society, Croatan children, like their white and black neighbors, attended public schools, albeit schools segregated by race. The discrepancy between national policies for Indian education and North Carolina's support of Croatan Indian schools is therefore a point of slippage between the national and the local. North Carolina's policies toward the Croatans can be understood as a local slippage point because the state did not have a specific agenda when it came to Indian education. That is, while North Carolina had an uneasy relationship with black public schools—many whites felt that their tax money should not support "Negro schools" and the black population should only be taught agricultural skills—the Indian schools of Robeson County were essentially a blank slate. Black schools, underfunded and overcrowded, were institutions that reflected systematic discrimination, but Croatan Indian schools were open spaces; this allowed for significant agency on the part of Indian leaders, who fought to make these schools the middle rung in Robeson's three tiers of segregation. Even when the Indian schools ranked below black schools in terms of funding and overall conditions, Indian leaders worked to convince their community that these were institutions of *distinction* rather than *discrimination*. Located at a slippage point between the national and the local and within the local, the Indian schools of Robeson County offered the Croatans a unique opportunity: the chance to take control of their educational system and to shape expressions and representations of their Indian identity.

## NOTES

1. The Croatan Indians were a state-recognized Indian community concentrated in Robeson County, North Carolina. Although the Croatans did not have a treaty history with the U.S. government, the community caught the attention of government officials through its active campaign for federal recognition. In 1956 the Croatans achieved federal recognition and were designated as the Lumbee Indians; however, a vocal minority identifies itself as Tuscarora. Studies of the evolving identity of this community include Karen I. Blu, *The Lumbee Problem: The Making of an American Indian People* (New York: Cambridge University Press, 1980); Gerald Sider, *Living Indian Histories: Lumbee and Tuscarora People in North Carolina* (Chapel Hill: University of North Carolina Press, 2003);

Christopher Arris Oakley, *Keeping the Circle: American Indian Identity in Eastern North Carolina, 1885–2004* (Lincoln: University of Nebraska Press, 2005).

2. Burnt Swamp Baptist Association, *Minutes of the Annual Session of the Burnt Swamp Baptist Association* (Raleigh, NC: Edwards and Broughton & Co, 1897), 7.

3. In the 1870s, churches became the first institutions to separate Indians from blacks. See Jospeh Michael Smith and Lula Jane Smith, *The Lumbee Methodists: Getting to Know Them* (Raleigh, NC, Commission of Archives and History, NC Methodist Conference, 1990).

4. The Democrats' support for Croatan education can be traced back to 1885, when a local Robeson Democrat, Hamilton McMillan, sponsored the legislation for separate schools and recognition of the Croatan Indians in 1885 and the creation of the Normal school in 1887.

5. Burnt Swamp Baptist Association, *Proceedings of the Annual Session of the Burnt Swamp Baptist Association* (Lumberton, NC: Robesonian Printing House, 1910), 10.

6. H. Leon Prather, *Resurgent Politics and Educational Progressivism in the New South, North Carolina 1890–1913* (Rutherford, NJ: Fairleigh Dickinson University Press, 1979), 9.

7. North Carolina, Department of Public Instruction, *Biennial Report of the State Superintendent of Public Instruction of North Carolina for the Scholastic Years 1898–99 to 1889–1900* (Raleigh, NC: Edwards & Broughton and E.M. Uzzell, State Printers, 1900), 155, 286, 288.

8. Prather, 40.

9. *Biennial Report, 1898–1900*, 155, 278, 279.

10. Ibid., 140.

11. In the elections of 1894 and 1896, the coalition of poor, white Populists and black Republicans captured the governorship, general assembly, and local offices in what became known as "fusion rule." Democrats were so incensed by fusion victories that their 1898 campaign was marked by racist appeals and threats of violence. After winning the 1898 election by fraud and intimidation, the Democrats in Wilmington, North Carolina—frustrated that municipal offices were not up for election and remained in the hands of Fusionists—stormed through the city, armed with guns and torches. A race riot ensued. See David S. Cecelski and Timothy B. Tyson, eds. *Democracy Betrayed: The Wilmington Race Riot of 1898 and Its Legacy* (Chapel Hill: University of North Carolina Press, 1998) and Glenda Elizabeth Gilmore, *Gender and Jim Crow: Women and the Politics of White Supremacy in North Carolina, 1896-1920* (Chapel Hill: University of North Carolina Press, 1996).

12. John D. Bellamy, *Memoirs of an Octogenarian* (Charlotte, NC: Observer Printing House, 1942), 134.

13. Ibid., 135.

14. Ibid., 135. It is impossible to confirm if the Croatans voted for Bellamy in such numbers, because the vote was not broken down by race.

15. John D. Bellamy, *Remarks of Hon. John D. Bellamy of North Carolina, in the House of Representatives, Thursday, February 1, 1900* (Washington, DC: GPO, 1900).

16. According to Bellamy, his speech was "copied in almost every newspaper in the United States." Bellamy, *Memoirs*, 127.

17. "The White Supremacy Club," *Robesonian*, 22 June 1900.

18. T. C. Henderson, "A Card from Prof. Henderson," *Robesonian*, 3 July 1900.

19. W. H. Humphrey, "A Card," *Robesonian*, 26 June 1900.

20. O. R. Sampson, "Strong Argument for the Amendment," *Robesonian*, 17 July 1900.

21. A. N. Locklear, "Another Croatan for the Amendment," *Robesonian*, 27 July 1900.

22. *Robesonian*, 26 June 1900.

23. Prather, *Resurgent Politics and Educational Progressivism in the New South*,194.

24. Charles Aycock, as quoted in Edgar W. Knight, *Public Education in North Carolina* (Boston, New York: Houghton Mifflin, 1916), 332–33.

25. North Carolina, Department of Public Instruction, *Biennial Report of the State Superintendent of Public Instruction of North Carolina for the Scholastic Years 1904–1905 to 1905-1906* (Raleigh, NC: Ashe & Gatling, 1907), 34.

26. Robeson County, North Carolina, Minutes of the Board of Education, *Statistical Report 1906–1907*(Raleigh, NC: State Archives).

27. Burnt Swamp Baptist Association, *Proceedings of the Annual Session of the Burnt Swamp Baptist Association* (Lumberton, NC: Robesonian Printing House, 1906), 6.

28. Burnt Swamp Baptist Association, *Proceedings of the Annual Session of the Burnt Swamp Baptist Association* (Lumberton, NC: Robesonian Printing House, 1910), 10.

29. A. N. Locklear, "The MACS of Robeson," *Robesonian*, 6 August 1908.

30. "A Great Day," *Robesonian*, 15 November 1909.

31. Robeson County, North Carolina, Minutes of the Board of Education, *Statistical Report 1911–1912* (Raleigh, NC: State Archives). Value of schoolhouses is for rural schools.

32. See Robeson County, North Carolina, Minutes of the Board of Education. *Apportionment of School Funds for January 1911*. (Raleigh, NC: State Archives), and North Carolina, Department of Public Instruction, *Biennial Report of the Superintendent of Public Instruction of North Carolina to Governor W.W. Kitchin for the Scholastic Years 1910–1911 to 1911–1912* (Raleigh, NC: Edwards and Broughton Printing, 1913), 41.

33. "Indian Tribal Names: Croatans of Robeson Seek to Change Name to Cherokee: Most Unique Committee Hearing in Recent Years," *Robesonian*, 6 February 1911.

34. "Educational Rally: Annual Gathering of Indians at Pembroke: State Supt. Joyner Speaker of the Occasion," *Robesonian*, 24 October 1910.

35. A. S. Locklear, "A Protest," *Robesonian*, 14 February 1910.

36. "Indian Tribal Names: Croatans of Robeson Seek to Change Name to Chero-
    kee," 6 February 1911. In January of 1910, Representative Hannibal Godwin
    proposed legislation to the house of representatives to change the name of the
    Croatans to Cherokee. The bill did not pass; community leaders may have then
    shifted their focus to state recognition as Cherokee.

37. Although Industrial education was designed for the black population in this era,
    the Croatans viewed the establishment of an Industrial school as an opportunity
    to equalize their educational opportunities. As their congressional representa-
    tive, Hannibal Godwin testified, "The colored and the white races have far the
    advantage over the Indians because the whites in North Carolina have their col-
    leges; agricultural and mechanical colleges and academic institutions, through-
    out the State, and so do the colored people . . . but the Indians have no colleges."
    U.S. Congress. House. Committee on Indian Affairs. *Hearings before the Com-
    mittee on Indian Affairs House of Representatives on S.3258 to Acquire a Site and
    Erect Buildings for a School for the Indians of Robeson County, N.C., and for Other
    Purposes, February 14, 1913* (Washington, DC: Government Printing Office,
    1913), 6. Hereafter cited as Hearing. For the link between the black population
    and Industrial education in North Carolina, see Gilmore, *Gender and Jim Crow.*

38. Charles Pierce, "The Croatan Indians of North Carolina," *Indian School Journal*
    13 (March 1913): 305.

39. Ibid., 303.

40. Ibid., 305.

41. Ibid., 306.

42. Hearing, 12.

43. Ibid., 6.

44. Ibid., 10.

45. Ibid., 10.

46. Ibid., 16.

47. Ibid., 19.

48. Ibid., 25.

49. O. M. McPherson, *Indians of North Carolina: Letter from the Secretary of the Inte-
    rior Transmitting in Response to a Senate Resolution of June 30, 1914. A Report on
    the Condition and Tribal Rights of the Indians of Robeson and Adjoining Counties
    of North Carolina* (Washington, DC: GPO, 1915), 7.

50. See North Carolina, Department of Public Instruction, *Biennial Report of the
    Superintendent of Public Instruction of North Carolina for the Scholastic Years
    1914–1915 and 1915–1916* (Raleigh, NC: Edwards &Broughton State Print-
    ers, 1917), 228; Robeson County, North Carolina, *Minutes of the Board of Edu-
    cation, Apportionment for the School Year 1915–1916, from General School Fund*
    (Raleigh, NC: State Archives), 249.

51. Robeson County, North Carolina. Minutes of the Board of Education. *Statisti-
    cal Report, 1915–1916* (Raleigh: State Archives).

52. H. L. Edens, "Indian Race Problems: True Cause of frequent Contentions among
    Indians of Robeson over Indians' School Matters: Fighting Amalgamation:

Eternal Vigilance Price of Racial Preservation: A Suggestion," *Robesonian*, 16 April 1914.

53. Ibid.

54. A. A. *Goins, W. W. Goins and W. D. Goins vs. the Board of Trustees of the Indian Normal Training School at Pembroke, North Carolina*, Transcript of Trial, No. 296 (North Carolina Supreme Court, Fall Term, 1915) (collection of North Carolina Department of History and Archives, Raleigh, NC, Supreme Court Records), 27. Hereafter cited as Case transcript.

55. Ibid., 55.

56. Ibid., 24.

57. Ibid., 35.

58. Ibid., 34.

59. Ibid.

60. Ibid., 1.

61. Ibid., 2.

62. Ibid., 44.

63. The concepts of reputation and association were used frequently in court cases involving the determination of racial identity. See Peter Wallenstein, *Tell the Court I Love my Wife: Race, Marriage, and Law—an American History* (New York: Palgrave Macmillan, 2002), and Ariela Gross, "Litigating Whiteness: Trails of Racial Determination in the Nineteenth-Century South," *The Yale Law Review Journal* 105, no. 1: 109–88.

64. Case transcript, 23.

65. Ibid., 24.

66. Ibid., 23.

67. Ibid., 23. Emphasis mine.

68. Ibid., 25.

69. Ibid.

70. Ibid., 27.

71. Ibid., 28.

72. Ibid., 33.

73. Ibid., 35.

74. Ibid., 36.

75. Ibid., 32.

76. Ibid., 36.

77. Evelyn Nakano Glenn, *Unequal Freedom: How Race and Gender Shaped American Citizenship and Labor* (Cambridge, MA: Harvard University Press, 2002), 5.

78. For Indian education and assimilation, see David Wallace Adams, *Education for Extinction: American Indians and the Boarding School Experience, 1875–1928* (Lawrence, KS: University Press of Kansas, 1995), and M. C. Coleman, *American Indian Children at School, 1850–1930* (Jackson, MS: University Press of Mississippi, 1993).

# CHAPTER 4

# SEARCHING FOR AMERICA: A JAPANESE AMERICAN'S QUEST, 1900–1930

## EILEEN H. TAMURA[1]

What is there for us to be ashamed of being a Jap? To be born a Jap is the greatest blessing God has bestowed on us . . . [T]o die as Jap under the protection of the Japanese Flag which has weathered through many national storms without a defeat for 2600 years is the greatest honor a man can ever hope to cherish. I, in the name of the Niseis [second-generation Japanese Americans] proclaim ourselves Japs, 100 per cent Japs, now, tomorrow, and forever.

Tenno Hei Ka Banzai! Banzai! Banzai!
Dai Nippon Teikoku Banzai! Banzai! Banzai!
Zai Ryu Dobo Banzai! Banzai! Banzai![2]

SUCH WERE THE INCENDIARY WORDS OF THE NISEI JOSEPH YOSHISUKE Kurihara, World War I veteran and leading dissident at Manzanar, one of ten U. S. Relocation Centers in which West Coast Nikkei—ethnic Japanese—were forced to live during World War II.[3] Kurihara's fighting words, proclaimed in 1943, reflected his stance during the war and contrasted markedly with his attitude and behavior before the war. What had catalyzed his radical change in attitude was the incarceration of law-abiding Nikkei, who were forced to leave their homes and occupations and made to live in isolated camps surrounded by barbed wire. His bitterness increased when he realized that his status as U.S. veteran of the First World War was of no import to the government. Confronting Kurihara was the betrayal of American ideals that he had taken to heart. The intensity of his bitterness and his subsequent rejection of America was a reflection of the intensity of his disillusionment. In 1944, after two years of incarceration during the war, Kurihara renounced his American citizenship, and the following year, at age fifty, boarded a ship bound for Japan, a country he had not previously visited. He never returned to the United States.

Kurihara is the vehicle through which this essay explores the themes of education, identity formation, and marginalization. During the early decades of the twentieth century, Kurihara made a "deliberate, systematic, and sustained effort to . . . acquire knowledge, attitudes, values, [and] skills" that would enable him to live a satisfying life as an American.[4] He charted a path for himself, enrolling in schools that he believed would provide quality education within a Western framework, embracing Christianity, enduring anti-Japanese hostility directed at him, and fighting as a soldier in the U. S. Army during World War I. This dogged pursuit in making a place for himself as an American enabled him to become conversant in Western modes of thinking and behavior, and as a result, he was able to bridge two worlds, Japanese American and European American.

The notion of Nisei-as-bridge emerged during the 1910s and '20s in the context of anti-Japanese hostility on the U.S. West Coast and in Hawai'i. This hostility resulted in legal barriers demonstrating that the Japanese were unwelcome. The most notable legal blocks were (1) alien land laws in California and other Western states that prohibited Japanese from owning or leasing land, (2) the 1922 U.S. Supreme Court decision in *Ozawa v. the United States* that denied naturalization rights to Japanese immigrants, and (3) the 1924 immigration law that closed the doors to further Japanese migration to the United States.[5] Although the 1924 law barred all Asians, it targeted the Japanese because other Asians had already been essentially excluded by earlier laws.[6]

In the scholarly literature on Japanese Americans, a few studies examine the biculturalism of the Nisei,[7] and some studies discuss the role of the Nisei as bridges, a role made possible by their bicultural identities. The notion of Nisei as bridge was a central theme and a major educational goal that parents had for their children. This was because Japanese immigrants were forbidden naturalization rights, while their children were U.S. citizens because of their place of birth.[8]

The bridge idea encompassed two overlapping aspects. One emphasized internationalism, placing the Nisei in the role of intermediaries between the countries of Japan and the United States. With this in mind, immigrant parents in the 1930s encouraged their American-born children to relocate to Japan to live and study there.[9] The other aspect saw the Nisei who never set foot on Japanese soil as nevertheless having dual identities and Japanese immigrants thus encouraged their children to embody the best of Japanese and American cultures.

Kurihara personified this second aspect. In his search for America, Kurihara did not reject his ethnic community but sought to be part of it at the same time that he would be part of the larger community. In this sense he would serve as a bridge of understanding between the two societies.[10] As his personal journey illustrates, however, despite the grand rhetoric of embracing two different worlds, the path was often rocky and difficult to navigate. His experiences bring to life the personal dimension of the struggles of a young man as he attempted to straddle the gulf separating two sociocultural worlds.[11]

## EARLY SCHOOLING

Kurihara was born in Hawai'i in 1895. This was two years after the overthrow of the Hawaiian monarchy and three years before the U.S. government annexed the islands.[12] His father, Kichizo Kurihara, was among the many farmers in southwestern Japan who had been hit hard by the economic transformations brought about by the Meiji government.[13] Like many others from Yamaguchi prefecture, he responded positively to the call for plantation workers. He and his wife Haru arrived in Hawai'i in the late 1880s.[14]

They were among the first wave of migrant workers from Japan. A few women like Haru accompanied their husbands, but the overwhelming majority were men. During the next twenty years, tens of thousands more from Japan, most of them male, would follow this first group.[15]

In Lihue Plantation on the island of Kaua'i, Kichizo Kurihara performed backbreaking labor for ten to twelve hours a day under the scorching sun, amid dusty air, razor-sharp cane leaves, and buzzing wasps and yellow jackets.[16] He worked alongside other Japanese as well as Chinese, Native Hawaiians, South Pacific Islanders, Portuguese, and a few Spaniards. Germans, too, worked for the Lihue Plantation, not as field laborers, but as more highly paid skilled workers and field foremen.[17] The couple lived in a Japanese camp that was segregated from laborers of other ethnic groups. This was a common practice on the sugar plantations. They slept in a simple room with other laborers in a barrack that the plantation provided. They had no kitchen facilities and little privacy.[18]

After three years and with a growing family, Kurihara's father left the plantation. In 1897, when Kurihara was two years old, his family moved to Honolulu—the seat of government of the Republic of Hawaii and the urban center of the island of Oahu.[19] A year later the United States annexed the Hawaiian Islands and in 1900 incorporated them into the union as a territory. When the Kurihara family relocated to Honolulu, it was a bustling little city of 29,000 inhabitants, holding almost a third of the population of the island chain.[20]

The family rented a simply constructed wooden cottage, one of many clustered together in the Palama district of the city. The Kurihara home was surrounded by homes of other struggling, working-class families. People cooked on wood-burning stoves and filled their lamps with kerosene.[21] Ox carts and horse carriages traveled the unpaved dirt roads, which sloshed with mud during and after heavy rains.[22]

In 1900, an out-of-control Chinatown fire that had been set to eradicate bubonic plague—part of a worldwide pandemic that had hit the city—left five thousand low-income people without their businesses and homes. Their subsequent relocation into the Palama district caused overcrowded conditions and water, sewer, and sanitation problems.[23]

Despite this setback, Palama maintained a vibrancy all its own. During the first decade of the twentieth century, the district—a mile from busy Honolulu Harbor, which accommodated increased shipping of raw sugar to mainland markets—offered a rich amalgam of rural and urban life. It included small businesses, family-owned shops, wooden cottages, tenement houses, and acres of sugar cane.[24]

Kurihara's father worked as a hack driver, one of many drivers of horse-drawn cabs that transported passengers to their destinations.[25] After a few years he became a drayman, an independent businessman who transported heavy loads.[26] A few years later he opened a new business as a contractor for stone wall and cement work.[27]

Kurihara's family, like many other immigrant families in Honolulu, sent their children to public grammar school. For Kurihara, this meant Kaiulani School, which was less than a mile away from his home. The school was named after the heir apparent to the Hawaiian kingdom, Princess Kaiulani, who died in 1899, the year the school opened. With 407 students enrolled in its first year, the school helped to ease the overcrowding of other Honolulu schools.[28]

Kaiulani School was an attractive two-story brick and stucco structure with large windows. This solid, contemporary-styled school building, like others constructed in the islands at the turn of the twentieth century, helped to demonstrate that Hawai'i was no backward way station but, on the contrary, was in step with the United States.[29] Such evidence supported the efforts of the Republic's European American political and business leaders, who had orchestrated the overthrow of the Hawaiian monarchy and subsequently pushed to achieve annexation and then territorial status for the archipelago.[30] As part of their attempt to show that Hawai'i was Americanized, political leaders of the republic had also enacted a law that made it compulsory for children six to fifteen years of age to attend either public or private schools. This law also provided for free public schooling and authorized the Department of Public Instruction to furnish all books at cost.[31]

The efforts of the republic's leaders saw fruition when Congress passed a joint resolution, signed by President William McKinley in 1898, that annexed the islands. The resolution authorized the creation of a commission that would make recommendations and draft an Organic Act. In its report, the commission concluded that the school system already in place was "very satisfactory" and "peculiarly American," and recommended that it "remain in force."[32] Congress heeded this advice and as a result the Organic Act, which in 1900 became the fundamental law of the territory, made few references to education.[33] In 1905, when the Hawai'i territorial legislature passed a set of school laws, it kept the essential features of the public school system established by the Republic of Hawaii.[34] It was in this setting that Kurihara began his schooling.

When his first day of school arrived, on a September morning in 1903, eight-year-old Kurihara walked barefoot to Kaiulani School.[35] That year the school was one of nineteen public grammar schools in a city of 39,000 inhabitants. There was also one public high school and thirteen private schools.[36]

Like his classmates, many of whom were also children of immigrants, Kurihara was an American citizen because of his place of birth. In many ways, however, he and other Asian Americans were treated as non-Americans or as "new" Americans. In the first half of the twentieth century, the word "American" referred to European American. The territory's public school reports, for example, included teachers' names and their "nationality." The term American was reserved for European Americans, while Asian Americans were designated as Japanese or Chinese.[37]

As a first-grader, Kurihara shared his teacher with forty other students. By today's standards, such a student-teacher ratio would be considered abysmal. But Kurihara was more fortunate than his peers in other densely-populated urban neighborhoods who sat in classrooms with as many as sixty students.[38] By the time Kurihara reached the eighth grade in 1910, overcrowding had become an even greater problem, with some classrooms in urban Honolulu having as many as fifty to eighty students in a room.[39] Kaiulani School's student body, which grew from 569 to 952 during the first decade of the twentieth century, reflected this increase in the number children attending school.[40]

Kurihara's teachers were white and female, which was the norm in the territory's public schools. His classmates were predominantly Native Hawaiian and Chinese, and some Japanese students. This reflected the ethnic breakdown of this urban school's student body and of the surrounding neighborhood.[41] While the particular proportions among ethnic groups varied from school to school, the predominant groups enrolled in the territory's schools during the first two decades of the twentieth century were, in order of numerical size, Japanese, Native Hawaiians, Portuguese, and Chinese. As this indicates, Japanese immigrants and their children constituted the largest ethnic group in the islands during this period; they lived primarily in rural areas, in or near the sugar plantations. Other groups, including Caucasians—as distinguished from the Portuguese who were recruited for plantation work—were also enrolled, although in fewer numbers.[42]

This new American territory included a unique combination of ethnic groups, but ethnic diversity in schools in the country's major cities was not unusual during this period. In 1908, 72 percent of all students in New York City schools were immigrants or children of immigrants; the percentages in other cities were also high: 67 percent in Chicago, 64 percent in Boston, 60 percent in Cleveland, and 58 percent in San Francisco.[43] In matters of curriculum, too, Hawai'i's public schools reflected national trends. During each of his grammar school years, Kurihara's course of study included language use, arithmetic, nature study, geography, physiology and hygiene, reading, writing, manual work, calisthenics, and music. In his fifth through eighth grade years, history was also part of the curriculum.[44] In addition to schoolwork, Kurihara and his classmates enjoyed playing together at recess and after school, and on occasion indulging in small treats. One former Kaiulani School student recalled how she savored the buttered roll and soda that she sometimes bought for lunch for ten cents at a bakery near the school.[45]

When Kurihara was sixteen years old, he completed the eighth-grade at Kaiulani School. He likely spent the next two years working in order to continue his schooling. Then in September 1913 he entered the Catholic all-male St. Francis School; tuition was a dollar per month.[46] In his autobiographical essay, Kurihara does not explain why he decided to enroll in a private school that required tuition. McKinley High School, the only public high school on the island at the time, was noted for its high academic standards and was accessible by trolley car. It is likely that Kurihara was by then attracted to Catholicism.

Situated near his home at the corner of College Walk and Kukui Street, St. Francis was connected to St. Louis College, a high school run by the Brothers of Mary and known to give its students a sound education.[47] Brother Henry served as principal of the two schools, which sat side by side.[48] In his class of forty-six students, Kurihara was the only one of Japanese descent, but there were many other Asian Americans, namely Chinese Americans, who constituted 44 percent of his classmates, while 37 percent were European Americans and 17 percent were Native Hawaiians.[49] The Chinese had arrived a generation earlier than the Japanese and were more open to Christianity.

This ethnic makeup of Kurihara's class reflected the student body of the school and its senior school, St. Louis College. In 1913–14, for example, only 9 of the 726 males who were enrolled at the two schools were ethnic Japanese.[50] Father Reginald Yzendoorn, in his history of the Catholic mission in the islands, noted the relatively few ethnic Japanese students at Catholic schools in the first two decades of the twentieth century, in contrast to the more numerous ethnic Chinese students. As more Japanese American children reached school age in the 1920s and '30s, however, their numbers in Catholic schools grew, and some of them converted to Catholicism. Nevertheless, those attending Catholic schools remained a small minority of Japanese American students.[51]

Thus, Kurihara was an anomaly. He was the only one in his family of Buddhists to attend a Catholic school, and after moving to San Francisco, he "embraced" Catholicism.[52] These actions reflected his push to adopt Western ways.

Kurihara left St. Francis School in March 1914.[53] By then he had decided to become a doctor and continue his schooling on the U.S. West Coast. Knowing that his family could not support his educational aspirations, Kurihara worked for a year in road construction in South Kona, on the island of Hawai'i, in "probably the most uninhabited section of the island."[54] When he had earned enough money for transportation to and resettlement in California, he quit this job.

### SCHOOLING IN SAN FRANCISCO

In July 1915 Kurihara left for an eight-day journey to San Francisco aboard the steamship *Sierra*, one of several ships of the Oceanic Steamship Company of San Francisco and one among many that serviced the busy seaport of Honolulu. With Kurihara were twelve other passengers as well as mail and cargo.[55]

Upon arrival in the Bay area, Kurihara needed a job so that he could "accumulate as much as possible" in order to attend school. Learning that the Sacramento valley farms needed laborers, he went there. He found himself toiling "under the over-bearing heat" alongside other seasonal workers, most of them Nikkei—people of Japanese descent.[56] During the 1910s, farm labor was the type of work most available to the Nikkei, and among the western states, California dominated farming. Many of the employers were Japanese who leased the land. In the Sacramento Delta, where Kurihara worked, Japanese farmers leased 27 percent of the cultivated land, growing onions, beans, asparagus, celery, and deciduous fruits.[57] Once employed there, Kurihara found food plentiful. Although the work was strenuous, he enjoyed his life there because fruit, fish, and game were abundant.[58]

Life in the city of Sacramento, however, was a shock to him. "While walking on K Street . . . a fairly well-dressed person came and kicked me in the stomach for no reason whatever . . . I watched his next move, maneuvering into position to fight it out the best I could."[59] "My nature," he admitted, would "not permit me to let it go unchallenged."[60] The fight would have proceeded, had another man not stepped in to stop it. In another instance, youths threw rocks at him and his Japanese American friend as they were walking down a residential street in Sacramento. "No such thing ever happened where I came from," he noted.[61]

Although he was surprised at such treatment, hostility in the form of stoning, assaults, and vandalism toward the Nikkei was not unusual in California.[62] Kurihara had entered an environment where whites—immigrants and American citizens—had little or no tolerance for people of color. What happened to him in Sacramento reflected the palpable enmity in California and other western states toward the relatively small number of ethnic Chinese and Japanese, whether American citizens like Kurihara or alien residents, who were prohibited from becoming U.S. citizens. Like the Chinese who arrived earlier, the Japanese were needed as laborers for farms, railroads, lumber mills, salmon canneries, and coal and copper mines at the same time that they were despised as outcasts.[63]

In September Kurihara relocated to San Francisco, the "financial and social center of the West," growing rapidly and teeming with merchants, financiers, professionals, small-business people, trades people, laborers, sailors, fishermen, and a host of other workers. The city had recently recovered from the devastation caused by the 1906 earthquake and subsequent inferno that had destroyed 28,000 buildings and left 650 people dead and 400,000 homeless. As proof of its recovery, San Francisco in 1915 marked the inauguration of the Panama Canal by holding the Panama-Pacific International Exposition, which opened just a few months before Kurihara's arrival to the city. Despite war in Europe, the exhibitions welcomed 20 million visitors.[64]

In San Francisco, Kurihara found support among like-minded Nikkei at St. Francis Xavier Japanese Catholic Mission. Located on Buchanan Street, among Japanese businesses and residences in the city, the mission was established two years before Kurihara's arrival. In November 1915, Father Julius von Egloffstein, who administered to the spiritual needs of the small congregation of San Francisco's Japanese Catholics, baptized Kurihara.[65] It is interesting to note that Kurihara did not choose to become a Protestant. In his view, Catholicism was part of mainstream America, in contrast to Buddhism, his family's religion.

Upon baptism, Kurihara took the name Joseph. He was twenty years old.[66] During the early- to mid-twentieth century, changing one's given name was common among children of immigrants, especially as they grew older. This allowed them to fit in more easily and to accommodate

Americans who were unaccustomed to non-English names. In addition, Joseph—which has a similar-sounding first syllable as Yoshisuke—was an appropriate name for a Catholic.

In San Francisco, Kurihara enrolled at the college-preparatory St. Ignatius High School. Established in 1855, this Jesuit school prided itself in its academic rigor, emphasizing the ancient classics of Latin and Greek.[67] Kurihara attended classes in a box-like, utilitarian, and drafty building on Hayes and Shrader Streets. This "temporary" structure—used from 1906 to 1927 and nicknamed "the shirt factory"—was constructed quickly after the devastating earthquake and fire of 1906 demolished the school.[68]

Kurihara lived on Fulton Street in a residential neighborhood several blocks from the school. To pay for his tuition and room and board, he maintained a boiler for the apartment building in which he lived. The pay "was so small . . . [but] I was satisfied because . . . I wanted an education which I was unquestionably getting." In the evenings, he cut firewood for the boiler, and on weekends, he swept the building's hallways, polished the brass work, and scrubbed the back stairs.[69]

Kurihara's teachers were priests, brothers, and missionaries, both Italians and Americans.[70] His courses included religion, Latin, English precepts, composition, history, elocution, science, and mathematics. His academic grades compared favorably with those of his classmates: they were good but not spectacular. Conversely, his "conduct" grade was outstanding; he was the only student in his first- and second-year classes who received 100 every month. This meant that he exhibited the school's virtues of gentlemanly behavior, punctuality, "strict obedience," and "blameless conduct." This reflected his strong desire to do what he thought was right.[71]

Enrollment at St. Ignatius High School during the second decade of the twentieth century ranged from 140 to 250 students. As in the 1800s, during the first decades of the twentieth century, students were predominantly white. In 1915–16, when Kurihara was a first-year student at the school, he was the only nonwhite in his section. There was a black student in the other section of his class, but the rest of the 188 students enrolled in the school were white. In the following school year, Kurihara was the only nonwhite among the 186 students enrolled.[72]

On the one hand, this was a far cry from the ethnic diversity in his former schools in Hawai'i. On the other hand, the fact that St. Ignatius admitted Asian Americans was noteworthy in a city that maintained a segregated public school for Chinese, to which the school board had attempted, although unsuccessfully, to direct Japanese youths.[73] White reaction against the Japanese, and the Chinese before them, was well out of proportion to their numbers. During the first two decades of the twentieth century, the Chinese population decreased from 2.5 to 1.5 percent, while the Japanese constituted 1.1 percent of San Francisco's residents.[74] Unlike the Chinese, who were concentrated in the city's Chinatown area, the Japanese maintained their shops and homes in small Japanese communities scattered in various parts of the city.[75]

As in Sacramento, the "atmosphere" in San Francisco could be unpleasant. During the two years he lived in the city, he had to endure "the distasteful word, 'Jap.'" Kurihara's sojourn in California occurred during a period of rabid anti-Japanese agitation. Led by San Francisco mayor James D. Phelan, labor unions, and the Asiatic Exclusion League, white Californians pushed for barring Japanese from entering the United States. Although unsuccessful in that endeavor, they were able to convince the California legislature to pass an alien land law in 1913 that was aimed at the Japanese, who were gaining a foothold in farming. The law prohibited "aliens ineligible for citizenship"—a phrase referring to Japanese immigrants, who were prohibited from naturalizing as U.S. citizens—from owning land and limited their leasing of land to three years. More stringent amendments were added in 1920 and 1923.[76]

## FROM SOLDIER TO UNIVERSITY STUDENT TO SMALL BUSINESSMAN

Given this environment, it is not surprising that Kurihara responded favorably to the idea of relocating to Michigan to continue his schooling. His friend persuaded him to move, convincing him that people there would be friendlier and kinder than they were in California. In June 1917, the two young men took a train to Chicago and upon their arrival saw a "Japanese boy . . . walking down the street with an American girl, arm in arm." Kurihara's friend exclaimed, "See what I told You? They don't discriminate . . . out here."[77]

Among the jobs open to them were dishwashing in Milwaukee and houseboy service in Minnesota. They chose instead to work as bellhops at Mt. Clemens Mineral Springs because of its relative proximity to the University of Michigan at Ann Arbor, where they intended to enroll that fall. While at Mt. Clemens, however, Kurihara "was seized with an intense desire to join the army."[78] The United States had entered the

Great World War in April 1917, and Congress a month later had passed the Selective Service Act. Kurihara decided that he would not wait to be drafted but instead enlist in the army. He later recalled that as a youth attending Japanese language school, he took to heart the notion of *koku on*, which he interpreted to mean "to be true to the country [the United States] to which [he owed his] living."[79] Here was an instance in which he was expected by the older generation to integrate a cultural notion from Japan into the American context.

After training for eight months at Camp Custer, Michigan, Kurihara was sent to France with the 85th Division, where he experienced the grueling life of a wartime soldier. After the war he served with the U.S. occupation forces in Germany.[80]

Upon his discharge, Kurihara moved to Los Angeles to continue his schooling. At this point, he decided to pursue a career in business instead of medicine. In 1920 he began taking bookkeeping courses at California Commercial College, so that he could work as a bookkeeper while continuing his education at a university.[81]

By 1920 Los Angeles had become a port city of well over half a million residents, primarily European Americans and European immigrants. The Nikkei constituted only 2 percent of the population. There were some Chinese and larger numbers of Mexican Americans and African Americans, but together nonwhites were only 9 percent of the city's inhabitants.[82] What was called "Little Tokyo" in downtown Los Angeles was an economically depressed area that included Japanese shops and small businesses, Buddhist temples, and residences. The Nikkei, who constituted 18 percent of the residents in Little Tokyo, lived in rental buildings and rooming houses among Mexicans and Mexican Americans, blacks, and foreign-born whites.[83] Kurihara lived on South Flower Street, not far from City Hall and about two miles away from Little Tokyo. Surrounding the apartment building in which he lived were numerous other apartment buildings, small hotels, and stores.[84]

The Nikkei in the Los Angeles area were able to survive, and some of them even prospered, by specializing in economic enterprises that others ignored or rejected—catching fish and abalone, and practicing labor-intensive farming that required less land. They cultivated fruits, vegetables, and flowers and created a distribution system to market these crops. More specifically, they dominated the growing of celery, peas, beans, cauliflower, and berries, selling the produce to Nikkei wholesalers who distributed the products to Nikkei retailers, who sold them at their numerous fruit and vegetable stands.[85]

Their success in these endeavors bred resentment; despite the fact that Japan had been an ally of the United States in the Great War, anti-Japanese sentiment in Los Angeles was unmistakable. Kurihara arrived in Los Angeles during a successful campaign to amend the California alien land law by placing further obstacles for Japanese farmers. A 1920 amendment forbade Japanese immigrants from leasing and corporations from owning agricultural land, and a 1923 amendment prohibited Japanese from sharecropping. Like other American citizens of Japanese ancestry, Kurihara and his friends helped immigrant farmers circumvent the law by having the leases placed under their names.[86]

In this racial climate, Kurihara was subjected to disagreeable encounters. "[M]any times I was turned out of restaurants catering to customers of the working class. . . . Practically in all of these restaurants . . . there [was] a sign reading, 'We reserve the right to refuse service to anyone.' Such things," he declared, "must not be allowed if America is to be the Democratic standard bearer of the world." In another instance, in an "electric train" heading southward to San Pedro, he took a seat beside a woman who told him, "I don't want a Jap to [sit] next to me." She moved when he retorted, "Sorry, madam, I paid my fare. If you don't like my looks, why don't you move?" In yet another instance, as he was walking to his bookkeeping class, one of three boys who passed him in the opposite direction spat at him. "Throwing my books down," he later recollected, "I jumped at his throat. He didn't expect such a sudden charge. The force threw him off balance and he fell backward, striking his head on the walk with a thump. He was wiggling and groaning with pain." Kurihara then "picked up [his] books and continued on [his] way." As these instances demonstrate, Kurihara had a fighting spirit, sense of justice, and forthrightness, which twenty-five years later administrators—at World War II camps holding Nikkei—would remark on and admire.[87]

Having completed his course at the commercial college, and taking the advice of his professor there, Kurihara decided to study accounting. He enrolled at Southwestern University while working part-time as a bookkeeper. He pursued his schooling with earnestness, passion, and determination: "Many, many times I went with only two meals a day. To work through school is not an easy task. It requires super-human determination to accomplish one's aim. . . . My body trembled and I experienced fainting spells frequently during those trying days. I saw boys and girls heading for picture shows while I had to stay in and study. I saw people going to a picnic party while I had to work. It really was discouraging at times but I felt and know, to succeed I must deny all pleasures however painful it may be."[88]

Southwestern University, then located on Spring Street, a short distance from Kurihara's residence, offered degrees in law and commerce. From its earliest days in 1911, the school had encouraged women and minorities to enroll.[89] In the 1921–22 academic year, Kurihara's first year at Southwestern's School of Commerce, 510 students were enrolled, of which 30 were women and 10 were Asian Americans.[90]

In addition to courses in accounting, Kurihara took classes in economics, finance, marketing, commercial law, and banking, as well as English, mathematics, and other general subjects. His thesis, "The Farmer and Politics," undoubtedly helped him understand California's anti-Japanese campaign and the rhetoric swirling about him in support of restrictive land laws proposed and enacted during the early 1920s.[91]

The "greatest and the most glorious day of my life," he later recalled, arrived in June 1924 when he received from the university a bachelor's degree in commercial science as well as a certificate of accountancy.[92] Kurihara graduated from Southwestern at a time when it was rare for Japanese Americans to attend a university. This was because most were born after 1910 and therefore not yet of college-age in the 1920s. Furthermore, older children had to work to help support their families. These older siblings often helped younger siblings financially when the latter graduated from high school and entered college. Kurihara was the fourth of five children and did not need to support younger siblings, but he did have to work his way through high school and college.

After graduation from Southwestern, Kurihara worked in a number of jobs in accounting and small business management. These jobs were bounded within the narrow economic sphere that ethnic Japanese were engaged in—food production and distribution. "No job was open to my kind," Kurihara explained years later, "and I had to make my living among the Japanese people the best I could."[93] Like their parents, second-generation Japanese Americans living on the U.S. West Coast during the first four decades of the twentieth century found their job opportunities limited to farming, fishing and other nonfarm labor, domestic service, and work that was related to food distribution. Most other areas of employment were closed to them, even for university graduates.[94]

Nevertheless, during the decade-and-a-half after his graduation from Southwestern University, Kurihara was able to achieve some degree of economic prosperity.[95] That he was able to achieve this relative prosperity was a result, in part, of his effort to negotiate his way outside the Nikkei community. While his work placed him in the heart of Little Tokyo, Kurihara chose to live elsewhere. In this way he kept one foot inside and the other outside the Japanese community.[96] As in San Francisco, where he attended a predominantly white Catholic school, and in Michigan and Europe, where he trained and fought as a soldier in the U.S. Army, in Los Angeles both his matriculation at Southwestern University and his jobs involved interactions with whites—school officials, classmates, business people, government officials, and others.[97] While not of the white world, he was relatively conversant in European American modes of thinking and behavior. This enabled him to bridge the Nikkei world with that of the larger society in which they lived.

Were it not for the events triggered by World War II, Kurihara's life would have continued in the direction that he had earlier set out for himself. At the outbreak of war between the United States and Japan, Kurihara—who was nearing forty-seven years old—had reached moderate economic success, and he would have likely continued to enjoy a reasonably satisfying life in the ensuing years, despite not being fully integrated into mainstream society. But with his wartime incarceration, along with others of Japanese ancestry living on the U.S. West Coast, his attitude made an about-turn. He became a leading dissident at the Manzanar Relocation Center, and as a result, he was labeled an "agitator" and "troublemaker." His patriotism had transformed into disillusionment and bitterness.

## CONCLUSION

Kurihara's attitude and behavior in the decades before World War II contrasted markedly with his perspective during the war, demonstrating the ways in which acts of injustice can completely overturn the movement toward the mainstream and the mind-set of a once-avowedly patriotic person. He had pursued his American education deliberately and systematically, selecting schools for their academic quality and converting to Christianity and more specifically, Catholicism. Especially in those early decades of the twentieth century, Buddhism was considered to be an alien religion, while Christianity was equated with Americanism and civilization.[98]

From his family, schools, and churches he acquired values, knowledge, and skills that he hoped would make him a productive and integrated member of American society. From his parents, he learned the value of hard work and perseverance. From his public schooling, his Catholic schooling, and Catholicism, he learned from the formal curriculum and catechism, while also becoming attuned to Western thinking, American mannerisms, and American ideals. During his interrogation at the World War II Leupp isolation camp for Japanese American dissidents, he responded to questions from the chief of internal security, Francis Frederick, by saying, "Is it not a fact that we were taught in school to think like Americans, live like Americans and standup and fight for our rights like Americans? So I have fought, and will fight for right and justice."[99]

Kurihara's story personifies the process of identity formation in its ethnic, cultural, social, and national dimensions. What he learned, how he learned, and how he interpreted the "text" before him were bound together with his experiences, his evolving self-image, and his ongoing re-creation of himself. Ironically, months after he had decided to renounce his U.S. citizenship, he continued to maintain an American identity, stating, "I will voice my conviction like a man and will fight like an American."[100]

Kurihara's story further personifies the contradictions between rhetoric and reality in American society. He tolerated the anti-Japanese hostility that he encountered in California, continuing to believe in his country and enlisting in the army when the United States entered The Great War. After returning home as a veteran, however, he could not accept the shock of incarceration—the final disillusionment that convinced him to reject the country that he had so passionately sought to be a part of. He had naively believed in the rhetoric of American democracy so much that when reality hit him, his disappointment was profound. He came to realize that he had been searching for an America that did not exist. This he could not accept.

Finally, Kurihara's story provides a window through which we see how later life experiences, perceived as contradicting the ideals that had been learned earlier, can reverse a once-promising trajectory toward mainstream society. It is a starkly visible example of the often invisible emotional scars that immigrants and children of immigrants can carry as they struggle to adjust and gain full acceptance from the larger society.

## NOTES

1. I would like to thank Father Michael Kotlanger, S. J., of the University of San Francisco Archives, for his generous help in my research. Many thanks to Mako Rova of the Xavier Catholic Mission in San Francisco; Linda Whisman of Southwestern Law School Library; Dore Minatodani of Special Collections and Ross Togashi of Map Collection, Hamilton Library, University of Hawai'i; Glen Creason of the Los Angeles Public Library; and Tami Suzuki of the San Francisco Public Library.

2. Joseph Y. Kurihara, "The Niseis and the Government," Charles and Lois Ferguson Collection, Japanese American National Museum, Los Angeles, script, (1943). Translation by Ruriko Kumano, 30 August 2005: Emperor 10,000 Years of Life! 10,000 Years of Life! 10,000 Years of Life! Great Imperial Japan 10,000 Years of Life! 10,000 Years of Life! 10,000 Years of Life! Remain Together Comrades 10,000 Years of Life! 10,000 Years of Life! 10,000 Years of Life!

3. In the literature on the incarceration of Japanese Americans during World War II, the name of Joseph Y. Kurihara appears as one of the leading dissidents who railed against the injustice of imprisoning innocent men, women, and children. This essay, which is part of a larger project that examines Kurihara and his resistance in Manzanar, is the first published piece on his life in the decades before World War II.

4. This definition of education is from Lawrence Cremin, *Public Education* (New York: Basic Books, 1976), 27.

5. Yuji Ichioka, *The Issei: The World of the First Generation Japanese Immigrants, 1885–1924* (New York: Free Press, 1988), 210–54. The emergence of the bridge idea is discussed in ibid., 252–54.

6. "National Origins Act: an Act to Limit the Immigration of Aliens Into the United States, and for Other Purposes, 26 May 1924," in *The Columbia Documentary History of the Asian American Experience*, ed. Franklin Odo (New York: Columbia University Press, 2002), 192–95; Roger Daniels, *Asian America: Chinese and Japanese in the United States since 1850* (Seattle: University of Washington Press, 1988), 96, 149–52.

7. For example, Lon Kurashige, "The Problem of Biculturalism: Japanese American Identity and Festival before World War II," *Journal of American History* 86 (March 2000): 1632–54; Yuji Ichioka "A Study of Dualism: James Yoshinori Sakamoto and the *Japanese American Courier*, 1928–1942," *Amerasia Journal* 13 (1986–87): 49–81.

8. Studies that discuss the bridge idea are Ichioka, *The Issei*, 252–54; Eiichiro Azuma, "'The Pacific Era Has Arrived': Transnational Education among Japanese Americans, 1932–1941," *History of Education Quarterly* 43, no. 1 (Spring 2003): 41–49; Eileen H. Tamura, *Americanization, Acculturation, and Ethnic Identity: The Nisei Generation in Hawaii* (Urbana: University of Illinois Press, 1994), 68–69; Jere Takahashi, *Nisei/Sansei: Shifting Japanese American Identities and Politics* (Philadelphia: Temple University Press, 1997), 49–53; David K. Yoo, *Growing Up Nisei: Race, Generation, and Culture among Japanese Americans*

*of California, 1924–1949* (Urbana and Chicago: University of Illinois Press, 2000), 31–32.

9.  Azuma, "'The Pacific Era Has Arrived,'" 39–73.

10. Kurihara did not use the word "bridge" to describe what he was attempting to do. My use of the term is based on his words and actions.

11. For other examples of difficulties in straddling two worlds, in particular, the resulting conflicts between parents and children, see Tamura, *Americanization, Acculturation, and Ethnic Identity*, 179–82; S. Frank Miyamoto, "An Immigrant Community in America," in *East across the Pacific: Historical and Sociological Studies of Japanese Immigration and Assimilation*, ed. Hilary Conroy and T. Scott Miyakawa (Santa Barbara, CA: ABC-Clio, 1972), 230; John Modell, *The Economics and Politics of Racial Accommodation: The Japanese of Los Angeles, 1900–1942* (Urbana: University of Illinois Press, 1977), 154–56; Koji Shimada, "Education, Assimilation, and Acculturation: A Case Study of a Japanese-American Community in New Jersey" (EdD diss., Temple University, Philadelphia, 1974), 149–55; Sandra O. Uyeunten, "Struggle and Survival: The History of Japanese Immigrant Families in California, 1907–1945" (PhD diss., University of California San Diego, 1988), 190–93.

12. The overthrow of the Kingdom of Hawaii in 1893 and the subsequent annexation in 1898 were illegal acts. These acts violated treaties between the United States and the Hawaiian Kingdom; therefore they violated international law on treaties and the U.S. Constitution, which states in Article VI that all treaties are the "Supreme Law of the Land." In 1993 Congress passed and President Bill Clinton signed PL 103-150, which admitted that the U.S. government illegally invaded and occupied the Kingdom of Hawaii. See Francis A. Boyle, "Restoration of the Independent Nation State of Hawaii under International Law," *St. Thomas Law Review* 7 (1994–95): 727–38; Rich Budnick, *Stolen Kingdom: An American Conspiracy* (Honolulu, HI: Aloha, 1992), 86–187; Michael Dougherty, *To Steal a Kingdom* (Waimanalo, HI: Island Style, 1992).

13. Alan T. Moriyama, "The Causes of Emigration: The Background of Japanese Emigration to Hawaii, 1885–1894," in *Labor Immigration under Capitalism: Asian Workers in the United States before World War II*, ed. Lucie Cheng and Edna Bonacich (Berkeley: University of California Press, 1984), 248–61.

14. Yukiko Irwin and Hilary Conroy, "Robert Walker Irwin and Systematic Immigration to Hawaii," in *East across the Pacific: Historical and Sociological Studies of Japanese Immigration and Assimilation*, ed. Hilary Conroy and T. Scott Miyakawa (Santa Barbara, CA: ABC Clio, 1972), 46–47. According to "Kichizo Kurihara family records," Consulate-General of Japan, Honolulu, no date, Kurihara's parents came from Ōshima district. Arrival date is in "Yoshisuke Kurihara Certificate of Hawaiian Birth," Office of the Secretary, Territory of Hawaii, 2 May 1910. For a discussion of contract labor in Hawai'i, see Edward D. Beechert, *Working in Hawaii: A Labor History* (Honolulu: University of Hawaii Press, 1985), 40–55.

15. Romanzo Adams, *Japanese in Hawaii* (New York: National Committee on American Japanese Relations, 1924), 11. A smaller group had arrived from

Japan in 1868, but ill treatment led the Japanese government to halt further recruitment until 1885, when Japan and Hawaii reached a new agreement. See Beechert, *Working in Hawaii*, 88.

16. Ronald Takaki, *Pau Hana: Plantation Life and Labor in Hawaii, 1835–1920* (Honolulu: University of Hawaii Press, 1983), 57–126.

17. Payroll book 1887–1891, Hawaiian Sugar Planters' Association Plantation Archives, LPC PV.4-14, University of Hawaii at Manoa Library Hawaiian Collection.

18. Beechert, *Working in Hawaii*, 102–3. For a discussion of plantation living and working conditions during the 1880s and '90s, see Tamura, *Americanization, Acculturation, and Ethnic Identity*, 11–17.

19. Payroll book 1887–1891; Joseph Y. Kurihara, "Autobiography," Japanese Relocation Papers, The Bancroft Library, University of California, Berkeley, typescript, (1945), 1.

20. *Polk-Husted's Directory of Honolulu and Territory of Hawaii* (Honolulu: Husted, 1898), 43, hereafter cited as *Polk's Directory 1898*. In the ten years after 1900, when Hawai'i became a U. S. territory, the population of Honolulu county increased 40.2 percent, to 82,028, which was 43 percent of the territory's population; at the same time the territory's population increased 24.6 percent, to 191,909. See U.S. Bureau of the Census, *Thirteenth Census, 1910: Statistics for Hawaii* (Washington, DC: GPO, 1913), 5–7, hereafter cited as Census 1910. By 1910 the dominant industry in the territory was sugar cane production, with rice and coffee also being produced. In the next few years pineapple would also grow to become a major industry. Census 1910, 37, 46; *Polk's Directory 1911*, 50; *Polk's Directory 1915*, 46. Territorial status had enabled raw sugar to enter the U.S. mainland duty free, resulting in a boom in the sugar industry.

21. George Houghtailing, interview by Michiko Kodama, 30 January 1984, Honolulu, transcript, in Ethnic Studies Oral History Project, *Kalihi, Place of Transition*, vol. 3, 1103 (Honolulu: ESOHP, University of Hawai'i Manoa, 1984). By the mid-1910s a fortunate few were able to benefit from the electricity that had arrived in the area.

22. Paula Rath, "Pioneers of Palama," *Honolulu Advertiser*, 25 September 2005, http://the.honoluluadvertiser.com/article/2005/Sep/25/il/FP509250321.html/?print=on (accessed 6 October 2005).

23. James C. Mohr, *Plague and Fire: Battling Black Death and the 1900 Burning of Honolulu's Chinatown* (New York: Oxford University Press, 2005), 3–4, 7–16, 29–34, 125–46; Robert H. Rath Sr., interview by Warren Nishimoto, 17 October 1996, Honolulu, transcript, in Center for Oral History, University of Hawai'i at Manoa, *Reflections of Palama Settlement*, vol. 1, 90–95 (Honolulu: COH, University of Hawaii Manoa, 1998); Paula Rath, "Pioneers of Palama."

24. Sanborn Fire Insurance Maps, Territory of Hawaii, Honolulu, 1914, sheets 7, 9–10, University of Hawaii Libraries, http://micro189.lib3.hawaii.edu:2534/sanborn (accessed 5 October 2005), hereafter cited as Sanborn Maps 1914; Albert Nawahi Like, interview by Warren Nishimura, 12 January 1984, Honolulu, transcript, in Ethnic Studies Oral History Project, *Kalihi, Place of*

*Transition*, vol. 2, 687–93 (Honolulu: ESOHP, University of Hawai'i Manoa, 1984); Joe A. Joseph, interview by Warren Nishimoto, 16 February 1984, Honolulu, transcript, in Ethnic Studies Oral History Project, *Kalihi, Place of Transition*, vol. 2, 501 (Honolulu: ESOHP, University of Hawai'i Manoa, 1984); Houghtailing interview, 1099–1106.

25. Niece of Joseph Y. Kurihara, interview by author, 21 September 2005, Honolulu; *Polk's Directory 1908*, 345.

26. *Polk's Directory 1914*, 421.

27. *Polk's Directory 1917*, 471.

28. Hawaii Republic, Department of Public Instruction, *Report of the Minister of Public Instruction, Biennial, 1897* (Honolulu: MPI, 1898), 17, hereafter cited as *Report of the Minister of Public Instruction*. For enrollment numbers at Kaiulani, see *Report of the Minister of Public Instruction, 1899*, 128. The name of Kurihara's grammar school is in Joseph Yoshisuke Kurihara, Individual Record, FBI Report, 8 July 1942, Department of Justice File No. 146-54-117, FOIA.

29. U.S. Department of the Interior, Bureau of Education, *American Schoolhouses*, Bulletin 1910, No. 5, Plates 31, 43, 85, 178 (Washington, DC: GPO, 1910); William C. Brubaker, *Planning and Designing Schools* (New York: McGraw-Hill, 1998), 1–5; Ben E. Graves, *School Ways: the Planning and Design of America's Schools* (New York: McGraw-Hill, 1993), 23–24. For information on materials used to construct Kaiulani School, see *Report of the Minister of Public Instruction, 1897*, 5. For a photo of the newly built Kaiulani school, see *Report of the Minister of Public Instruction, 1899*, 6. Other photos taken in 1900 of the school, showing it surrounded by trees, shrubs, grass, and walkways, are in the photo collection at the Hawaii State Archives. For a photo of another school, the Royal School, which was built during the same period, see *Report of the Superintendent, 1902–1904*, 1.

30. Noel J. Kent, *Hawaii: Islands under the Influence* (Honolulu: University of Hawaii Press, 1993), 56–68; Tom A. Coffman, *Nation Within: The Story of America's Annexation of the Nation of Hawai'i* (Kaneohe, HI: Epicenter, 1998), 245–61; Michael Dougherty, *To Steal a Kingdom* (Waimanalo, HI: Island Style, 1992), 141–80; Rich Budnick, *Stolen Kingdom: An American Conspiracy* (Honolulu, HI: Aloha, 1992), 83–190; James C. Mohr, *Plague and Fire: Battling Black Death and the 1900 Burning of Honolulu's Chinatown* (New York: Oxford University Press, 2005), 17–27.

31. Hawaii Republic, Act 57, Sections 23, 24, 32 in *Laws of the Republic of Hawaii Passed by the Legislature at Its Session, 1896*, 187, 189 (Honolulu: Republic of Hawaii, 1896).

32. U.S. Hawaiian Commission, *The Report of the Hawaiian Commission Appointed in Pursuant of the "Joint Resolution for Annexing the Hawaiian Islands to the United States," Approved July 7, 1898* (Washington DC: GPO, 1898), 10, 133, 136.

33. *U.S. Organic Act: An Act to Provide a Government for the Territory of Hawaii*, C 339, 31 Stat 141, with amendments up to 1958, no date for document, www.hawaii-nation.org/organic.html (accessed 8 February 2002); Richard C.

Pratt, *Hawai'i Politics and Government: An American State in a Pacific World* (Lincoln: University of Nebraska Press, 2000), 100–101; Benjamin O. Wist, *A Century of Public Education in Hawaii* (Honolulu, HI: Hawaii Educational Review, 1940) 142–43.

34. Hawaii Territory, "Revised School Laws, 1905" in *School Laws*, 1–35 (Honolulu: Department of Public Instruction, 1928).

35. During first two decades of the twentieth century, children in the territory often began first grade at age eight or older. Going to school barefoot was also common. Kurihara's walk was less than a mile, in contrast to rural children, who often had to walk four or more miles each way. See Tamura, *Americanization*, 95–96. For photos of barefoot students, see ibid., photograph following 161.

36. For Honolulu's population, see *Polk's Directory 1903*, 39. For the numbers and types of schools, see Hawaii Territory, Department of Public Instruction, *Report to the Governor and Legislature, 1902–1904* (Honolulu: DPI, 1905), 100–104, hereafter cited as *Report to the Governor, 1902–1904*.

37. See *Report to the Governor, 1910–1912*, 223–33. Before World War II, the Territory of Hawaii hired Asian Americans as public school teachers; there was a need for teachers and Asian Americans constituted a majority of young adults who filled this need. This practice contrasted with the U. S. West Coast, where local school districts refused to hire Asian Americans as teachers.

38. *Report to the Governor, 1902–1904*, 2, 103.

39. *Report to the Governor, 1908–1910*, 28.

40. For enrollment at Kaiulani School, see *Report to the Governor, 1902–1904*, 103; and *Report to the Governor, 1910–1912*, 209.

41. For the names and ethnic breakdown of Kaiulani teachers and teachers of all public schools, see, e.g., *Report to the Governor, 1902–1904*, 103, 120–38. For the ethnic breakdown of Kaiulani students, see Kaiulani School Term Report, September 1909, Department of Public Instruction, Hawaii Territory, Hawaii State Archives, Honolulu.

42. *Report to the Governor, 1910–1912*, 190–91; *Report to the Governor, 1920*, 205.

43. David B. Tyack, *The One Best System: A History of American Urban Education* (Cambridge, MA: Harvard University Press, 1974), 230.

44. *Report to the Governor, 1902–1904*, 64–77; *Report to the Governor, 1904–1906*, 31–45.

45. Mary Rios, interview by Michiko Kodama, 28 March 1984, in Ethnic Studies Oral History Project, *Kalihi: Place of Transition, vol. 3*, 809 (Honolulu: ESOHP, University of Hawaii, 1984).

46. S.F.S. #1, Bro. Leo Schaefer, 1913–14, "Tuition Records 1912–1916, St. Louis College and St. Francis School," file 307, SLC Records, St. Louis School Archives, Honolulu. St. Francis School was established in 1893 and ceased operations in 1916. See Reginald Yzendoorn, *History of the Catholic Mission in the Hawaiian Islands* (Honolulu, HI: Honolulu Star-Bulletin, 1927), 230; and Patricia Alvarez, "Weaving a Cloak of Discipline: Hawaii's Catholic Schools, 1840–1941" (PhD diss., University of Hawaii Manoa, 1994), 382.

47. Alvarez, "Weaving a Cloak of Discipline," 202, 265, 269–70.

48. *Polk's Directory 1910*, 73.

49. S.F.S. #1, Bro. Leo Schaefer, 1913–14, "Tuition Records 1912–1916."

50. S.F.S. #s 1–4, 1913–14, "Tuition Records 1912–1916, St. Louis College and St. Francis School," file 307, SLC Records, St. Louis School Archives, Honolulu; St. Louis Term Report, December 1913, Department of Public Instruction, Hawaii Territory, Hawaii State Archives, Honolulu.

51. In 1924 the first Japanese American in Hawai'i was baptized a Catholic, followed by more in the next several years; by 1927 there were six hundred Nikkei Catholics. See Yzendoorn, *History of the Catholic Mission*, 239. However, when compared to the 139,600 ethnic Japanese in the territory, most of whom were Buddhists, Japanese Catholics as well as Protestants remained a relatively small group. See Tamura, *Americanization*, 118; Alvarez, "Weaving a Cloak of Discipline," 268, 292. For numbers and percentages of ethnic groups in Hawai'i, see Andrew W. Lind, *Hawaii's People*, 3rd ed. (Honolulu, HI: University of Hawai'i Press, 1967), 28.

52. Kurihara, "Autobiography," 1.

53. Class Register September 1913 to March 1914, Brother Leo, Class Registers 1904–1916, First Class St. Francis School, file 140, SLC Records, St. Louis School Archives, Honolulu; S.F.S. #1, Bro. Leo Schaefer, 1913–14, "Tuition Records 1912–1916."

54. Kurihara, "Autobiography," 1.

55. Manifest of Alien Passengers from U.S. Insular Possessions, manifest no. 14498, National Archives Microfilm Publication M1410 (Passenger Lists of Vessels Arriving at San Francisco, May 1, 1893–May 31, 1953), Roll 83, National Archives Pacific Region, San Bruno, CA; *Polk's Directory 1908*, 63. In 1915 there were seventeen ship companies, each with a number of ships, servicing Honolulu Harbor. See *Polk's Directory 1915*, 1120.

56. Kurihara, "Autobiography," 2.

57. Masakazu, Iwata, *Planted in Good Soil: A History of the Issei in United States Agriculture*, vol. 1. (New York: Peter Lang, 1992), 221–34; Roger Daniels, *Asian America: Chinese and Japanese in the United States since 1850* (Seattle: University of Washington Press, 1988), 144. For a Japanese immigrant's perspective of Japanese "schoolboys" working temporarily on farms, see Henry Kiyama, *The Four Immigrants Manga: A Japanese Experience in San Francisco, 1904–1924*, translated, with an Introduction and Notes by Frederik L. Schodt (Berkeley, CA: Stone Bridge, 1999), 52–57.

58. Kurihara, "Autobiography," 2.

59. Dorothy Swaine Thomas and Richard Nishimoto, *The Spoilage: Japanese-American Evacuation and resettlement During World War II* (Berkeley: University of California Press, 1969), 365.

60. Kurihara, "Autobiography," 2.

61. Thomas and Nishimoto, *The Spoilage*, 366.

62. Roger Daniels, *The Politics of Prejudice: The Anti-Japanese Movement in California and the Struggle for Japanese Exclusion* (Berkeley: University of California Press, 1962), 33–34; Charles M. Wollenberg, *All Deliberate Speed: Segregation*

*and Exclusion in California Schools, 1855–1975* (Berkeley: University of California Press, 1977), 53. Other Japanese Americans recounted similar experiences in California in the 1920s and '30s. See William C. Smith, *Americans in Process* (Ann Arbor, MI: Edwards Brothers, 1937), 16–17, 24.

63. Daniels, *Asian America*, 29–66, 100–54; Sucheng Chan, *Asian Americans: An Interpretive History* (Boston: Twayne, 1991), 45–61. For a discussion of the types of jobs available to Japanese, see Iwata, *Planted in Good Soil*, 111–52.

64. Quote is from Doris Muscatine, *Old San Francisco: The Biography of a City* (New York: G. P. Putnam's Sons, 1975), 420. For occupations in San Francisco, see William Issel and Robert Cherny, *San Francisco, 1865–1932: Politics, Power, and Urban Development* (Berkeley: University of California Press, 1986), 57. On the earthquake, see Philip L. Fradkin, *The Great Earthquake and Firestorms of 1906: How San Francisco Nearly Destroyed Itself* (Berkeley: University of California Press, 2005); Oscar Lewis, *San Francisco: Mission to Metropolis*, 2nd ed. (San Diego: Howell-North Books, 1980), 192; Tom Cole, *A Short History of San Francisco* (San Francisco: Lexikos, 1981), 103–7. On the Exposition, see Cole, *A Short History*, 116–18; and Lewis, *San Francisco*, 222.

65. *Catalogus Provinciae Californiae, Societatis Jesu*, 1915, 21, RG 1 Box 19, University of San Francisco Archives; John Bernard McGloin, *Jesuits by the Golden Gate: The Society of Jesus in San Francisco, 1849–1969* (San Francisco: University of San Francisco, 1972), 182–83; Kyoko Matsuki, "Golden Era of Our Church," no pagination, unpublished typescript, St. Francis Xavier Japanese Catholic Mission, 1992; *Registrar's Book, 1906–1927*, St. Ignatius High School, RG1 Box 17, University of San Francisco Archives; Joseph Yoshisuke Kurihara, Certificate of Baptism, San Francisco, November 16, 1915. For discussions of Japantown in the early decades of the twentieth century, see Suzie Kobuchi Okazaki, *Nihonmachi: A Story of San Francisco's Japantown* ([San Francisco]: SKO Studios, 1985), 38–82; Kenji G. Taguma, "San Francisco Japantown Properties Up for Sale," *The Hawaii Herald*, 6, March 17, 2006. The mission was located on 2011 Buchanan Street. In the few months before he left San Francisco, Kurihara lived within a block of the mission, at 2041 Pine Street.

66. The records at St. Francis School in Hawai'i list him as Yoshisuke Kurihara. His certificate of baptism and the records at St. Ignatius School identify him as Joseph Y. Kurihara.

67. *Catalog of St. Ignatius University*, 1916–1917, 113–18, RG 4 Catalogs, University of San Francisco Archives.

68. McGloin, *Jesuits by the Golden Gate*, 96; Paul Totah, "Spiritus Magis: 150 Years of St. Ignatius College Preparatory, Part 1," *Genesis IV, The Alumni Magazine, History Supplement* 42, no. 1 (Spring 2005): 1–48, www.siprep.org/genesisIV/index.cfm33-36 (accessed 10 May 2005). In the nineteenth century the school was called St. Ignatius College. The school used the term "college" in the European sense of the word, a school for students six to eighteen years old. Beginning in the late nineteenth century, the school began to include high school and post-high school classes. At the turn of twentieth century, the school ended its elementary-level classes but continued to include grades 7 and 8 until 1918. In

1909 the high school division became known as St. Ignatius High School, and in 1912 the post-high school division was renamed University of St. Ignatius and still later University of San Francisco. See McGloin, *Jesuits by the Golden Gate*, 134–37; and Totah, "Spiritus Magis," 3, 7, 30, 42.

69. Kurihara, "Autobiography," 3–4. Kurihara lived at 2095 Fulton Street in a building that was still standing in 2006; the next year he moved to 931 Anza Street. Kurihara's addresses are listed in *Registrar's Book, 1906–1927*, 307–8, 331–32, 353–54.

70. Totah, "Spiritus Magis," 9. Until 1909, when native-born Americans joined the faculty, the priests, brothers, and missionaries who taught at St. Ignatius were from Italy.

71. For course grades, see Scholastic Records, 6th Grade 1912–1913 to Senior High School 1925–1926, St. Ignatius High School, RG1 Box 9, University of San Francisco Archives; and Scholastic Records, 7th Grade 1916–1917 to Senior College 1920–1921, St. Ignatius High School, RG1 Box 9, University of San Francisco Archives. For expectations of student behaviors, see Bulletin, St. Ignatius University, 1916–17, 10–11, RG 4 Catalogs, University of San Francisco Archives.

72. Photo Albums, St. Ignatius High School (1907–1925), University of San Francisco Archives. Lists of student names accompany the class photos.

73. Wollenberg, *All Deliberate Speed*, 29–47; Victor Low, *The Unimpressible Race: A Century of Educational Struggle by the Chinese in San Francisco* (San Francisco: East/West Publishing Co., 1982), 59–73. In 1885 the San Francisco school board had created a separate school for Chinese, which continued to operate through the 1930s. The creation of the school was in response to *Tape v. Hurley*, 66 California Reports 473–75 (1884–1885), in which the State Supreme Court upheld a lower court decision that allowed a Chinese American girl, Mamie Tape, to enroll in a regular public school. The court had reasoned that no state law prohibited the Chinese from attending school with whites. In response the California legislature passed a law that allowed school districts to establish segregated schools for "Mongolians." In 1906, when the San Francisco school board directed Japanese and Korean children to attend the Chinese school, uproar among the Japanese in San Francisco and Japan led to federal intervention by President Theodore Roosevelt, who feared a diplomatic crisis with the emerging Asian power. The result was the Gentleman's Agreement of 1907–1908, in which Japan agreed not to issue passports to laborers intending to travel to the U.S. continent. In turn, the San Francisco school board agreed to allow the few Nikkei (ethnic Japanese) youths in the city—93 of the 28,000 students—to attend regular public schools. Congress then passed a bill that allowed Roosevelt to issue an executive order that barred Japanese from entering the U.S. continent via Hawai'i, Canada, and Mexico. The Gentleman's Agreement stopped the flow of laborers but not family members, and as a result, wives and other family members arrived until a 1924 immigration law stopped their entry into the United States. See Wollenberg, *All Deliberate Speed*, 61, 67; and Daniels, *The Politics of Prejudice*, 43–44. It should be noted that some of

California's public high schools—somewhat more tolerant than its grammar schools—did admit Asian Americans. See Wollenberg, *All Deliberate Speed*, 44, 72–73. On the other hand, it was relatively rare in 1915 for Asian Americans to attend high school: Chinese Americans were relatively few as a result of the Chinese exclusion laws, and most children of Japanese immigrants were not yet of high school age.

74. "San Francisco Population from the 1920 Census and 1910 Census," 18 March 2005, San Francisco Public Library, http://sfpl.lib.ca.us/librarylocations/main/ gic/sfpop1920htm (accessed November 2, 2005); Kimiko Higashiuchi Jinbo, "Japanese Americans in California," M.A. thesis, Stanford University, 1955, 66.

75. Okazaki, *Nihonmachi*, 38–42.

76. Kurihara, "Autobiography," 3. California's 1920 land law forbade Japanese immigrants from leasing and corporations from owning agricultural land. A 1923 law further forbade Japanese from sharecropping. Between 1912 and 1923, Washington, Oregon, Idaho, Arizona, Texas, and Nebraska passed similar laws. See Daniels, *The Politics of Prejudice*, 46–54, 79–91; Yuji Ichioka, *The Issei: The World of the First Generation Japanese Immigrants, 1885–1924* (New York: Free Press, 1988), 153–56, 226–43; and Tamura, *Americanization*, 78. By 1913 the Chinese were no longer seen as a threat. They had been excluded in 1882 with the Chinese Exclusion Act, which was extended in 1892 and 1902 and made indefinite in 1904. During World War II, with China an ally of the United States, the law was rescinded, and Chinese were allowed to become naturalized citizens. See Sucheng Chan, *Asian Americans: An Interpretive History* (Boston: Twayne, 1991), 54–55, 122. Phelan, who attended St. Ignatius High School, was mayor from 1897 to 1903 and U.S. senator from 1913 to 1919.

77. Kurihara, "Autobiography," 4. You is capitalized in the original.

78. Thomas and Nishimoto, *The Spoilage*, 366.

79. Kurihara, "The Niseis and the Government," 19. The following translation is by Ruriko Kumano, 21 February 2006: *koku* is country, *on* is gratitude; *koku on* means "a deep sense of gratitude toward one's country."

80. J. Y. Kurihara, "I Was in the War," *Kashu Mainichi*, 19 May 1940 and 26 May 1940.

81. Kurihara, "Autobiography," 9.

82. In 1920 Los Angeles included 11,618 Nikkei, 2,062 Chinese, 21,652 Mexicans, and 15,579 African Americans. See John Modell, *The Economics and Politics of Racial Accommodation: The Japanese of Los Angeles, 1900–1942* (Urbana: University of Illinois Press, 1977), 23. Ten years later the nonwhite population was 14 percent: 21,081 Nikkei, 3,009 Chinese, 3,245 Filipinos, 97,116 Mexicans and Mexican Americans, and 45,000 African Americans. See Writers' Program, *Los Angeles: A Guide to the City and Its Environs*, (New York: Hastings House, 1941), 3.

83. Modell, *The Economics and Politics of Racial Accommodation*, 71–75. Information on the location of temples in Los Angeles is from Glen Creason, Map Librarian, Los Angeles Public Library, e-mail correspondence, 19 December 2005; and Writers' Program, *Los Angeles*, 146, 156–57.

84. "Payne's Heart of Downtown," 1931 map, Los Angeles Public Library, Los Angeles, California; "Sims Map of Metropolitan Los Angeles," 1926, Los Angeles Public Library, Los Angeles, California. Kurihara lived at 308 South Flower Street, 8 blocks away from City Hall. Address in Joseph Y. Kurihara, Transcripts, 1924, Southwestern University, Los Angeles, California.

85. Modell, *The Economics and Politics of Racial Accommodation*, 8–9, 70, 94–99; Iwata, *Planted in Good Soil*, 393–448.

86. Kurihara, "Autobiography," 12; Modell, *The Economics and Politics of Racial Accommodation*, 100–102; Daniels, *The Politics of Prejudice*, 46–54, 79–91; Ichioka, *The Issei*, 153–56, 226–43; Tamura, *Americanization*, 78. The land laws were ineffective in preventing Japanese immigrants from farming. Kurihara's experience was an example of how Japanese immigrants responded to the land laws: leasing or purchasing the land in the names of their children or friends who were American citizens. Moreover, little effort was made to enforce the laws. See Daniels, *The Politics of Prejudice*, 88; and Modell, *The Economics and Politics of Racial Accommodation*, 102.

87. Kurihara, "Autobiography," 9; Raymond R. Best, "Joe Kurihara, 'Repatriate,'" typescript, Japanese Relocation Papers, The Bancroft Library, University of California Berkeley, 19; Francis S. Frederick, "Case History, Joseph Yoshisuke Kurihara," 17 August 1943, World War II Internment Case File for Joseph Y. Kurihara, Box 2864, 5/68/56/4, Records of the War Relocation Authority, RG 210, National Archives, no page number. Raymond Best was director at the Tule Lake Relocation Center and Francis Frederick was chief of internal security at Leupp Isolation Center.

88. Kurihara, "Autobiography," 10.

89. "History of Southwestern," Southwestern University School of Law, 2005, no author, http://www.swlaw.edu/about/history (accessed 9 December 2005).

90. *Official Announcement of Southwestern University School of Commerce, 1922–1923* (Los Angeles: Southwestern University, n.d.), 35–39.

91. Joseph Y. Kurihara, Transcripts, 1924, Southwestern University, Los Angeles, California.

92. Kurihara, "Autobiography," 10; *Official Announcement of Southwestern University School of Commerce, 1925–1926*, 34–35; Kurihara, Transcripts, 1924.

93. Joseph Y. Kurihara, Renunciation of United States Nationality, 22 March 1945, Case File 146-54-117, U.S. Department of Justice, FIOA.

94. Modell, *The Economics and Politics of Racial Accommodation*, 130–33.

95. Kurihara, "Autobiography," 15–24; Grandnephew of Kurihara, interview by author, Honolulu, 21 September 2005.

96. Kurihara lived on 788 East Pico Blvd. See U.S. Bureau of the Census, *Fifteenth Census, 1930, Population Schedule*, Los Angeles, Sheet 33A; Joseph Yoshisuke Kurihara, Individual Record.

97. Kurihara, "Autobiography," 12–13, 18–24.

98. Louise H. Hunter, *Buddhism in Hawaii: Its Impact on a Yankee Community* (Honolulu: University of Hawaii Press, 1971).

99. Frederick, "Case History, Joseph Yoshisuke Kurihara," no page number.

100. Ibid.

# CHAPTER 5

# THE ROMANCE AND REALITY OF HISPANO IDENTITY IN NEW MEXICO'S SCHOOLS, 1910–1940

LYNNE MARIE GETZ

AFTER THE ACHIEVEMENT OF STATEHOOD IN 1912, THE HISPANOS OF New Mexico found themselves increasingly outnumbered by Anglos.[1] While they remained a force to be reckoned with in politics, Hispanos more and more felt the effects of a long and steady erosion of land ownership and economic power. In the isolated rural villages of northern New Mexico, Nuevomexicanos continued to predominate in numbers through the 1930s, but their existence became more precarious. The everyday lives of the people living in these quaint villages had been changing since the early decades of the century, when more men had been forced to migrate seasonally in search of work. The prospects for the young people of the villages grew dimmer as their schools failed to prepare them for a wider world. Meanwhile, Hispanos living in urban areas, though much fewer in number than their rural counterparts, faced stiffer competition for jobs and business opportunities from the rapidly expanding Anglo population. Spanish-speaking Nuevomexicanos heard more English spoken on the streets and in businesses and faced increasing incidents of discrimination for continuing to speak their native language and live their culture. All Hispanos, whether rural or urban, began to understand the full impact of an increasingly Americanized society. They had become a marginalized group, separated from the dominant Anglo society by language, culture, and economic power. In seeking ways of reducing the damaging effect of marginalization, many Hispanos resorted to a unique strategy of romanticizing Hispano identity, both to reinforce a positive self-image and to make their presence in American life seem less threatening to Anglos. The public schools became a central location for the construction of a romantic Hispano identity and its use as a tool for combating marginalization.

In the 1920s and 1930s, a number of educators in New Mexico, both Anglo and Hispano, worked to minimize the effects of marginalization in the schools and the broader society. By romanticizing certain aspects of Hispano culture, these educators hoped to decrease the harmful effects of marginalization by portraying Hispanos as having an attractive folk culture. In so doing, they believed they could counteract Anglo fears about the existence of a divergent culture within the larger social whole. Among the positive outcomes of this strategy were a measure of respect accorded the Hispano culture within New Mexico and the survival of many Hispano cultural patterns. New Mexico schools also experimented with some models of bilingual education and cultural pluralism that still seem remarkable today. On the negative side, however, these efforts did not succeed in eliminating discrimination, racism, or even segregation in schools, and they failed to provide young Hispanos with the educational training necessary to enable them to compete with middle-class Anglos in the wider economy.

## THE RISE OF THE ROMANTIC HISPANO IDENTITY

The process of pushing Hispanics aside had proceeded much less quickly in New Mexico than in California or Texas, other territories absorbed by the United States in the mid-nineteenth century.[2] Anglos found fewer incentives for moving to New Mexico, and so their numbers remained small during the nineteenth century. Hispanos used their concentrated population to retain political power and demand respect. As David Maciel and Erlinda Gonzales-Berry have said, "Nuevomexicanos entered the twentieth century with a strong sense of place and cultural identity."[3] Several factors contributed to the status of Hispanos as a population to be reckoned with in politics and social life. The elite families, or *los ricos*, of New Mexico retained considerable economic and political power well

into the twentieth century. Not only were they desirable business part-
ners, but they also commanded the votes of large blocs of poorer Hispanos, *los pobres*. The political and economic power of *los ricos* made
them important agents in a number of struggles involving the status and
conditions of the Hispano community. Working with Anglo allies, they
engaged in the campaign for statehood and worked to improve educational opportunities for all Hispanos. The issue of Hispano identity
entered into both struggles.

The efforts of New Mexicans to achieve statehood had been thwarted
several times before its successful passage in 1912. While many factors
complicated these various attempts, an underlying and recurring argument against statehood was that New Mexicans were racially inferior and
unable to meet the obligations of citizenship. Racially, Nuevomexicanos
derived largely from mestizo, or mixed Spanish and Native American
bloodlines. Few pure Spanish families settled in Spain's northern
province of Nuevo Mexico, and over time much intermarriage occurred
between the Spanish colonists and their Native American neighbors.
Nevertheless, Nuevomexicanos, especially the elite, tended to stress their
Spanish identity and to claim pure Spanish blood. This penchant for self-
identification as Spanish grew more pronounced in the late nineteenth
century in response to predominant pseudoscientific racial views that
characterized "mixed-blood" peoples as inferior and unfit for democracy.
Nuevomexicano editors and intellectuals embraced a view of racial identity that denied any Native American or mestizo heritage. Instead, they
promoted the "New Mexico legend," using such terms such as "hispano"
or "Spanish American" to refer to Nuevomexicanos and arguing that the
people of New Mexico and its culture derived directly from the pure-
blooded Spanish *conquistadores*.[4] As historian John Nieto-Phillips has
argued, "the Spanish ethos allowed Nuevomexicanos to lay claim to
whiteness as an argument for full inclusion in the nation's body politic."[5]
Self-identification as Spanish Americans, rather than as Mexican Americans, encouraged the romanticizing of New Mexico's colonial past and
preempted association with Mexican immigrants. While Anglo writers,
artists, and tourism boosters abetted this process for their own reasons,
Nuevomexicanos hoped that their culture would be interpreted in positive, nonthreatening terms rather than as a dissonant foreign civilization.
The promotion of the romanticized Hispano was not the only factor in
achieving statehood, but it did help to solidify a movement making wide
use of that identity.

Significantly, Anglos in the tourist industry in the late nineteenth century began to understand the usefulness of constructing an idealized identity for Hispanos centered on their Spanish colonial past. As early as 1880, New Mexico's Bureau of Immigration encouraged tourists to come to New Mexico Territory to experience the charm of the "exotic" Spanish colonial heritage. Fred Harvey lured visitors to his Alvarado Hotel in Albuquerque with the promise of Spanish ethnic crafts and colonial architecture. Harvey collaborated with the Santa Fe Railway to construct hotels and design tours to cater to the interest in the land of the conquistadores.[6] By the 1920s, a significant tourist industry had developed based on promotion of New Mexico as a place where exotic folk cultures lived on in the midst of a modernizing American society.

## CONTESTING MARGINALIZATION IN THE SCHOOLS

This movement to romanticize Hispanos, carried on by Anglos and Hispanos alike for different purposes, had noteworthy consequences for Hispanos living on the margins of American society. Not all who idealized Hispano culture did so for crass economic reasons. Some Anglos and most Hispanos who did so hoped that by emphasizing the positive and exotic aspects of Hispano culture, they would soften the oppression of Hispanos' marginalized status and enable them to improve their lives. Nowhere was this more in evidence than in education. When New Mexico became a state in 1912, it was unclear whether Spanish could be used as the language of instruction in the public schools. Recent Anglo arrivals preached Americanization for the Hispano population and intended to use the schools to achieve their goal of complete assimilation of all Nuevomexicanos.[7] A spirited contest ensued between Anglo and Hispano leaders over control of the schools. Until the early 1920s, New Mexicans engaged in a lively debate over language policy in the schools. Ostensibly a discussion about the best methodology for educating children, it masked a more profound question over cultural preservation and assimilation. The Nuevomexicano community itself reflected the deep sense of ambivalence that characterized the different perspectives in this debate. Many Nuevomexicano politicians, newspaper editors, educators, and parents wanted Nuevomexicano children to learn both English and Spanish to keep their cultural identity alive, while others were willing, albeit reluctantly, to sacrifice Spanish literacy in the belief that children would be better prepared for life in American society if they were fully assimilated.[8] For Nuevomexicanos, the language issue, and through it education, became a major location for contesting the marginalization of their culture.

The campaign to identify Nuevomexicanos as Spanish may have helped New Mexico gain statehood, but initially it did little to prevent the marginalization of Spanish-speaking children in the schools of the new state. In the 1920s, state officials promoted educational practices that effectively segregated Spanish-speaking children for pedagogical purposes. Although segregation was prohibited by the New Mexico state constitution, and segregation was never sanctioned by law, some schools followed the suggestions of the State Department of Public Instruction and placed Spanish-speaking children in separate classes to facilitate the teaching of English. In 1920 State Superintendent Jonathan Wagner encouraged schools to use intelligence tests to sort students into separate classes in their first year.[9] This endorsement, along with the 1921 New Mexico Course of Study recommendations for use of the Direct Method for teaching English, meant that many schools segregated Spanish-speaking children in the first few grades in order to teach them English.[10] The practice held back children a few years so they progressed through the grades, if at all, with younger classmates, thus adding social barriers that discouraged them from attending school. For many young Nuevomexicanos, segregation under such conditions was humiliating. The use of intelligence tests to sort children stigmatized them with the label of "retarded," while some teachers strictly enforced an English-only policy, even resorting to punishing students for using their native language.[11]

Had such efforts succeeded in imposing a standard approach to education across New Mexico, Nuevomexicanos would have been even further marginalized in their native land. Two factors worked against total standardization. First, local control of schools generally prevailed and the state educational establishment lacked the power and resources to determine what went on in every school district. Many rural schools, in particular, continued to be taught by Spanish-speaking teachers using Spanish as the language of instruction. Second, many prominent educators in the state, both Anglo and Nuevomexicano, embraced the movement to idealize the Spanish culture and Spanish colonial past. Nieto-Phillips uses the terms *hispanophiles* to refer to Anglos who romanticized all things Spanish, and *hispanistas* for those Nuevomexicanos who embraced the Spanish language, culture, and identity as a means of resisting marginalization.[12] The combined efforts of hispanophiles and hispanistas succeeded in implementing educational programs promoting cultural preservation in the schools.

Anglo hispanophiles and upper-class Hispanos had joined together to romanticize Spanish culture and history as early as the 1880s, but these efforts intensified in the 1920s and 1930s. Groups such as the Historical Society of New Mexico and the Spanish Colonial Arts Society depicted Hispanic New Mexico as a picturesque and unspoiled premodern society. These organizations emphasized folklore, crafts, religious art, and a sanitized history centered on the glorious deeds of swashbuckling conquistadores. They invented new traditions, such as the Santa Fe Fiesta, designed to draw tourists to the area and celebrate the newly discovered wonders of the Hispano culture.[13] Lost in all this romantic salutation, however, was any recognition of the struggle for political and economic hegemony that had occurred since the American conquest. The successful expropriation of Hispano identity carried out by the hispanophiles had the effect of portraying Nuevomexicanos as a nonthreatening and benign enclave within the larger society, but did little to explain the social and economic conditions of the average Hispano and even helped to rationalize their oppression.

## THE AGENT OF HISPANO IDENTITY: NINA OTERO-WARREN

For educators, the new emphasis on the positive artistic contributions of Nuevomexicanos made it easier to explore curricular innovations that incorporated cultural aspects of Hispano life in the schools. Educators such as Nina Otero-Warren, Loyd Tireman, Brice Sewall, and George I. Sánchez led efforts to experiment with bilingual education and vocational programs using traditional arts and crafts. Motivated by a sincere desire to improve the educational achievement of Hispanic children, these educators ironically chose to emphasize a Hispano identity that many might have considered the cause of marginalization of these children. Yet, they turned the source of marginality on its head, banking instead on the romantic appeal of Spanish culture as the basis for overcoming the antagonism between white society and Hispanos.

As one of the leading hispanistas of her day, Nina Otero-Warren stood as a critical power broker between the Hispano and Anglo communities of New Mexico. A descendant of two distinguished upper-class Hispanic families, Otero-Warren served as Santa Fe County school superintendent from 1917 to 1929. During this time, she balanced the county school budget; increased teachers' salaries, while raising certification standards; increased the school term; built several new high schools; and hired the county's first school nurse.[14] But her influence reached beyond Santa Fe, and indeed beyond the state, through her promotion of Hispanic culture and her ideas for incorporating cultural preservation into school curricula.

Otero-Warren became a leading proponent of the New Mexico legend of Spanish origins with the publication of her book *Old Spain in Our Southwest* in 1936. The book reflected a lifetime of collecting the stories, plays, songs, and traditional lore of Hispanic New Mexico. Otero-Warren depicted the colonial past of New Mexico as an idyllic time when both *ricos* and *pobres* lived "close to the soil and to nature. They cherished their traditions, inherited from Spain and adopted to their new life. Theirs was a part of the feudal age, when master and man, although separate in class, were bound together by mutual interests and a close community of human sympathy."[15] By simplifying the past and ignoring the history of discrimination and hardship endured by many Nuevomexicanos since 1848, Otero-Warren managed to suggest that New Mexico still remained the harmonious and tranquil society it had been in her romanticized colonial past. It was a view of New Mexico that Anglos could accept. Otero-Warren promised accommodation and loyalty, as long as Nuevomexicanos were allowed to retain their cherished cultural traditions.

Otero-Warren's work struck a note that characterized the overall strategy for educators wishing to minimize the negative effects of marginalization for Hispano children. Reflecting the conflicted role she played as an upper-class Hispano advocate, Otero-Warren aimed to establish a balance between accommodation and cultural preservation. As a pioneer cultural broker in this direction Otero-Warren implemented her approach in the Course of Study for the Santa Fe County elementary schools in 1929. She emphasized accommodation to the dominant culture to the extent that children had to learn the language, skills, and values that they would need to succeed in Anglo society. A solid grounding in English was necessary as the first step to acquiring other skills. But she also recognized that the forceful and often punitive approach taken in teaching English too often alienated the Spanish-speaking children, thus undermining their overall academic prospects. Therefore she advocated a two-pronged strategy for teaching native Spanish speakers.

First, Otero-Warren encouraged teachers to take a sympathetic approach to teaching young Nuevomexicanos. She believed that teachers should manifest a "feeling of comradeship, friendliness, and mutual belief so that the child may be freed from embarrassment and self consciousness." The Spanish-speaking child "is extremely sensitive and timid, though he is actuated by the same attention as all children, and responds in the same way to right teaching procedures and treatment."[16] In advocating a compassionate attitude toward Nuevomexicano children, Otero-Warren used her own standing and influence to champion decent treatment for her people. But she went further in demanding respect for the Nuevomexicano community by insisting on the inclusion of Spanish culture in the schools as well.

In the second part of her strategy for improving education for Nuevomexicanos, she proposed that traditional games, songs, folklore, arts and crafts should be incorporated into the school curriculum. Not only would this instill pride in the native culture, but it would also help to preserve traditional village life, Otero-Warren thought. Sincerely believing that children of New Mexico's villages would remain in those villages, Otero-Warren believed they could continue to make a living there only if traditional activities such as weaving, pottery, tinwork, woodwork, and other crafts were passed on to the younger generation. As she said, "The industries of people who have lived in this country for so long should not be allowed to disappear or become modernized."[17]

In this respect, Otero-Warren also epitomized the fatal flaw in the romantic strategy for avoiding marginalization of Nuevomexicanos. Promoting traditional arts and crafts as the key for future economic success depended on a number of factors that proved to be highly unrealistic. A village economy based on arts and crafts needed viable markets for those products. While Anglo-based organizations such as the Spanish Colonial Arts Society attempted to generate a sustainable market for these items, sufficient demand never materialized to support the population.[18] The residents of New Mexico's northern rural villages found it increasingly difficult through the 1920s and 1930s to make a living through subsistence farming or traditional home industries. Historian Sandra Deutsch has shown that a pattern of migrant labor developed with Nuevomexicano men leaving the villages for seasonal work in the fields and mines of Colorado.[19] Furthermore, the emphasis on traditional crafts industries ironically limited the opportunities for Nuevomexicano children by failing to prepare them to pursue other activities, particularly those requiring a college education. These limitations would eventually undermine this strategy for overcoming marginalization.

Otero-Warren's ideas nevertheless became the model for other educators to follow. In the 1930s, several leading Anglo educators adopted strategies similar to those of Otero-Warren. To their credit, these educators treated Nuevomexicanos with respect and compassion and undoubtedly believed that their efforts would help Hispanos improve their lives. Their shortcomings, however, mirrored those of Otero-Warren in that they believed the idealization of Hispano culture would be sufficient to avoid marginalizing the population within the larger society. They failed to recognize that Hispanos could not reap the full benefits of participation in American society by remaining within their traditional village structure.

### THE ANGLO ALLIES: LOYD S. TIREMAN, MARY AUSTIN, AND BRICE SEWALL

Loyd S. Tireman arrived in New Mexico in 1927 as a young assistant professor of education at the University of New Mexico and quickly established himself as a leading authority on pedagogical practice and curricular reform. Like many Anglos who had moved to New Mexico, he fell in love with the place. He soon adopted the romanticized view of Nuevomexicanos typical of the hispanophile. To him the New Mexico past was a history of a charming but primitive civilization that had much to teach modern Americans about beauty, filial piety, and courtesy.[20] But he also believed that benevolent Anglos had a duty to instruct Nuevomexicanos on how to live in American society. Although he found much to admire in the culture, he attributed Hispanos' lack of educational achievement to the impoverished home environments that characterized so many Nuevomexicanos. While Tireman made this observation in the spirit of scientific objectivity, it was often interpreted as criticism aimed at Hispanos, particularly since Tireman also tended to play down factors of discrimination and conflict that had contributed to the economic conditions of the Hispano population. Tireman thus left a contradictory legacy, one that epitomizes this ambiguous pattern of well-meaning Anglos and Hispanos attempting to overcome the subordination of Nuevomexicanos by emphasizing their cultural distinction.

In educational practice, Tireman proposed innovative methods that were intended to boost the confidence and self-esteem of Spanish-speaking children. Working closely with community leaders and parents, Tireman established two experimental schools where he modeled good teaching methods and tried out innovative curricula. In the San José district of Albuquerque, his experimental school pioneered several new pedagogical practices aimed at increasing the child's interest in school. In contrast to many other educators in New Mexico, Tireman understood that any situation that segregated the Spanish-speaking children from their English-speaking counterparts was likely to discourage them and inculcate feelings of inferiority, even if the segregation was purely based on pedagogical reasons. For those students who required special instruction, therefore, Tireman took measures to reduce the stigma associated with separate classes. Some of the methods he used later became standard instructional practice in teaching students from non-English-speaking and lower socioeconomic families. For instance, instead of keeping students in first grade for several years while they learned English, the San José School began the practice of preschool classes for children before they reached the age for regular school attendance. For students already in school, Tireman had his teachers divide their classes into sections for individualized instruction, then bring the entire class together for other activities. Older students were not kept in the lower grades, as was the nearly universal practice in New Mexico's schools, but instead they attended the "Opportunity Room" to receive special instruction with other older children, and then returned to their regular classes as soon as possible.[21]

Tireman's concern for the self-esteem of his students emerged also in his advocacy of bilingual instruction, one of his most innovative ventures in an era when bilingual instruction was almost unanimously rejected. The experiment in bilingual instruction appealed to Tireman because he thought it would help students learn English more readily, but he also justified it on cultural grounds as well. In 1932 the teachers of the San José school began to include thirty-minute sessions of Spanish language instruction daily in the first five grades. Tireman declared that the study of Spanish as a subject would help Hispano children by "awaken[ing] in them an appreciation of their lingual heritage." And in an interesting twist, Tireman suggested that having native Spanish and English speakers studying Spanish together would offer "a competitive field in which group advantages and disadvantages are more or less equalized and in which group barriers can be effectively broken down." Tireman hoped to prove that "the bi-lingual tendencies that now operate as an educational handicap to Spanish-American children in general, can be transformed into an educational asset by the simple process of teaching Spanish along with English in the lower grades."[22]

Along with efforts to boost self-esteem through sensitive teaching and bilingual instruction, Tireman also initiated vocational programs designed to reinforce Hispanic cultural traditions. As Otero-Warren had done in the Santa Fe County schools, Tireman brought traditional New Mexican arts into the curriculum, including tinwork, weaving, dying, and tanning. These two educators embraced the inclusion of traditional arts and crafts for different reasons, however, and the contrast in their motivations points to a distinction between the Hispano agent and the Anglo ally. While Otero-Warren envisioned a future with economically viable Hispano villages, she expressed little interest in encouraging Hispanos to leave the villages. Clearly Otero-Warren felt a great deal of ethnic pride in her heritage and wanted in part to preserve her native culture for its own sake and for the reinforcement it gave to her own identity. Tireman, while he valued Hispano culture for many reasons, advocated the crafts curriculum as vocational training designed to provide wider economic opportunities for Hispanos, who might very well leave their villages and seek opportunities elsewhere. They both identified the traditional arts and crafts curriculum with the Spanish colonial past, but Otero-Warren's pride in that past tended to blind her to the real needs of modern students.

Tireman's ability to work with persons with whom he had subtle differences was also demonstrated by his recruitment of Mary Austin. Tireman enlisted the help of the well-known regional author to assist him in publicizing the work of the San José School. Austin joined the board of directors of the school and wrote several articles promoting its work.[23] In bringing Austin on board, Tireman allied himself with one of the leading lights of the Spanish Colonial revival movement. Austin, who had settled in Santa Fe in 1924, became a vocal champion of the effort to conserve the region's native arts and handicrafts before her death in 1934.[24] In her enthusiastic support for the San José School, she demonstrated, perhaps to a greater degree than any other individual, how the idealization of a culture, while meant to overcome marginalization, actually contributed to it. In many ways the cooperation between Austin and Tireman seems ironic and suggests some naïveté on his part, since she took a condescending attitude toward him and his views of Hispano culture.[25]

Austin's views of Hispano culture, as well as her perspective on Native American societies can only be characterized as primitivist. Recently, historians such as Margaret Jacobs have highlighted Austin's role in idealizing Pueblo Indians. Austin celebrated the premodern nature of their culture and suggested that modern, industrialized society would benefit from following Native American examples. She approached Hispano culture with the same antimodern assumptions.[26] In contrast to Tireman, who believed that modernization was not only possible but desirable for Hispanos, Austin hoped to preserve traditional Hispano communities as they were. While she may have believed that she was portraying them in a positive light, she nevertheless assumed certain racial characteristics about both groups that she did not expect could be overcome by environment. Austin thought a traditional reading-based curriculum would be wasted on them because Hispanos had never "acquired the habit of receiving their education from the printed page," and so they would not benefit from book learning. They learned best through doing, she declared, because "the Spanish speaking peon derives from both lines of his descent the capacity to make things requiring a high degree of artisan skill, and to make them beautifully and well." Ironically, Austin believed that to turn the tables on racism, all that was needed was to reinforce the artisanship of the Hispano—a stance that actually relied heavily on racist assumptions regarding Hispanos' natural aptitudes. With proper instruction and encouragement from Anglos, Austin asserted, "the despised peon class could become the superior hand-craftsmen of the western world."[27] Unlike Tireman, Austin agreed with Otero-Warren that the schools could be used as vehicles for restoring traditional village life in New Mexico. The schools had been guilty of destroying village life by trying to acculturate Nuevomexicanos to American life, almost to the point of extinguishing "all that is dramatic, entertaining, poetic, and generally cultural in the social life of the native New Mexican village."[28] For Austin, restoration of the traditional village would preserve a vital premodern existence and serve as an antidote to the oppressive standardization of modern life. Austin's embrace of the village had more to do with her primitivist urge to counter the forces of modern life than with her genuine concern for the livelihood or progress of Nuevomexicanos. She did not wish to see Hispanos assimilated into modern American life.

Nevertheless, Mary Austin became a close collaborator with educators whose goals ultimately aimed for the assimilation of Hispanos in certain respects. Austin's role on the board of the San José School illustrates the close collaboration between the Spanish Colonial revival movement and educational leaders in the state. This partnership was further solidified in 1932 when the state Department of Public Instruction adopted the vocational curriculum of the San José School and accepted Mary Austin's

recommendation of Brice Sewell as state supervisor of trade and industrial education. Praising Sewell, a young sculptor who had arrived in New
Mexico in 1930, Austin said, "I have had him closely under my eye . . . I
think he is admirably fitted for that work, and that he realizes . . . the
need for rehabilitating native culture along with the most successful
vocational training."[29]

Indeed, Sewell adopted many of Austin's views on Nuevomexicanos
and what they needed from an education, but he also saw vocational education in the same light as Tireman did. They did not benefit from a traditional academic curriculum, he believed, and their high dropout rates
proved that the standard American curriculum did not hold their interest. Instead, they should be trained in activities that they would recognize
as belonging to their own heritage, the "village hand-craft industries
which utilize local raw materials and convert them into finished products." Students would only respond to a curriculum based on "what is
demanded by the community and is deemed practical from the stand-
point of giving a fair assurance of the students' being able to follow and
earn a living from the trade." These activities, incorporated into the state
vocational course of study, included carpentry, woodworking, weaving,
tanning, spinning, and needlework.[30] Unlike Austin, however, Sewell
tempered his romantic appreciation of Spanish colonial aesthetics with a
pragmatic understanding of the economic difficulties faced by villagers.
He supported efforts to develop adult education programs in Chupadero
and other villages for training in tanning, woodworking, spinning, and
harness making. Within two years the Chupadero workshop, which was
operated as a community cooperative, received more orders than it could
fill.[31] Sewell's efforts thus reinforced what Tireman was trying to do in his
experimental schools—train students for viable economic activities that
coincided with their cultural heritage.

### THE IMPACT OF CULTURAL IDEALIZATION
### ON THE HISPANO COMMUNITY

Despite Tireman and Sewell's efforts, the movement to preserve the traditional New Mexican village, closely connected to the Spanish colonial
arts revival, ultimately failed to provide Hispanos with sustainable livelihoods. A few individual artists flourished in the midst of the brief renais-
sance of interest generated by the Spanish Colonial Arts Society in the
mid-1930s, but even that handful of artisans turned to supplementary

activities to support themselves and their families. Few villages experienced the rebirth anticipated by the leaders of the revival movement.[32] The combined effort of Anglos and Hispanos alike to stave off economic marginalization for rural Nuevomexicanos by reinvigorating traditional arts and crafts was based on an inflated estimation of the volume of demand for such products.

Deeper flaws in this thinking have become apparent only with the benefit of hindsight. The attempt to revive traditional village life rested on a basic assumption that Hispano culture was inherently valuable and worthy of respect, as long as it conformed to the definition of Spanish colonial identity determined by Anglos and upper-class Hispanos. Not only did this stifle new cultural innovation, but it also ultimately served the interests of Anglos and upper-class Hispanos more than those of impoverished Hispano villagers. It implied that Hispanos would be valued and respected only as long as they remained nonthreatening to Anglos or upper-class Hispanos. Their marginalized status would be smoothed over by granting them a highly sentimentalized acclaim, but they were not to be encouraged to enter any arena where they might compete directly with their presumed social superiors. The movement to romanticize and preserve Hispano culture served the status quo.

Another flaw in the assumptions of many romantic cultural preservationists was their neglect of the aspirations of many Hispanos themselves. Few Nuevomexicanos wanted to reject their entire cultural and linguistic heritage, but neither did they wish to be deprived of the tools necessary to compete in modern American society. They wanted their children to learn English, even if they could not, and they wanted the next generation to succeed. It was generally assumed by antimodern romantics that Hispanos possessed no sense of ambition, or that quality of "get-ahead-edness" usually associated with Yankees. To the contrary, however, even the most humble of Hispano villagers would speak longingly of their desire that their children should have better opportunities. Andreita Padilla, for example, remembered how difficult it had been for her to learn English when she had been a schoolgirl in the 1920s; she wanted her own children to experience more success: "The teachers, they were all *Anglos*. There was no Spanish at all. It was hard, because when I needed to go to the bathroom, I didn't know what to say. I just put up my hand and I told them, you know, but it was hard. I thought, 'Maybe if I try I can learn it. If I try to break my head learning it, I can understand it.' And it wasn't too long to learn. But that's why I taught my family English, so they don't be so ignorant."[33]Some Hispanos feared that clinging to their Hispanic heritage and Spanish language would marginalize their children, and tragically they might have encouraged the abandonment of precious cultural practices. This loss was what the antimodernists sought to prevent, but such pragmatic parents undoubtedly had a more realistic view of their children's prospects.

Those Hispanos who wanted the schools to provide their children with the skills necessary for equal competition with Anglos had few options. The most innovative programs undertaken in New Mexico to improve the schools were those of Tireman, Otero-Warren, and Sewell. While all three stressed viable methods of learning English and basic reading skills, they differed in degree on what the future for Hispanos should be. Otero-Warren stressed preservation of Hispano village culture over modernization and complete assimilation. Sewell thought village life should be preserved but economic opportunities enhanced. Tireman believed that cultural preservation was possible within an assimilationist framework. None of them, however, believed that the schools should try to prepare Hispano children for education beyond high school, and this certainly was their greatest shortcoming. Working-class Nuevomexicanos, while welcoming cultural programs in the schools and participating in village arts when it proved profitable, nevertheless clamored for greater opportunities than those being touted by upper-class Hispanos and their Anglo allies. This made a place in the educational politics of New Mexico for a cultural broker who bridged the divide between two opposing groups of Hispanos. This role was filled for a brief time by George I. Sánchez.

### THE MAVERICK: GEORGE I. SÁNCHEZ

Sánchez was one of the few New Mexico educators who resisted the temptation to romanticize the past while at the same time refusing to absolve Anglos and Hispanos alike for failing to provide equal educational opportunities. His true constituency was not those Hispanos who were willing to collaborate with Anglos in allowing a culturally pluralistic curriculum while sacrificing a rigorous academic preparation. Rather he spoke for the many voiceless poor Hispanos who simply wanted their children to have better opportunities, even if that meant giving up some of their traditions. In the end, Sánchez failed to achieve the goals he sought, mainly because he refused to ignore blatant discrimination and thus drew the fire of too many political opponents.

A native Nuevomexicano, Sánchez worked his way through the University of New Mexico (UNM) by teaching in small rural schools around Albuquerque. By the time he had earned his B.A. in 1930, he had also captured the attention of some influential Anglo patrons, including UNM president James F. Zimmerman. Zimmerman saw in the young man a native who had leadership potential and the ambition to improve the educational conditions of his people. The college president helped Sánchez get a scholarship to the University of Texas, where Sánchez completed his master's degree. Later Sánchez went on for the doctorate in education at the University of California at Berkeley.[34] In 1931 Sánchez joined the New Mexico Department of Public Instruction as the director of the Division of Information and Statistics, a position that he himself had proposed and that was funded by the General Education Board.[35]

What distinguished Sánchez from romantic primitivists like Austin, or even other progressive educators like Tireman, was his willingness to confront the realities of social and economic inequality. Few regional observers even acknowledged the seemingly obvious systemic discrimination that haunted the Hispanic population across the Southwest, and fewer still offered incisive analyses of the problem.[36] Sánchez put forward both an analysis of the problems faced by Nuevomexicanos and a potential solution, equal educational funding for the schools of New Mexico. Neither made him popular with the wielders of power in New Mexico.

In 1940 Sánchez published his most important work on the Hispanos of New Mexico, *Forgotten People*, a study of the socioeconomic conditions of Rio Arriba County in northern New Mexico. While acknowledging the proud past of New Mexico, Sánchez offered a different assessment of traditional village life. The culture and character of Spanish villagers had been valuable in the past as the means that enabled this people to survive in a harsh and isolated environment. But these "age-old patterns" did not work in the modern setting and instead prevented Hispanos from competing successfully with Anglos. Hispanos, he said, "battle their own cultural inadequacy. They are unprepared to act in their new environment—unprepared because of centuries of isolation. They have no tradition of competition, of education, or of Western civilization beyond the sixteenth century. The New Mexican is not yet an American culturally, the Treaty of Guadalupe notwithstanding."[37]

Instead of idealizing the vestiges of the colonial past, Sánchez argued that the very retention of some aspects of that culture impeded Hispano progress. The fault, however, lay not simply with Hispanos themselves, but with Anglos who had systematically denied Hispanos the tools necessary to assimilate and participate on an equal basis in American society. Anglos had been content to ignore the economic and educational conditions of most Hispanos, blaming Nuevomexicanos for their own misfortune and expecting them to make up for their own deficiencies. Hispanos had to overcome their own "cultural inertia," Sánchez declared, but the state and county governments, controlled by Anglos and upper-class Hispano allies, had to bring to an end the inequitable policies that had discriminated against the mass of Hispanos since the American takeover.[38] In Sánchez's analysis, the lack of equal educational opportunity lay at the heart of the woes of rural Hispanos. Not only could they not compete for higher-paying jobs, but without adequate education, they did not fully understand the political process and could easily be taken advantage of by bosses and cynical politicians who courted their vote but ignored their interests. Health conditions suffered as well with continued reliance on traditional medicine, home remedies, and patent medicines.[39]

While Sánchez decried certain cultural practices as detrimental to Hispano progress, he did not condemn the culture wholesale, nor did he advocate total assimilation to Anglo practices. Without romanticizing Hispano culture, he identified many worthy aspects of tradition that would make valuable contributions to American civilization. "His ability to contribute, and the nature of the contribution," Sánchez asserted, "is suggested by the tenacity with which he has maintained himself, his economy, and his social structures on this forbidding frontier for more than three centuries. That contribution might well embody worthy elements of his culture—language, music, folklore, architecture, foods, crafts, and customs. The New Mexican's filial respect, his love of home and of country, and his fortitude in the face of adversity are potential resources to Americanism. The democracy inherent in New Mexican culture bespeaks these peoples' preparedness to enhance American life.[40]

The solution to the desperate conditions of Hispano life had to incorporate the positive aspects of the culture while addressing the serious deficiencies that had resulted from neglect and isolation. Sánchez's multifaceted proposal for reform was radical. First, he suggested that the federal government should purchase the former common lands that had once belonged to the Hispano villages and return the land to the villages.

He pointed out that the government had set a precedent for a similar land program in creating reservations for Native Americans. With a return to a larger land base, Hispano agriculture would have a better chance of sustaining the communities. To ensure prosperity, state and federal government must implement a broad-ranging program of economic and educational development aimed at instructing the villagers in modern agricultural practices, including the use of farm machinery, improved breeds of livestock, and fertilizers. Similar efforts would have to be directed toward improving the health, diet, and sanitation of the villages and providing credit and banking facilities. Finally, the schools had to offer a curriculum for both children and adults that took into account the culture and circumstances of the village.[41]

*Forgotten People* might have been received more positively had its author not already established himself as a thorn in the side of the establishment. Sánchez's book came at the end of a decade during which he had repeatedly attacked the state government for its shortcomings when it came to education for Hispanos. It was particularly galling for political and educational leaders that Sánchez supported all his arguments with sound statistical and scientific evidence. He proved conclusively that the state discriminated against Hispano-dominated counties in the apportionment of state school funds. He pestered the legislature to pass an equalization bill, but by the time it was signed into law in 1935, it had been so watered down that it gave most control for its implementation to state officials beholden to railroad and landowner interests. Sánchez never forgave the politicians for succumbing to cronyism, and the politicians, in turn, saw to it that Sánchez's position in the state Department of Public Instruction lost its funding.[42] In 1940 Sánchez accepted a position on the faculty of the University of Texas and left his home state. By the end of his career, he had become one of the most well-respected and honored advocates of equal educational opportunity for Hispanics in the Southwest.

## IDENTITY, MARGINALIZATION, AND CITIZENSHIP

Sánchez's efforts to infuse a dose of reality into the contest over Hispano identity failed to hit home in New Mexico. To Sánchez the issue of identity masked a larger problem of equal educational and economic opportunity for the Hispano population, and he tried to focus attention on these more practical problems. The solutions for Hispanos' woeful conditions would have entailed an even greater commitment on the part of federal and state government than occurred under the New Deal. During the 1930s, efforts were made in New Mexico to reinvigorate the economy, schools, and social life of northern New Mexico, but these fell far short of the broad changes that Sánchez thought would be necessary to create equal opportunities for Hispanos. It is an open question whether Sánchez might have eventually influenced other educators such as Otero-Warren, Tireman, or Sewall to abandon or accommodate the identity-based strategy they had pursued through the 1930s and to focus more on economic issues. Sánchez was forced out of the state, and soon after the great developments associated with World War II eclipsed New Deal programs in their effect on the lives and livelihoods of Nuevomexicanos. Like Americans everywhere, New Mexicans would emerge from the war in the midst of different circumstances entirely. The work of George Sánchez and other educators such as Nina Otero-Warren, Loyd Tireman, and Brice Sewell came to a rather abrupt end as a result of the war, and so we cannot evaluate their long-range effect. Rather, they represent significant and unusual approaches to the problem of marginalization that remain intriguing despite their obvious elitist and primitivist underpinnings.

The movement to romanticize Hispanos in New Mexico reflected the use of identity for different purposes, depending on whose perspective we consider. Hispanos could embrace the construction of an identity based on their Spanish colonial past for a number of reasons. It was, in fact, a heritage to be proud of, one that portrayed them as deriving from noble roots and offered a history of sturdy and brave pioneers adapting to a harsh environment and triumphing over adversity. They could feel justly proud of their artistic and architectural contributions, and not be ashamed of their language and culture. Anglos, conversely, seemed to have adopted the use of a romantic Hispano identity for a greater range of reasons. Some simply wished to promote tourism in New Mexico, and the Spanish colonial identity offered an exotic and appealing attraction. Others sincerely wished to improve the reputation of Hispanos and boost their self-esteem. Still others hated modern industrial society and saw in traditional Hispanic culture an antidote to the ills of modernity. All of these views, Hispano and Anglo alike, represented a tacit assumption that New Mexico's Hispano community was unique and needed to be distinguished from the specter of Mexican immigrants.

The romanticizing of Hispano identity, whoever used it, did have the potential to reduce the burden of marginalization by encouraging respect for Hispanos and by promoting cooperation between Anglos and Hispanos. Upper-class Hispano leaders, such as Nina Otero-Warren, both sought out Anglo allies and were courted by Anglos in the effort to improve schools and promote the Spanish colonial heritage. Some Anglos, such as Loyd Tireman, devoted their careers to improving the lives of Hispanos. And few public officials or politicians in New Mexico dared ignore the Hispano community or treat them with blatant disrespect.

Ironically, however, the praise heaped on the Hispano community in the process of making it seem romantic and attractive came at a price. George Sánchez exposed that price, and in the end, he paid dearly. He worked with Anglos his entire career and was even considered a potentially effective cultural broker who could uplift his people through his cooperation with the established system. But he broke the unspoken rule of the whole New Mexican game: he named the broken promises, he listed the failures, he read the record of discrimination out loud. He revealed the fallacy at the heart of the effort to bring the two peoples together under the guise of romance. Idealization of the Spanish colonial identity was the consolation prize for acceptance of second-class citizenship.

What this episode says to us about the exercise and recognition of citizenship is the larger lesson to be drawn from the contest over Hispano identity. In a most fundamental way, the issue for Hispanos was whether or not they could exercise full citizenship in a sense that has recently been characterized as "cultural citizenship." Evelyn Nakano Glenn defines cultural citizenship as "the right to maintain cultures and languages differing from the dominant ones without losing civil or political rights or membership in the national community."[43] Hispanics across the Southwest believed in 1848 that the Treaty of Guadalupe Hidalgo had guaranteed them cultural as well as civic citizenship. Well into the twentieth century they were still struggling to achieve it, and today the question still resonates with newly arrived immigrant populations.

New Mexico's Hispano elites, who were in a position to act as agents on behalf of the state's poor and powerless Hispanos, chose to embrace a romanticized racial and cultural identity. They hoped that Anglos would no longer feel threatened by the presence of a supposed alien culture within their midst and thus would not stand in the way of full participatory citizenship by Hispanos. But the strategy failed to address the problem of exclusion from full participation in American life. Part of the reason why it failed was that the strategy, and its agents, only demanded cultural inclusion, instead of demanding full political and economic participation. It also failed because it depended on a moral obligation on the part of Anglo power brokers to follow through with education, economic opportunities, and political power, having accepted the cultural identity of Hispanos. In the 1930s they were not willing to do this. The experience of World War II changed the entire landscape, giving the Hispano community a much greater sense of inclusion as citizens because of their wartime service, but also leaving them with a greater willingness to pursue assimilation. Only with the militant Chicano movement of the 1960s and '70s did young Hispanos demand not only their full political and economic rights as citizens, but also the right to embrace with pride their true mestizo identity.

## NOTES

1.  The terms *Hispano* and *Nuevomexicano* will be used interchangeably throughout this essay to refer to New Mexicans of Spanish descent. The terms were in use at the time and are commonly used by historians today. The terms *Mexican* and *Mexican American* were generally rejected by New Mexicans. The term *Chicano* was used as a pejorative by New Mexicans until the Chicano movement of the 1960s and even then was embraced more by young activists than by older New Mexicans. The term *Spanish American* was used commonly from the late nineteenth century through the present, although I have chosen not to use it here, except in reference to the identity campaign from which it derived. When I use the term *Hispanic*, I am referring to any persons of Spanish descent, whether they live in New Mexico, California, Texas, etc. The terms *Californio* and *Tejano*, which were more common in the mid-nineteenth century, were much less in use by the 1920s and 1930s, and so I avoid using them when referring to Hispanics in California and Texas.

2.  See Charles Montgomery, *The Spanish Redemption: Heritage, Power, and Loss on New Mexico's Upper Rio Grande* (Berkeley: University of California Press, 2002), 48–53; Leonard Pitt, *The Decline of the Californios: A Social History of Spanish-speaking Californians, 1846–1890* (Berkeley: University of California Press, 1966), 7–11, 85–86; Douglas Monroy, *Thrown among Strangers: The Making of a Mexican Culture in Frontier California* (Berkeley: University of California Press, 1990), 207–19; Albert Camarillo, *Chicanos in a Changing Society: From Mexican Pueblos to American Barrios in Santa Barbara and Southern California, 1848–1930* (Cambridge, MA: Harvard University Press, 1979); and Matt S. Meier and Feliciano Rivera, *The Chicanos: A History of Mexican Americans* (New York: Hill and Wang, 1972), 88–95.

3. David R. Maciel and Erlinda Gonzales-Berry, "The Twentieth Century: Overview," in *The Contested Homeland: A Chicano History of New Mexico,* ed. Erlinda Gonzales-Berry and David R. Maciel (Albuquerque: University of New Mexico Press, 2000), 84.

4. John Nieto-Phillips, "Spanish American Ethnic Identity and New Mexico's Statehood Struggle," in *The Contested Homeland,* 123–25.

5. John Nieto-Phillips, *The Language of Blood: The Making of Spanish-American Identity in New Mexico, 1880s–1930s* (Albuquerque: University of New Mexico Press, 2004), 49.

6. Nieto-Phillips, *The Language of Blood,* 118–35.

7. For a discussion of the struggle over control of schools prior to statehood in New Mexico, see Lynne Marie Getz, *Schools of Their Own: The Education of Hispanos in New Mexico, 1850–1940* (Albuquerque: University of New Mexico Press, 1997), 13–47.

8. Erlinda Gonzales-Berry, "Which Language Will Our Children Speak? The Spanish Language and Public Education Policy in New Mexico, 1890–1930," in *The Contested Homeland,* 169–85.

9. Educators in the 1920s enthusiastically embraced intelligence tests as a tool for determining the abilities of children. Unfortunately, they did not take into account the cultural and class biases of IQ tests and therefore came to conclusions that most nonwhite groups were racially inferior to whites. Thus IQ testing reinforced racist beliefs and justified low expectations for nonwhite children, including Hispanics. Later social scientists, including George I. Sánchez, exposed the biases of IQ testing, which led to efforts to develop bias-free tests. On the issue of intelligence testing, see Leon J. Kamin, *The Science and Politics of IQ* (New York: John Wiley and Sons, 1974); Paul Ehrlich and S. Shirley Feldman, *The Race Bomb: Skin Color, Prejudice and Intelligence* (New York: Quadrangle Books, 1969); and Amada M. Padilla, "Early Psychological Assessment of Mexican-American Children," *Journal of the History of the Behavioral Sciences* 25 (Jan. 1988): 111–16.

10. *New Mexico Common Schools Course of Study* (Santa Fe, NM: State Board of Education, 1921), 89–90; and *New Mexico Course of Study for Elementary Schools* (Santa Fe, NM: State Department of Education, 1930), 40, in Department of Education Papers, Exp. 50, New Mexico State Records Center and Archives, Santa Fe (hereafter NMSRCA).

11. Joan M. Jensen, "Women Teachers, Class and Ethnicity: New Mexico, 1900–1950," *Southwest Economy and Society* 4 (Winter 1978–79): 7–9; and Nan Elsasser, Kyle MacKenzie, and Yvonne Tixier Y Vigil, *Las Mujeres: Conversations from a Hispanic Community* (Old Westbury, NY: Feminist, 1980), 25, 87.

12. Nieto-Phillips, *The Language of Blood,* 145–49, 171–76.

13. Marta Weigle, "The First Twenty-Five Years of the Spanish Colonial Arts Society," in *Hispanic Arts and Ethnohistory in the Southwest,* ed. Marta Weigle (Santa Fe: Ancient City, 1983), 182-183; and Montgomery, *The Spanish Redemption,* 172–77.

14. News clippings re: Nina Otero-Warren, #105, and Scrapbook #6—Nina Otero Warren's congressional campaign, #122, Bergere Family Collection, NMSCRA; and Charlotte Whaley, *Nina Otero-Warren of Santa Fe* (Albuquerque: University of New Mexico Press, 1994), 64–66, 73–75.

15. Nina Otero-Warren, *Old Spain in Our Southwest* (New York: Harcourt Brace and Company, 1936), 51.

16. Adelina Otero Warren, "Curriculum for the Elementary Schools of Santa Fe County," 1929, 2, File #42, Bergere Family Collection, NMSCRA.

17. Ibid., 2.

18. Weigle, "The First Twenty-Five Years of the Spanish Colonial Arts Society," 188, 190–91; and Suzanne Forrest, *The Preservation of the Village: New Mexico's Hispanics and the New Deal* (Albuquerque: University of New Mexico Press, 1989), 53–54.

19. Sarah Deutsch, *No Separate Refuge: Culture, Class, and Gender on an Anglo-Hispanic Frontier in the American Southwest, 1880–1940* (Oxford University Press, 1987).

20. Loyd S. Tireman, "Mi Amigo el Hispano," 5, 7–8, 1033.1, Box 599, Folder 631, General Education Board Papers, Rockefeller Archives Center, Pocantico Hills, New York (hereafter GEB).

21. Loyd S. Tireman, "First Annual Report of the San José Training School," 1931, 2–4, in 1033.1, Box 599, Folder 6361, Ser. I. 4, GEB.

22. L. S. Tireman, Mela Sedillo Brewster, and Lolita Pooler, "The San José Project," *New Mexico Quarterly* 3 (November 1933): 214.

23. Loyd S, Tireman to Leo M. Favrot, 3 December 1931, in 1033.1, Box 598, Folder 6358, Ser. I.4, GEB.

24. Esther Lanigan Stineman, *Mary Austin: Song of a Maverick* (New Haven: Yale University Press, 1989), 152–54, 176.

25. Montgomery, *The Spanish Redemption*, 179, 282 fn 56.

26. For a recent discussion of Mary Hunter Austin's role in idealizing Pueblo Indian culture, see Margaret D. Jacobs, *Engendered Encounters: Feminism and Pueblo Cultures, 1879–1934* (Lincoln: University of Nebraska Press, 1999).

27. Mary Austin, "Mexicans and New Mexico," *Survey* 66 (1931): 144, 187.

28. Mary Austin, "Rural Education in New Mexico," *University of New Mexico Bulletin*, Training School Series, 2 (I) (December 1931), 28–29.

29. Mary Austin to Governor Arthur Seligman, 28 January 1933, in State Department of Education, Governor Arthur Seligman Papers, NMSCRA.

30. Brice Sewell, "Vocational Education: Do You Know?" *New Mexico School Review* 12 (May 1933): 23; and *Report of the Superintendent of Public Instruction for the Fourteenth Biennium Period Beginning July 1, 1936, and Ending June 30, 1938* (Santa Fe, NM: State Superintendent of Public Instruction, 1938), 38.

31. Brice H. Sewell, "A New Type of School," *New Mexico School Review* 14 (October 1935): 49–50.

32. Forrest, *Preservation of the Village*, 140–50; and Montgomery, *The Spanish Redemption*, 185–86.

33. Elsasser, MacKenzie, and Tixier y Vigil, *Las Mujeres*, 25.

34. James Nelson Mowry, "A Study of the Educational Thought and Action of George I. Sanchez" (PhD diss., University of Texas, 1977), 23–26; and Gladys R. Leff, "George I. Sanchez: Don Quixote of the Southwest" (PhD diss., North Texas State University, 1988), 36–37, 111–12.

35. The General Education Board was founded in 1902 by John D. Rockefeller. Intended primarily to provide assistance for improving education for blacks in the South, the GEB extended aid to New Mexico as a result of the entreaties of New Mexican educators, suggesting that both the GEB and New Mexicans saw parallels between education for blacks in the South and Hispanics in New Mexico. GEB agents emphasized technical education and the nurturing of "cultural brokers," individuals who would promote cooperation between the races. Raymond B. Fosdick, *Adventure in Giving: The Story of the General Education Board* (New York: Harper & Row, 1962), 8–9, 83–85; James D. Anderson, "Northern Foundations and the Shaping of the Southern Black Rural Education, 1902–1935," *History of Education Quarterly* 18 (Winter 1978): 374, 378–81; W. W. Brierly to Georgia Lusk, State Superintendent, 24 April 1931, and Georgia Lusk, John Milne, and J. F. Zimmerman to General Education Board, 6 March 1931, in NM I, Box 100, Folder 900, Ser. I, GEB.

36. Montgomery, *The Spanish Redemption*, 202.

37. George I. Sánchez, *Forgotten People: A Study of New Mexicans* (Albuquerque: University of New Mexico Press, 1940), 13. Sánchez is referring here to the Treaty of Guadalupe Hidalgo of 1848, which ended the Mexican-American War and ceded the territories of New Mexico, Arizona, and California to the United States. Under the Treaty the former Mexican citizens who chose to become U.S. citizens were guaranteed the protection of their civil, property, religious, and cultural rights. Unfortunately, this proviso was widely and blatantly disregarded throughout the Southwest. See Matt S. Meier and Feliciano Rivera, *The Chicanos: A History of Mexican Americans* (New York: Hill and Wang, 1972), 69–73.

38. Sánchez, *Forgotten People*, 38–39.

39. Ibid., 34–35, 37.

40. Ibid., 97–98.

41. Ibid., 89–98.

42. "Progress of the N.M.E.A. Legislative Program," *New Mexico School Review* 14 (December 1934): 8; "N.M.E.A. Legislative Program Compared with Educational Legislative Enactments," *New Mexico School* Review 14 (March 1935): 8–9; Leff, "George I. Sanchez," 167–69; *Santa Fe New Mexican*, 8 February 1935, 9 February 1935, 11 February 1935, 20 March 1935; Tom Wiley, *Public School Education in New Mexico* (Albuquerque: Division of Government Research, University of New Mexico, 1965), 53–56.

43. Evelyn Nakano Glenn, *Unequal Freedom: How Race and Gender Shaped American Citizenship and Labor* (Cambridge, MA.: Harvard University Press, 2002), 54.

# CHAPTER 6

# USING THE PRESS TO FIGHT JIM CROW AT TWO WHITE MIDWESTERN UNIVERSITIES, 1900–1940

RICHARD M. BREAUX

IN 1937, CHARLOTTE CRUMP, A BLACK STUDENT AT THE UNIVERSITY OF Minnesota (UM), published a series of letters to her sister Marsha titled "The Free North," which appeared in the UM quarterly review and later in the National Urban League's monthly journal, *Opportunity*. In these letters she described her and other black students' struggles against discrimination at UM. University policy barred black students from campus dormitories, barred and then segregated them in the School of Nursing, and prohibited black men from intercollegiate baseball and basketball teams. Crump became increasingly frustrated by the arbitrariness of campus and off-campus racism. As the title of her series suggests, this was life in the free North, not the segregated South. Moreover, the source of this racism and discrimination was the so-called gifted, educated, and enlightened whites, not the stereotypical poor, ignorant, rural white person. "Why," asked Crump, "did I think that white college students would be different from other white people?"[1]

Crump's article was, in part, credited with bringing an end to black students' exclusion from UM's dormitories in 1938. Her writings, along with protest by the university's Negro Student Council, revealed the contradiction between America's and UM's professed ideals of equality for all, and the realities of Jim Crow for many black collegians on America's predominantly white college campuses.[2]

In this essay, I argue that black students at the University of Minnesota and the University of Kansas (KU), and their supporters, used the black press and at times the white press to expose and challenge racial discrimination and segregation on their respective campuses. These alternative newspapers and magazines (1) published black students' thoughts and frustrations about the ways white students, faculty members, and administrators marginalized them; (2) printed evidence that demonstrated that black students were the intellectual equals of whites; and (3) challenged written and unwritten campus policies that barred blacks from, or segregated them in, the classroom, academic disciplines, and academic clubs and honor societies. While stories of black students' struggles occasionally found room in the mainstream white press, it was the local, regional, and national black press and the alternative white press—in tandem with the efforts of civil rights activists—that "extended democracy" and made university and state government officials more "accountable to the people."[3]

In their works on college student life, Helen Lefkowitz Horowitz and Paula Fass describe black college students on predominantly white colleges as the quintessential outsiders and well outside the mainstream of those who participated in or created college-youth culture.[4] This was never wholly the case at KU and UM, because local and regional black newspapers played an important part in informing black readers of these collegians' achievements and contributions to student culture. Many of these early students experienced a mixed reception from their white peers and white administrators, and campus student newspapers were equally as likely as the black press to report positive as well as negative incidents involving these students. The racism and discrimination faced by the likes of students such as Blanche K. Bruce (KU, 1885) and Andrew Hilyer (UM, 1882) made news, but very little was recorded concerning the ways in which these pioneering black students protested their campuses' conditions.[5] One of the earliest indications of black student protest at either of these institutions came in 1898, when McCants Stewart, an UM law student, filed charges against the owner of a Minneapolis restaurant for violating the state's civil rights statute. According to witnesses, Stewart entered the restaurant, seated himself at a vacant table, and waited over forty-five minutes before the owner, John Flangstad, refused to take Stewart's order.[6] After Flangstad insulted Stewart several times, Stewart collected the names of witnesses, left the restaurant, and later successfully sued on the claim that the state's civil rights law had been violated.[7]

Such bold and successful battles against Jim Crow rarely occurred among black collegians at white colleges and universities in the immediate aftermath of the *Plessy v. Ferguson* decision, but as once-liberal colleges and universities such as Oberlin, Harvard, KU, and UM became entangled in the national web of federally and state-sanctioned Jim Crow, black students' protests against racial discrimination began to occur more frequently.[8]

What started as an annoying issue for white college administrators from the 1890s to the 1910s grew into a serious problem by the 1920s and 1930s. Campus racism as well as discrimination against black collegians in places of business near university campuses began to increase around 1912, when the number of black students at both UM and KU remained just large and persistent enough to maintain black student groups and black fraternities and sororities. Changes in these universities' administrative personnel, increases in white student enrollment, and the nation's worsening racial climate also played roles in the upsurge in racist practices. In 1919, the year twenty-six race riots erupted in northern and southern cities, KU began to bar black men from intercollegiate athletic teams, intramural sports, and the military sciences; black women from the school of nursing; and blacks from the clinical years of medical school and from the teaching practicum needed to be certified as public school teachers. Blacks at KU were also forced to sit in sections designated for "blacks only" at university concerts; they were barred from campus housing and segregated at tables and in restrooms in the student union building. At UM, whites made similar but less successful attempts to bar black men from certain sports and the clinical years of medical school, to prevent black women's enrollment in nursing and home economics, and to prohibit blacks from residing in campus dormitories.

In 1926 the black-owned *St. Paul Echo* ran a story about five UM black women students who brought a civil suit against the owner of The Oak Tree restaurant when they were refused service. Like Stewart did twenty-eight years earlier, the five black coeds argued that The Oak Tree owner, Robert Kanze, had violated the state's civil rights law that was upheld in 1898 in the Stewart case.[9] Rachel Gooden's mother filed the case, but no existing records reveal the outcome of the complaint. In 1929–30, a biracial committee of the campus YMCA and YWCA found that of thirty-four restaurants frequented by UM students, twenty-six "showed little or no discrimination," three restaurants flatly refused to serve any African Americans, and others varied on their discriminatory treatment from "pointed slow service," to the use of unusually large amounts of spice on black patrons' foods. The student group also found that larger groups of black students faced greater discrimination than a single black patron or mixed groups of black and white student patrons.[10]

## THE BLACK AND ALTERNATIVE PRESS

For many blacks in the country, black newspapers affirmed their existence, their struggle, and their sense of humanness. Black newspapers, news magazines, and other "race publications" placed black culture, achievements, struggle, and defeat directly in the spotlight. In the documentary *The Black Press: Soldiers without Swords*, Vernon Jarret recalled that blacks did not exist in the white press unless they committed a crime. "We were neither born, we didn't get married, we didn't die," Jarret protested, "we didn't fight in any wars, we never participated in any kind of a scientific achievement." The black press, however, affirmed blacks' existence, "We did get married. They showed us our babies being born. They showed us graduating. They showed our PhDs."[11]

Black newspapers were not only filled with stories about black collegians' lives, experiences, and cultures at white colleges, these periodicals also became a place where many young black college-educated journalists began their careers. Conservative and militant black journalists and politicos like Roy and Earl Wilkins (UM), Marie Ross (KU), Charlotte Crump (UM), Homer Smith (UM), Doxey Wilkerson (KU), and a number of lesser-known students worked part-time, full-time, or as freelancers for the local and regional black newspapers. By the 1930s, the *Kansas City Call*, the city's middle-class and politically moderate black newspaper, issued an open invitation to black collegians who attended black and white colleges and universities in Kansas, Nebraska, Missouri, and Texas to contribute to its regular weekly column, "College News." Black students at KU, the University of Nebraska, Parsons Community College in Kansas, Kansas State Agricultural College, Kansas State Teachers College, Tillotson College, Western College, and Prairie View College took the opportunity to hone their newspaper-writing skills, while keeping readers abreast of the culture, politics, and progress of black colleges and collegians.[12]

Local and regional black newspapers have been one of the most underused sources in studies on black collegians at white colleges and universities before World War II. These papers, and the students who were often covered in their pages, occupy such a marginal place in the history of higher education that many are likely to believe that all black collegians before 1940 attended exclusively black colleges such as Fisk, Howard, Lincoln, and Tuskegee, or white heavily-endowed institutions like Oberlin, Harvard, the University of Chicago, and New York University. Most historians of education, following the model of W. E. B. Du Bois's *Crisis*, have focused on blacks in Ivy League institutions, blacks at black colleges, or blacks at public or private universities in major urban areas like New York City and Chicago. This essay focuses on blacks at UM, a predominantly white university in the twin cities of Minneapolis-St. Paul and blacks in the much smaller city of Lawrence, Kansas.

Three black Twin City newspapers provided regular coverage of events involving black UM students: the *St. Paul Echo* (1925–27), the *Twin City Herald* (1927–40), and the *Minneapolis Spokesman* (1934–present). The Topeka *Plaindealer* (1899–32) and Missouri's *Kansas City Call* (1919–present) proved to be equally effective in covering stories by and about black students enrolled at KU. The publications of black Greek-letter organizations, like Alpha Kappa Alpha's *Ivy Leaf*, Alpha Phi Alpha's *Sphinx*, Kappa Alpha Psi's *Kappa Journal*, and white radical student newspapers, like KU's *Dove*, also provided information on the ways blacks students voiced their thoughts and asserted themselves.

The perspective these papers offered usually mirrored the views of their editors. For example, the *St. Paul Echo* contained a variety of light-hearted and serious news items of concern to blacks locally and nationally. It did not shy away from criticizing President Calvin Coolidge on race issues. It provided extensive coverage of black life at UM, especially when local restaurants, university professors, or other university personnel discriminated against black students. Because Earl Wilkins, a black UM alumnus and former student newspaper editorial board member, edited the *St. Paul Echo*, news of the successes and trials of blacks at UM appeared regularly in the paper.[13] Cecil Newman edited the *Twin City Herald* until 1934 and then founded the *Minneapolis Spokesman* that same year. Newman's passionate commitment to black labor and civil rights meant that the papers he worked for or established, more than any other in Minneapolis-St. Paul, covered blacks' struggle to desegregate UM's School of Nursing, the clinical phase of the medical school, and campus dormitories.[14] In Topeka, the hot-tempered civil rights maverick Nicholas Chiles edited the controversial *Plaindealer* and the more mild-mannered, but equally dedicated Chester A. Franklin established, printed, and edited the *Kansas City Call*. Franklin pulled off a major coup d'état when he lured reporter Roy Wilkins, the future *Crisis* writer, NAACP executive director, UM alumnus, and brother of Earl Wilkins, away from the floundering *St. Paul Appeal* in 1923.[15]

Cases of racial exclusion or extreme campus racism began to receive national attention with the publication of the *Crisis*, the magazine of the National Association for the Advancement of Colored People (NAACP). Drawing on his early interest in black higher education, the *Crisis* editor, W. E. B. Du Bois, began to record the graduation of blacks from black and white colleges and the trials and tribulations students endured to achieve the personal and collective milestone of a college degree. While the annual education issue of the *Crisis* tended to focus on black student achievement, it did not take Du Bois very long to notice that "northern white colleges" had "ceased to encourage Negro students, and in many cases, actively discouraged them" from pursuing a college education.[16] Nonetheless, the reports from predominantly white campuses that appeared in the *Crisis* were rarely documented in detail. Only the most abhorrent cases of discrimination at KU and UM found their way into black national magazines such as the *Crisis*.

The campus dailies at UM and KU, the *Minnesota Daily* and the *University Daily Kansan*, varied in the coverage of black student life. These periodicals were politically moderate and generally sympathetic to black students' difficulties. While they covered protests against racial discrimination on campus, however, they—unlike the local and regional black press—offered very little on black student life on a regular basis. Like the national black periodicals, campus dailies tended to print only the most sensational racial episodes on campus.

Most publications that catered to a predominantly white readership either wholly ignored stories about blacks or printed the most sensational stories about black crime. The exception tended to be newspapers published by white radicals or progressives who sought to draw class alliances. In Kansas, for example, the publications of Emmanuel and Marcet Haldeman-Julius, the *Haldeman-Julius Weekly* and *Haldeman-Julius Monthly*, championed black civil rights and the rights of black students on a number of the state's predominantly white campuses. The radical white press, however, like the national black press, tended to cover black student protest and white campus racism only when incidents reached a feverish pitch.

While the more widely circulated Haldeman-Julius publications have received greater attention from historians, KU's *Dove* (1925–51)—technically published off campus—demonstrated a longer and more sustained commitment to black students' rights. The *Dove* was KU's pink, progressive newspaper; it rarely shied away from serious political debates. It was born immediately after the post–World War I "Red Scare," survived through World War II, and lasted until the witch hunts of the McCarthy era brought on its demise. It was a clear alternative to the more mainstream *University Daily Kansan*; it was antiwar, antifraternity, pro–civil rights, pro-labor, and pro–women's rights when these stances were largely unheard of in the mainstream press.[17] Most important for black students, it not only reported on campus racism but it also gave black students a venue to voice their opinions and included several black students, including Doxie Wilkerson, Sterling Owens, and Dolores Estues, on its staff or editorial board.

### BLACK STUDENTS WRITE ABOUT WHITES AND RACISM

In 1925 black KU student Doxey A. Wilkerson penned the article, "Wonder What the Negro Thinks About," in the *Dove*. Wilkerson's soliloquy exposed and explored the arbitrariness and inconsistency of white racism at KU. According to the article, white KU students spoke to and worked with black students in class but pretended not to know these same black students around campus. Many white students spoke to black students to get homework assignments and borrow pencils but pretended black students were invisible around campus. Whites who spoke "vehemently" against racism in class might speak to blacks in informal settings, but they apologetically explained to their white friends that they only spoke to blacks out of an obligation to fulfill course requirements.[18]

This was one of many articles about campus racism that would appear in the *Dove* over the next decade. Such press coverage of black student protest and campus racism at KU culminated in a Kansas House of Representative investigation of Jim Crow at KU in 1934 and the desegregation of the KU School of Medicine in 1938.[19]

Slightly less than a year before the desegregation of KU's medical school, black students began to demand greater changes at UM. Charlotte Crump's article, "The Free North," discussed in this essay's introduction, inverts the popularly studied concept of the black image in the white mind: Crump instead exposes the white image in the black mind. Her reflections reveal problems black students experienced in local stores and restaurants and the efforts of black students to draw interracial alliances with white students. Most important, Crump sheds light on black students' efforts to organize among themselves to rid UM and other colleges of Jim Crow once and for all. "The Free North" complicates our understanding of how so-called racial outsiders related to white students and vice versa. Crump maintained that there were three kinds of white students: (1) those who attended multiracial events and went to extreme lengths to speak to blacks to show their concern for the so-called "Negro Problem"; (2) those who demonstrated little interest in thinking about racism or discrimination because they felt it was not their problem; and (3) whites who were overtly "antagonistic" toward all nonwhites.[20]

While a substantial amount of history and literary criticism has investigated the real and imagined, and the distinct and distorted, images of blacks in the white mind and popular culture, historians and literary scholars have only recently began to examine how black Americans have perceived white Americans.[21]

The essays by Wilkerson and Crump lay bare the frustrations of blacks on predominantly white campuses during the 1920s and 1930s. Their writings both confront state and university-sanctioned Jim Crow as contradictory to northern and midwestern civil rights law and highlight the more exhausting "little things" that frustrated black and nonblack interactions on a daily basis.

## BLACK GREEK-LETTER ORGANIZATIONS

Black fraternities and sororities at KU and UM demonstrated that they could successfully compete academically with white Greek-letter organizations, and the national periodicals of black fraternities and sororities highlighted these achievements. Most U.S. colleges and universities that had fraternities and sororities ranked them academically each year. Administrators would divide the sum of the grade averages (GPAs) of each group's members by the total number of members to obtain a group grade-point average. As a group, black fraternities and sororities rode the roller coaster of academic rankings along with white fraternities and sororities. In some years, black Greek-letter groups ranked dead last, while in other years they ranjed higher than their white classmates. In most years, black fraternities and sororities ranked neither at the top nor the bottom, but near the middle. At times, they flexed their intellectual muscle. As early as 1922, KU's Upsilon chapter of Alpha Phi Alpha placed second in the standing for highest GPA among national Greek-letter fraternities on campus. A report in KU's *University Daily Kansan* noted, "Some of the social problems arising from the race have resulted in situations and practices that are intrinsically unjust to" blacks students. Blacks paid students fees for university-affiliated events and student parties from which whites barred them, yet whites respected and admired black students' "self-sufficient and pleasant social life" and blacks' "academic achievement."[22]

Reports on black achievements by black and alternative white papers sometimes advocated, but often inadvertently printed evidence, that blacks were whites' intellectual equals. In 1926, members of the Psi chapter of Kappa Alpha Psi at UM were able to maintain a "B" average.[23] During the 1927–28 academic year, Alpha Kappa Alpha at KU placed sixth out of twenty sororities. In the same year, the *Ivy Leaf,* Alpha Kappa Alpha's national monthly, reported that the Eta chapter of Alpha Kappa Alpha at UM placed first among sororities, although in the previous year it had placed a dismal twenty-first.[24] The *Ivy Leaf* and the *Dove* reported that in 1928–29 the Delta chapter of Alpha Kappa Alpha at KU ranked first among all sororities on its campus, black or white, but then fell to last place in the following school year, and then "reclaimed [its] throne" in 1930–31.[25] The year that Alpha Kappa Alpha resurfaced as KU's top sorority, the *University Daily Kansan* noted that Delta Sigma Theta ranked a dismal last among fifteen sororities on campus, and Alpha Phi Alpha and Kappa Alpha Psi at KU ranked eighteenth and twenty-third out of twenty-four national fraternities.[26] Meanwhile, *Minnesota Daily* reported that Eta chapter of Alpha Kappa Alpha at UM fell to thirteenth out of twenty-seven in 1930 but regained the top-ranked slot in the fall of 1931. Likewise, Alpha Kappa Alpha's brother organization at UM, the Mu chapter of Alpha Phi Alpha, ranked first among thirty-eight fraternities. As these examples demonstrate, black Greek-letter organizations and their journals emphasized the idea that black academic work and achievements were as important as those of white fraternities and sororities.[27]

The black press, campus papers, and departmental bulletins high-lighted the accomplishments of a few black scholars in particular areas of study, especially when black students received academic awards in the social sciences and sciences. In 1924, for example, the *Crisis* reported that Hugh Brown received a number of scholarships and prizes at KU for his work in zoology.[28] The *Haldeman-Julius Weekly* noted in 1927 that another black student received the Harmon Prize for achievement in Engineering.[29] In 1928 students at KU tapped Georgia Caldwell for *Pi Mu Epsilon*, a mathematics honor society, and KU's chapter of Alpha Kappa Delta, a sociology honor society, had selected Willie A. Strong, a black woman from Oklahoma and a member of Delta Sigma Theta, for membership.[30] The Alpha Kappa Alpha sorority monthly, *Ivy Leaf*, reported that in 1929 Florence Webster won KU's John T. Stewart Schol-arship for outstanding achievement in music, and classmates selected her for membership into the honorary music society Pi Kappa Lambda.[31] One year later, according to the *Ivy Leaf*, an honorary sociology sorority, Sigma Delta Gamma at UM, inducted Alpha Kappa Alpha member and baseball standout Pearl Renfroe. In 1934 the Kansas Pharmaceutical Society awarded Hamilton Perkins, a black KU student, first prize and "an engraved master pharmacist's diploma in its Prescription Com-pounding Contest."[32] Two years later members inducted John Hodge into Phi Mu Epsilon mathematic society and Dorothy Hodge into Sigma Delta Chi journalism society. *Phi Beta Kappa* (PBK) at KU selected the Hodge siblings for membership as well. In 1938 Beulah Payne, a member of *Alpha Kappa Alpha* at KU, received several honors: she was named on the dean's list, initiated into the *Iota Sigma Pi* hon-orary chemistry sorority, and inducted into PBK.[33] These achievements demonstrate that black students at UM and KU were white students' intellectual equals. Furthermore, the black press and progressive white press made a point to highlight these achievements as examples of racial uplift and advancement.

## NURSING SCHOOL

Black students on white campuses expected to be excluded from white social clubs, but many assumed that they would have a fair chance in aca-demic departments and in the classroom. However, these students encountered arbitrary expressions of racial discrimination. For example, black students were welcome in most disciplines in the humanities and social sciences, but they were discouraged from pursuing degrees in the sciences. In all disciplines, blacks faced segregated seating assignments and white professors who never gave black students grades higher than a C. Black students found the medical sciences the most difficult to enter, not because of these disciplines' academic standards, but because many hospital administrators claimed that white patients would never agree to physical examinations by black doctors or nurses.

Nursing was one of the few science-related areas in which university officials actually encouraged women, that is, white women, to enroll in unlimited numbers, believing that nursing suited women because of their so-called natural mothering abilities. Although black women showed an interest in nursing, KU generally barred them from nursing school, while UM initially barred them from nursing school and later, when they allowed a few to enter, discriminated against them with regard to the school's residential policy and clinical requirements.

Compared to UM, nursing administrators at KU were unwavering in regard to the politics of the color line; in the years before World War II, KU did not graduate any black nursing student. One black woman, however, Charlotte K. May, received three years of her training at KU before going to Kansas City's all-black General Hospital No. 2 for further training.[34] May was the exception rather than the rule. When the Kansas House of Representatives in 1935 investigated black students' complaints about racial discrimination at KU, legislators learned that, in addition to discrimination in KU's swimming pool and medical school, "Negro girls [were] denied the privilege of taking courses in nurse training at the University Hospital."[35]

At UM, one of the earliest documented cases involving the admission of a black woman to the UM School of Nursing arose in 1925 when Dorothy Waters, already a registered nurse in Illinois, applied and was accepted to undertake postgraduate work at UM. Waters received notice from the School of Nursing that she would be assigned to St. Paul Hospital. When she arrived at St. Paul Hospital, however, hospital administrators notified her that, because she was black, she would not be permitted to complete her assignment. Waters complained to Gertrude Brown, manager of Minneapolis' all-black Phyllis Wheatley Settlement House, which doubled as a community center for black Twin Citians and blacks at UM, that no special provisions or prohibitions directed at black students appeared in the UM enrollment contract. If they had, she would not have resigned from her position in Chicago. Angered by the bar against black women in nursing, Waters's mother and friends attempted to persuade her to get a lawyer to "make a strong effort for justice."[36] Only a conversation with Brown, a black clubwoman who had developed relationships with white clubwomen in Minneapolis, prevented Waters from launching a full assault.

Brown contacted Mrs. James Paige, president of the Woman's Christian Association, and convinced her to inquire on Waters's behalf to UM dean Elias P. Lyon. Paige pleaded Waters's case, pointing out that Waters had given up her home and was in dire "straits."[37] Lyon forwarded the letter to UM president Lotus D. Coffman, and Coffman replied that if he had known that Waters was black, he would have "advised her against coming" to Minneapolis. The university sent students to the hospital, but hospital administrators made the final decision on which students it accepted or rejected. Because St. Paul's Miller Hospital and the other hospitals affiliated with the School of Nursing were private and made no provisions for blacks, Coffman maintained that the university, "no matter how liberal its policies," could not "force colored nurses on white people."[38] When Lyon responded directly to Paige, he, too, laid the blame at the hospital's door. He claimed that the hospital and its patients, not the university discriminated against blacks. Lyon's suggestion that blacks follow the lead of the late Booker T. Washington and build their own institutions, not "force their way into white social institutions," reveals that the prejudice was not solely in the hospitals.[39] Indeed, Lyon apologized, but prevented Waters from continuing her course of study despite the presence of Louise Algee, another black student, in the public health nurse program.[40]

The UM School of Nursing controversy did not end with Dorothy Waters. Four years later, Lyon and Coffman developed more sophisticated, but less successful methods for keeping black women out of the nursing program. The university would make distinctions between black medical students and black nursing students, and it would also maintain that one of the reasons it rejected black nursing school applicants rested on the fact that the women who applied were not residents of Minnesota.

In 1928 Frances McHie, a black student from Minneapolis, applied to the School of Nursing. Lyon and Coffman collaborated on a letter stating that after an unsuccessful attempt to place a nursing student in the past, they could not provide any black nursing students with the required clinical experience. Lyon and Coffman suggested that the students go to Provident Hospital in Chicago, and UM's dean and president went to great pains to highlight the hospital's connection to the University of Chicago and its wonderfully equipped facilities. Lyon and Coffman's detailed letter outlined the other areas of study at UM (medicine and teacher education) that presented problems for UM when black students applied to these programs. They noted that certain areas of medicine remained closed to women, black or white. Nursing, which had nearly all women enrolled, and medicine, almost entirely male, posed similar but slightly different problems for UM when black students sought admittance. Medical students came in much less physical contact with white patients than nursing students. Black medical students were sent to one of a number of black hospitals around the country to complete their internships. UM did not have a similar process for black nursing student; instead, Lyon and Coffman preferred to recommend black women to black nursing colleges.

The left-leaning black alumnus Homer Smith and the local NAACP came to McHie's defense and helped her challenge UM's segregationist policy. Smith, who later joined the Communist Party and moved to Russia, only to become disillusioned by the Communism under Stalin, sent a letter to Coffman, demanding an explanation for UM's refusal to admit McHie to the nursing program.[41] When Coffman sent a reply with explanations that Smith deemed unsatisfactory, Smith had the communications reprinted in a local black paper, the *Twin City Herald*. Smith also fired off an indignant editorial in which he charged UM administrators with missing the opportunity to use fairness and their political power to combat "the Color problem."[42]

Soon the local chapters of the NAACP put their full weight behind McHie's efforts and pressed one of its white members, Sylvanus A. Stockwell, who also happened to be a member of the Minnesota legislature, to appeal to the governor. Stockwell also flexed his political muscle and in April 1929 discussed McHie's case on the floor of the legislature, invited McHie and Gertrude Brown to make an appearance, and convinced legislators to draft a letter to the UM regents to overturn McHie's rejection.[43]

The Minneapolis NAACP readied itself to file suit to bring about justice for McHie. It asked McHie to submit a second application for admission into the UM School of Nursing and local offices buzzed with anticipation as attorneys prepared briefs for the mounting case. With the threat of legal action and public embarrassment, however, President Coffman relented.

One year after McHie enrolled, another black student named Theresa Jones, who had been denied admission earlier, reapplied to the School of Nursing. Because of the residency requirement for nursing students, administrators assigned Jones to live with McHie, who was living in a segregated room in the Minneapolis General Hospital's nurse's home. Frances McHie graduated from UM in 1932.[44] There is no information on whether Theresa Jones graduated.

## MEDICAL SCHOOLS

The admission of blacks, and particularly black men, to UM's and KU's medical schools was also fraught with race and gender politics. Generally, medical school officials encouraged men interested in science to become doctors, but this was not the case for aspiring black physicians. One of the UM's and KU's greatest concerns was the clinical portion of medical school, which included obstetrical and gynecological work. White medical doctors and administrators cringed at the thought of black men examining white women.[45] Historian Raymond Wolters notes that this was a concern for black medical students at Harvard and the University of Vermont as well.[46] At KU an unwritten policy kept blacks from completing their internships and residencies in university-controlled or affiliated hospitals.[47] Policies toward black student enrollment in schools of medicine at other universities varied from a complete bar to admittance with strict quotas on the number of blacks who could be enrolled at any one time. Blacks, however, fought for equal access to publicly funded educational institutions, and they eventually brought down arbitrarily practiced Jim Crow at UM and hard-line Jim Crow at KU.

Black prospective medical students' efforts to enter clinical courses, internships, and residencies caused major problems for university administrators, despite the graduation of two blacks: W. B. Holmes, a light-skinned African American who later passed for white, graduated in 1894, and W. D. Bloom graduated in 1903.[48] Most black students interested in the human-related sciences who attended UM between 1903 and 1921 studied pharmacy.

White medical school administrators at UM dragged their feet on the issue of allowing black students to complete their entire course of study at UM. In 1925 William Brown, a native of Minneapolis, received his degree from UM, but UM medical school administrators and local hospital officials forced Brown to complete his internship at the all-black

Meharry Medical School in Nashville, Tennessee.[49] It took five more years before Walter Minor and John Chenault successfully challenged a St. Paul hospital superintendent's claim that blacks were not suitable to work as interns in the hospital. In 1930 one of the student's fathers filed a formal complaint with the county board of commissioners. Rather than face an expensive lawsuit and more negative publicity, the county board passed a resolution that outlawed discrimination on the basis of "race, creed, or color," and Dean Elias P. Lyon appointed the students to internships at UM's hospital. Both men graduated in that same year.[50]

For almost fifteen years, KU administrators consulted administrators at UM about how to address student, alumni, and regional black leaders' demands to desegregate KU's nursing and medical schools.[51] However, no administrator at KU could have anticipated the upsurge in student protests against campus discrimination in the late 1920s.

In 1923 Nicholas Chiles wrote an editorial in the *Topeka Plaindealer*. Chiles, the editor of the *Plaindealer*, charged that the bar against blacks disgraced black students and the university. He also blasted, "If you cannot be fair to all, then resign and go south where the devil and his angels favor persecuting colored people. John Brown died that Kansas might be free and it is not for you or your kind to change it. Get right, Brother Lindley, or get out." Chiles maintained that KU was a public state university supported by white and black taxpayers. As such, he proclaimed, "these institutions belong to the people, and the people demand fair treatment for all."[52]

Similar sentiments were written by Loren Miller in his essay, "Unrest among Negro Students," published in the August 1927 issue of the *Crisis*. Miller, who left KU after one year, blamed Chancellor Ernest H. Lindley for his perpetuation of racial inequalities through institutionalized racism. Although Lindley had championed the cause for a women's dormitory, he claimed that the enrollment of "so many Southern students" at KU prohibited black women from taking up residency in these facilities. Miller maintained that Lindley proudly proclaimed his family's abolitionist background but degraded every black student at KU.[53] White leftist publishers Marcet and Emmanuel Haldeman-Julius leaped at the chance to interrogate Lindley and other administrators about a number of issues including black students' exclusion from the last two years of medical study.

Black and white students and a few white professors joined the battle. Josephine Burnham, an assistant professor of English, wrote to Emmanuel

Haldeman-Julius that Jim Crow at the medical school remained one of the biggest problems at KU. Burnham argued that a racist general public, not administrators, remained the greatest roadblock to black students' medical school admission.[54] Black students like Sterling V. Owens, Florence Webster, John Bell, and Doxey Wilkerson and white students Paul Porter and Noel Gist organized a research team that supplied Marcet and Emmanuel Haldeman-Julius with information to write articles in their monthly and weekly journals. The *Haldeman-Julius Weekly* reprinted Miller's *Crisis* article with a commentary by Emanuel Haldeman-Julius. Haldeman-Julius emphasized the injustice endured by blacks who paid their state taxes but were not allowed to complete a medical degree at KU.

After visits to KU and to state campuses in Manhattan, Emporia, and Pittsburgh, and with help from her student research teams, Marcet Haldeman-Julius published a stinging thirty-page indictment of state tax-supported institutions: While administrators of these institutions claimed that racial prejudice only existed in social situations, they prevented blacks from their teaching practicum and the last two years of medical school. Haldeman-Julius said that she could empathize with Chancellor Lindley, but she also noted that neither he nor any other KU administrator did anything but pass the proverbial buck in which "the School of Medicine can blame the administration; the administration can blame the Regents; the Regents can blame the legislature; and the legislature can blame the people." The medical school dean, Harry R. Wahl, argued that patients who paid for their treatment in the university-owned hospital, which had 120 beds and took no free patients, could not be forced to have a black doctor or nurse. Haldeman-Julius recommended that, as a solution, the university convert an empty former hospital building in Kansas City into a separate hospital for blacks. Then the KU medical school could increase its black and white enrollment of medical students and assign black and white interns to nonpaying patients.[55] Although the editorials by Marcet and Emmanuel Haldeman-Julius, and the initial articles by Chiles and Miller, did not immediately change things for prospective black medical students, the research that supported these protests spawned a number of multiuniversity surveys and reports on the condition of black students at public universities in the Midwest.[56] Information from the editorials, surveys, and reports—concerning Jim Crow in KU's swimming pool and the barring of blacks from the teacher-training program as well as the nursing and medical schools—was used by the Kansas House of Representatives when it met for a special session in 1933 and again in March 1934. The legislative hearings confirmed black students' complaints and shined negative light on the state's once-liberal university, but it failed to make any significant changes or recommendations.

As the campaign against racism at KU continued, those who had been waging the war since Miller's *Crisis* article appeared in 1927, began to see some results. Between 1934 and 1939, three different black students applied for admission to the KU medical school, and finally, with assistance from a number of black communities in Kansas, the NAACP, and a newly elected governor, the wall fell that separated black medical students in their first two years of medical school in Lawrence from their subsequent years at the Rosedale campus in Kansas City. Donald S. Ferguson, a Kansas resident with bachelor's and master's degrees, applied and was denied admission to KU's medical school several times between 1934 and 1939. Another student, Geraldine Mowbray, who was a Kansas native and graduate of Howard University, applied to the medical school in 1937, and administrators similarly denied her admission. Despite these two rejections, the political environment was changing. In 1936 blacks had turned out to the polls and elected a politically moderate Democrat to the governor's office. At the same time, the Kansas City and Topeka chapters of the NAACP continued to apply pressure on KU's medical school. As a result, the wall of segregation cracked, and in 1938 Edward V. Williams entered KU's medical school for the complete four-year course of study. Williams graduated in 1941.[57]

## CLASSROOMS AND PROFESSORS

The victories for black medical students at KU and UM resulted from the combined efforts of black students, local blacks, and civil rights organizations. These, however, were probably easier victories because the prejudices against black collegians were so obvious. Racial discrimination in the classroom and as practiced by individual professors was in some ways more difficult to prove, confront, and change.

Classroom racism included segregated seating charts, racist comments directed at black students, professors' ignoring the raised hands of black students, and suggestions by advisers that blacks choose different majors. One professor at KU sought to discourage black students from pursuing a career in journalism when he commented, "I see we have a darky in the class."[58] Marie Ross, who wrote for the *Kansas City Call* as a student and later for the *Iowa Bystander*, remembered that the head of the journalism department suggested that she wasted her time learning how to write for newspapers that did not hire blacks. This professor insisted that there was nowhere that a black reporter could find work, and therefore, Ross should reconsider her career plans. A resistant and determined Ross later presented "a stack of black newspapers like the *Kansas City Call*" to her presumptuous professor.[59] She later asked Roy Wilkins, a black UM graduate and editor of the *Kansas City Call*, to be a guest speaker in her class.[60]

Engineering professors at KU marched in mental lock step with their peers in other departments, according to an article by Haldeman-Julius, when they advised black students to withdraw from the School of Engineering because there was no room for blacks in the field.[61] In his 1925 article published in the KU student newspaper, *Dove*, the black student Doxey Wilkerson pondered sarcastically whether the professor intentionally ignored his raised hand or if the library attendant purposefully served black students after whites on nearly every occasion.[62] Black students repeatedly complained of biased treatment by KU's professors. In February 1927, Wilkerson reported in the *Dove* that Chelsey Posey, a professor in the Department of Geology, ordered a group of black women enrolled in his course to sit together, segregated, in the corner of the classroom.[63]

At UM, Jeremiah Young, a professor of political science, omitted the name of a black student from his alphabetically arranged seating chart. Young told Willard Morrow, the only registered black student in his class, that he "could take a seat at either side or in the rear of the room." Outraged at the professor's suggestion, Morrow demanded that he be allowed to sit in alphabetical order among the white students or he would drop the course. When Professor Young appeared unmoved by Morrow's threat, the young black student asked if his classmates could vote on the matter. When Professor Young agreed, the class voted that Morrow had a right to be assigned as any white student and he assumed his rightful place in class.[64] But the story was not over. When the Minneapolis branch of the NAACP got word of the incident through the local press, newly appointed branch president, W. Ellis Burton, fired off a letter to UM president Lotus Coffman, voicing the NAACP's concern with racial prejudice in a University supported, in part by black and white taxpayers. Burton also encouraged UM administrators to "promptly suppress any act of" discrimination practiced by faculty or any representatives of UM.[65] How President Coffman handled the matter remains unclear;

however, it was obvious that the Minneapolis branch of the NAACP would not stand for race discrimination in a state-owned institution. If they could not win the war against racism, they would at least strike a blow against racial prejudice and injustice.

These and other instances demonstrate that black collegians' struggles at KU and UM to gain equal access to these universities' academic, professional, and intellectual resources were fraught with frustrations. Racial discrimination was arbitrary, difficult to document and often specter-like. Although the laws in these states supported the rights of blacks to have equal access to these institutions and their resources, more often than not, black students on white campuses had to fight for these rights. In using the press to help them challenge campus discrimination, these students and their supporters made significant inroads toward the goal of achieving equality for black collegians. Furthermore, these pioneers paved the way for greater access and better treatment for black and other nonwhite students who attended midwestern universities in the decades after World War II.

### NOTES

1. Charlotte Crump to Marsh (Marcia Crump), reprinted as "The Free North," *Opportunity* (September 1937), 271, 272, and 285. Crump graduated and worked for the *Pittsburgh Courier*. Earl Spangler, *The Negro in Minnesota* (Minneapolis: Denison, 1961), 116.

2. *Minnesota Spokesman*, 3 February 1938, newspaper clipping in the Presidential Correspondences, folder 1937–39, University of Minnesota Archives, Minneapolis, MN. Here after cited as UMA.

3. Henry Lewis Suggs, *The Black Press in the Middle West, 1865–1985* (Westport, CT: Greenwood, 1996), 350. A handful of studies have examined black protest on white public universities before 1940. See, for example, Raymond Wolters, *New Negro on Campus: Black College Rebellions in the 1920s* (Princeton, NJ: Princeton University Press, 1978); Kristine McCusker, "The Forgotten Years of America's Civil Rights Movement: University of Kansas, 1939–1961" (masters thesis, University of Kansas, 1994); Amber Reagan-Kendrick, "Ninety Years of Struggle and Success: African American History at the University of Kansas, 1870–1960" (PhD diss., University o f Kansas, 2004). Space constraints prevent me from including in this essay the successes and failures of black students at KU and UM to desegregate campus housing, student unions, and athletics.

4. Helen Lefkowitz Horowitz, *Campus Life: Undergraduate Cultures from the End of the Eighteenth Century to the Present* (Chicago: University of Chicago Press, 1987), 14; Paula Fass, *The Damned and the Beautiful: American Youth in the 1920s* (New York: Oxford University Press, 1977), 7–8.

5. Spangler, *The Negro in Minnesota*, 76; Tim Brady, "Almost Perfect Equality," *Minnesota Magazine* (September–October 2002), http://www.alUMi.UM.edu/printview/fd18e044-3823-47e6-9f00 (accessed on 9 July 2005); *University Courier*, 12 February 1866; Chuck Marsh, "First Black Graduate Was Acclaimed Tutor," *Kansas Alumni* 83, 5 (February 1985): 11; Robert Bruce Slater, "The First Black Graduates of the Nation's Flagship State Universities," *Journal of Blacks in Higher Education* (Autumn 1996): 78.

6. "Color Line Drawn: McCann Stewart Couldn't Get a Meal at Flangstad's Restaurant," *Minneapolis Tribune*, 18 March 1898, clipping in Personal Newspaper Clips No. 1, Stewart—Flippin Papers, Box 97-3, folder 53, Manuscripts Division, Moorland-Spingarn Research Center, Howard University, Washington, DC.

7. "Guilty! John Flangstad Convicted of Violating the Civil Rights Law," *Minneapolis Tribune*, 19 March 1898, clipping in Personal Newspaper Clips No. 1, Stewart—Flippin Papers, Box 97-3, folder 53, Manuscripts Division, Moorland-Spingarn Research Center, Howard University, Washington, DC.

8. Raymond Wolters, *The New Negro on Campus: Black College Rebellions in the 1920s* (Princeton, NJ: Princeton University Press, 1975), 313–33; W. E. Bigglestone, "Oberlin College and the Negro Student, 1865–1940," *Journal of Negro History 56, no. 3* (July 1971): 198–219; James O. Horton, "Black Education at Oberlin College: A Controversial Commitment," *Journal of Negro Education* 54, no.1 (1985): 477–99; Cally L. Waite, "The Segregation of Black Students at Oberlin after Reconstruction," *History of Education Quarterly* 41, no. 3 (Fall 2001): 344–64; Werner Sollors, Caldwell Titcomb, and Thomas A. Underwood, eds. *Blacks at Harvard: A Documentary History of African-American Experience at Harvard and Radcliffe* (New York: New York University Press, 1993); Linda Perkins, "The African American Female Elite: The Early History of African American Women at the Seven Sister Colleges, 1880–1960," *Harvard Educational Review* 67, no. 4 (Winter 1997): 718–56.

9. "Restaurant Refuses Co-eds: $500 Lawsuit to Be Brought by One Mother," *St. Paul Echo*, 2 October 1926. The students were Rachel Gooden, Zelma Jackson, Marjorie Wormley, Beulah Stephens, and Ruth Brown.

10. Maurine Boie, "A Study of Conflict and Accommodation in Negro-White Relations in the Twin Cities-Based on Documentary Source" (master's thesis, University of Minnesota, 1932), 54–55.

11. *The Black Press: Soldiers without Swords* (San Francisco, CA: California Newsreel, 1998).

12. "Among the Universities and Colleges of Kansas and Missouri," *The Call*, 29 November 1929; "College News," *The Call*, 26 November 1930, 7 October 1930, 21 November 1930, 12 December 1930, 30 January 1931, 27 February 1931, 22 January 1932.

13. Spangler, *The Negro in Minnesota*, 211; "Earl Wilkins of Xi," *The Oracle* (March 1925): 19; "University of Minnesota—Xi Chapter," *The Oracle* (March 1925): 21–22; Henry Lewis Suggs, "Democracy on Trial: The Black Press, Black Migration, and the Evolution of Black Culture and Community in Minnesota,

1865–1970," in Henry Lewis Suggs, ed. *The Black Press in the Middle West, 1865–1985* (Westport, CT: Greenwood, 1996), 177; Boie, "A Study of Conflict and Accommodation in Negro-White Relations in the Twin Cities-Based on Documentary Source," 62.

14. Suggs, "Democracy on Trial," 177–196; Spangler, *The Negro in Minnesota*, 210 and 211; Boie, "A Study of Conflict and Accommodation in Negro-White Relations," 47–50.

15. For more on Chiles, see, Dorothy V. Smith, "The Black Press and the Search for Hope and Equality in Kansas, 1865–1985," in *The Black Press in the Middle West, 1865–1985*, ed. Henry Lewis Suggs (Westport, CT: Greenwood, 1996), 118-119; For more on C. A. Franklin and the *Call*, see George Everett Slavens, "Missouri," in *The Black Press in the South, 1865–1979*, ed. Henry Lewis Suggs (Westport, CT: Greenwood, 1983), 217-241.

16. "Colleges and Their Graduates in 1914," *Crisis* (July 1914): 129.

17. "Plenty Hot, But Not Scorching," KU History; http://www.kuhistory.com/proto/story-printable (accessed 9 July 2005).

18. Doxey A. Wilkerson, "Wonder What a Negro Thinks About," *Dove* (April 1925): 2.

19. "Probe Discrimination at KU," Kansas City *Call*, 9 March 1934; "Prejudice at Kansas University," Kansas City *Call*, 9 March 1934; Nancy J. Hulston "The Desegregation of the University of Kansas School of Medicine, 1938," *Kansas History* 19, no. 2 (1996): 88–97; "There Is Too Much Talk Here about Segregation," http://www.kuhistory.com/proto/story.asp?id=337 (accessed 9 July 2005).

20. Crump, "The Free North," 271 and 272.

21. Mia Bay, *The White Image in the Black Mind: African-American Ideas about White People, 1830–1925* (New York: Oxford University Press, 2000); Jane Davis, *The White Image in the Black Mind: A Study of African American Literature* (Westport, CT: Greenwood, 2000), 2 and 3–9. Jane Davis argues that four "types" of whites have filled black literature and writing: (1) the overt white supremacist; (2) the hypocrite, (3) the good-hearted weakling, and (4) the liberal.

22. "Kansas Commends Colored Students for Grades," *University Daily Kansan*, 24 November 1922; Griffin Notes UA/ SH/ 85/ PP/ 14/ Box 22, University of Kansas Archives, Kenneth Spencer Research Library, University of Kansas Libraries, Lawrence, KS. Hereafter cited as KUA.

23. William L. Crump and C. Rodger Wilson, *The Story of Kappa Alpha Psi: A History of the Development of a College Greek Letter Organization, 1911–1971*, 2nd ed. (Philadelphia: Kappa Alpha Psi Fraternity, 1972), 76 and 77.

24. "Eta Chapter, University of Minnesota," Ivy *Leaf* 6 (1927–1928): 20–21.

25. Amy Delores Estues, "Leaving Their IQ Behind," *The Dove*, 21 November 1929; "Report of Delta Chapter, Lawrence Kans.," *Ivy Leaf* 6 (1927–1928): 16–17; "Delta Doings," *Ivy Leaf* (December 1931): 12–13; "Negro Sorority Awarded First in Scholarship Rankings," *University Daily Kansan*, 11 October 1931.

26. "Negro Sorority Awarded First," *University Daily Kansan*, 11 October 1931.

27. "All-U. Grades Hit New Mark Second Time with 1.223; 12 Fraternities Miss 'C' Average," *Minnesota Daily*, 29 September 1931;"Greeks Set High Scholastic Marks," *Minnesota Daily*, 1 October 1930; Charles H. Wesley, *The History of Alpha Phi Alpha: A Development in College Life*, 15th ed., (Chicago: Founder, 1991), 223; "Eta," *Ivy Leaf* (December 1937): 30.

28. "The Year in Higher Training," *Crisis* (July 1924): 108.

29. E. Haldeman-Julius, "How Kansas University Kicks the Negro," *Haldeman-Julius Weekly*, 20 September 1927.

30. "K.U. Girl Elected to Sociology Frat," *Omaha Monitor*, 1 June 1928.

31. "Delta," *Ivy Leaf* (June 1929): 19; "Delta," *Ivy Leaf* (June 1930): 5 and 11.

32. "Eta Chapter," *Ivy Leaf* (June 1930): 8; "Pearl Renfroe," *Gopher* (1930): 125; "Pharmacy News Letter Identifies a Colored Student, As Colored," *UK School of Pharmacy News Letter*, 1 June 1934, Griffin Notes, KUA.

33. "Georgia A. Caldwell, Delta," *Ivy Leaf* (May 1928): 34; "Delta," (June 1929): 19; "Soror Beulah Payne Elected to Phi Beta Kappa," *Ivy Leaf* (June, 1938): 9; Résumé of Dorothy Hodge Johnson, Dorothy H. Johnson papers, RG#94-12-9, biography folder, Box 2, KUA; "John E. Hodge Elected into Phi Beta Kappa" and "John and Dorothy Hodge Receive Honors at KU," news clippings in Dorothy H. Johnson Papers, RUMS 549.1.3, folder Report Cards 1923, 1933–35, KUA.

34. Adah Thoms, *Pathfinders: A History of the Progress of Colored Graduate Nurses* (New York: Kay Print House, 1929), 54.

35. *Journal of the Kansas House*, 5 March 1935, 3.

36. Mrs. James Paige to E. P. Lyon, 21 October 1925, Presidential Correspondences, folder 1921–35, University of Minnesota Archives, Elmer L. Anderson Library, University of Minnesota, Minneapolis, MN. Hereafter cited as UMA.

37. Mrs. James Paige to E. P. Lyon, 21 October 1925, folder 1921–35, Presidential Correspondences, UMA.

38. President L. D. Coffman to Mrs. James Paige, 30 October 1925, folder 1921–35, Presidential Correspondences, UMA.

39. Elias P. Lyon to Mrs. James Paige, 2 November 1925, folder 1921–35, Presidential Correspondences, UMA.

40. "Public Health Nurses," *Gopher* (1926): 76.

41. For more on Smith's views on Communism and his experiences in Russia, see Homer Smith, *Black Man in Red Russia* (Chicago: Johnson Publishing, 1964), chapter 4.

42. H(omer) S(mith), "How the Color Problems Are Created," *Twin City Herald*, 22 June 1929, folder 1921–35, clipping in Presidential Correspondences, UMA.

43. Ann Juergens, "Lena Olive Smith: A Minnesota Civil Rights Pioneer," *William Mitchell Law Review* 28, no. 1 (2001): 433–45.

44. "Francis McHie Rains, Nurse and Educator," http://www.startribune.com/viewers/story.php (accessed 24 February 2003). None of the above cases appear

in James Gray, *Education for Nursing: The History of the University of Minnesota School* (Minneapolis: 1960).

45. Phillip G. Hubard, *New Dawns: A 150-Year Look at Human Rights at the University of Iowa* (Iowa City, University of Iowa Sesquicentennial, 1996), 13.

46. Wolters, *The New Negro On Campus*, 330–31.

47. Hulston, "'Our School Must Be Open to All Citizens," 88–97 and note 17; In the 1920s UM reversed its policy on black nursing students.

48. "William Leonidas Ricks," *Appeal*, 10 June 1905; Tim Brady, "Almost Perfect Union," *Minnesota Magazine* (September–October 2002), http://www.alumni .umn.edu/printview/fdi8e044-3823-47e6-9f00-d8 (accessed 9 July 2005).

49. A. Henmina Poatgieter, "Biographies of Black Pioneers," *Gopher Historian* (1968–1969): 21.

50. Boie, "A Study of Conflict and Accommodation in Negro-White Relations in the Twin Cities," 48–49.

51. Malcolm Wiley to Raymond Nicholas, 19 March 1934, EHL Papers, RG # 2/9/1, General Correspondence folder N, Box 2 K-O, KUA.

52. Editor to Chancellor Lindley, "The K.U. Trustees Should Look after Chancellor Lindley," *Topeka Plaindealer*, 16 November 1923.

53. Loren Miller, "The Unrest among Negro Students," *Crisis* (August 1927): 187 and 188.

54. Ibid., 187; Josephine M. Burnham to Mrs. (Marcet) Haldeman-Julius, 21 November 1927, Haldeman-Julius Correspondence, folder 1927-11-28, Emanuel and Marcet Haldeman Julius Papers, Pittsburg State University, Pittsburg, KS. Hereafter cited EMJH Papers.

55. Haldeman-Julius, "How Kansas University Kicks the Negro"; Emanuel Haldeman-Julius to Lawrence Clem, 1 November 1927, Haldeman-Julius Correspondence, folder 1927-11-1,EMHJ Papers; Florence Webster to Marcet Haldeman Julius, 8 November 1927, Haldeman-Julius Correspondence, folder 1927-11-8, EMHJ Papers; Paul Porter to Marcet Haldeman Julius, 28 November 1927, Haldeman-Julius Correspondence, folder 1927-11-28, EMHJ Papers; "Race Question in Kansas, Discussed," clipping from the *Emporia Bulletin*, 25 October 1927, Haldeman-Julius Clippings, folder 1927-10-25, Haldeman-Julius Papers; Marcet Haldeman-Julius, "What the Negro Student Endures in Kansas," *Haldeman-Julius Monthly* (January 1928): 157–58.

56. "Data on "The Status of the Colored Student on Nine Middle Western University Campuses," 1928, RG#2/9/5, Box 1, Correspondence Dept—DOW, folder 1927/28, EHL Papers, KUA.

57. Hulston, 'Our School Must Be Open to All Citizens," 96–97.

58. Elaine Davis, "A Pioneer in the News Is Now a Story," *Kansas City Star*, undated clipping from the Black History file, Watson Community Museum, Lawrence, KS.

59. Davis, "A Pioneer in the News."

60. Jerri Niebaum, "Ross Devotes Career to Call for Equity," *Kansas Alumni Magazine*, (June/July 1993): 44; "Roy Wilkins, The Call's New Editor, Addresses K.U. Journalism Classes," *The Call*, 6 May 1927.

61. Haldeman-Julius, "How Kansas University Kicks the Negro."

62. Doxey A. Wilkerson, "Wonder What a Negro Thinks About," *Dove* 1, no. (29 April 1925): 6–7.

63. D. A. W., *Dove* 2, no. 4 (15 February 1926): 1.

64. "Equal Rights Voted for Negro Student," Minneapolis *Journal*, 21 April 1921, clipping in folder, 1921–1936, Presidential Correspondences, UMA.

65. W. E. Burton to Lofts Coffman, 27 April 1921, folder 1921–1936, Presidential Correspondences, UMA.

# CHAPTER 7

# BREAKING BARRIERS: THE PIONEERING DISABILITY STUDENTS SERVICES PROGRAM AT THE UNIVERSITY OF ILLINOIS, 1948–1960

STEVEN E. BROWN[1]

DURING THE PAST TWO CENTURIES, MANY AMERICANS BELIEVED INDIVIDuals with disabilities were deviant, or worse. Those with disabilities were cast aside, like criminals, away from public view.[2] In 1948 a determined young man named Tim Nugent intended to overturn such thinking. From 1948 to 1960, he shepherded a program that succeeded in shattering longstanding, pervasive institutional, physical, economic, psychological, and other barriers that marginalized and ostracized people with disabilities.[3] As the first director of the University of Illinois Disability Resources and Educational Services (DRES) program,[4] Nugent did everything in his power to ensure its survival. He battled prevalent negative social attitudes, university bureaucracy, and an inaccessible environment. He cajoled, badgered, and encouraged many students who were unprepared for postsecondary success. As a result, the Illinois program became an oasis in the desert of prevailing societal ostracism toward persons with disabilities, especially those considered to have the most severe

impairments, including people with spinal cord injuries, post-polio disabilities, and genetic conditions such as muscular dystrophy and cerebral
palsy. This essay places the program in historical context, discusses the
implementation of the program, and explains how Nugent and the Illinois program assisted other universities to support students with disabilities. The program therefore helped not only students with disabilities,
but all individuals with disabilities, to move from almost total isolation
and powerlessness to becoming productive, contributing members of
society.

## EDUCATION, REHABILITATION, AND ADVOCACY IN THE FIRST HALF OF THE TWENTIETH CENTURY

The problem of the crippled is very different from that of the normal child.
Unlike the latter, the crippled or deformed youngster is a lonely creature,
unable to join in the sports of other children, and constantly reminded of his
disability. This frequently develops an abnormal psychology, a moroseness,
self-consciousness, so affecting his point of view as to add to an unfortunate
physique a mental peculiarity.[5]

Criminals who broke the law were sentenced to prison terms. Individuals with disabilities were cast indefinitely into asylums.[6] Communities
purposely constructed the classic asylum, sometimes better known as a
state hospital, as physically isolated as possible from mainstream society.
The best location was on a rural road miles from town. The institution
would be plopped in the middle of the highest available hills if any
existed.[7]

An exception to the asylum came in the form of schools specialized for
distinct populations. The American School for the Deaf was founded in
Hartford, Connecticut, in 1817, and the Perkins School for the Blind in
Boston opened its doors to its first two students in 1832.[8] At the postsecondary level, today's Gallaudet University, for deaf, hard-of-hearing,
and hearing individuals interested in deafness issues, was first incorporated in 1857 as the Columbia Institution for the Instruction of the Deaf
and Dumb and Blind.[9]

The above instances proved the exception to the rule. Education for
individuals with disabilities, especially higher education, was rarely considered. Why would there be a need for those barred from mainstream
social structures to acquire an education?

Some attitudinal changes toward disability occurred after World War I, which both increased the numbers of individuals with disabilities, as a result of war wounds, and produced medical advances. In 1918 Congress passed the Smith-Sears Veterans Vocational Rehabilitation Act, establishing federal vocational rehabilitation for disabled soldiers. Two years later, in 1920, lawmakers passed the Fess-Smith Civilian Vocational Rehabilitation Act, creating a vocational rehabilitation program for disabled civilians.[10]

During the ensuing two decades, Vocational Rehabilitation (VR), which now combined veteran and civilian programs, struggled to legitimize its role, endeavoring to persuade state governments of its utility while maintaining a minimal funding base. In 1939 VR moved to the Federal Security Agency, created in one of many periodic governmental reorganizations. At the Federal Security Agency, VR became part of a team that included New Deal work programs such as the Civilian Conservation Corps and the National Youth Administration, and agencies like the Public Health Service and the Social Security Board, which worked, at least in part, with individuals with disabilities. Rehabilitation workers liked working with these agencies because they felt that their role of placing people with disabilities in the workforce required a multitude of skills and networks.[11]

A year later, in 1940, Congress extended vocational rehabilitation services to people with disabilities working in sheltered workshops. Charities established these workshops where workers were paid pennies on the hour for assembling piecemeal products. VR, for the first time, also served homebound individuals and laborers in need of VR services to remain employed. This broader responsibility set the stage for a decade of greater funding and responsibilities. In 1943 a stand-alone Office of Vocational Rehabilitation was created within the Federal Security Agency. VR funding increased 75 percent in 1940, and both fiscal allocations and services continued to expand throughout the 1940s.[12]

While VR grew, it still did not serve those with the most severe disabilities. Individuals who did not seem likely to find employment did not fit into the system. In addition, VR, like other programs for those with disabilities, instructed individuals with disabilities about what they could or should do, rather than listening to, or working in concert with them. This led, in the middle of the twentieth century, to the appearance of nascent disability rights organizations.

In 1940 the country's first cross-disability (composed of people with all kinds of disabilities) national political organization was formed: the American Federation of the Physically Handicapped. To meet its objective of ending job discrimination, the organization lobbied for various activities, including a National Employ the Physically Handicapped Week. Legislation supporting such a week became a reality in 1945[13] and evolved eventually into today's annual October National Disability Employment Awareness Month.

Two other notable groups began in the mid-1940s. The Paralyzed Veterans of America and the President's Committee on Employment of the Handicapped formed shortly after World War II. Lawmakers also provided significant incentives to veterans to facilitate their reentry into society and the workforce. Whereas programs after World War I concentrated on reintegration into the workforce, post–World War II legislation included broader social enticements. For example, a 1948 piece of housing legislation provided veterans with service-connected disabilities, a $10,000 grant, and a $10,000 loan to purchase, build, or modify a house.

These isolated pockets of change marked incipient changes in social values. In Los Angeles, for example, four World War II veterans began classes at UCLA in 1946, where they were assisted by a group of California veterans (CAL-VETS) volunteers who carried the vets into inaccessible buildings.[14] In 1947 the Paralyzed Veterans of America formed, the first meeting of the President's Committee on Employment of the Physically Handicapped occurred, and the World War II veteran and double-hand amputee Harold Russell earned two Oscars for his role in the 1946 movie, *The Best Years of Our Lives*, a portrait of how difficult it could be for someone wounded in war to reintegrate into society.[15] In addition, this movie was an excellent presentation of how difficult it was for all veterans, not just those with disabilities, to reenter society. It also demonstrated the impact all veterans had on post-World War II society.

Just as all veterans affected the culture to which they returned, the lives of veterans with disabilities had an effect on individuals with disabilities who had not gone to war. For example, modern mid-twentieth-century medicine, which saved the lives of many veterans who would have died from similar wounds in previous battles, also benefited others with disabilities. Moreover, the need to employ returning vets, especially those with disabilities, showed that all those with significant physical disabilities could work and be productive. In addition to these changes and evolving attitudes, the G.I. Bill, which opened doors for veterans with and without disabilities to enter colleges, influenced the development of the University of Illinois program for students with disabilities.

## TIM NUGENT COMES TO ILLINOIS

"When you embark on something new, there are those that oppose what you are doing out of honest beliefs and convictions. When you prove your points, they become among your strongest supporters"[16]

World War II's impact on American life is hard to overstate. Millions of Americans fought and died on battlefields, while multitudes were wounded. Many of the wounded became disabled veterans. Politicians were extremely sensitive to the power of these veterans. One reason for this heightened awareness resulted from the memory of the 1932 "Bonus March" in Washington, D.C., in which approximately twenty thousand World War I veterans, with and without disabilities, protested a delayed bonus promised by a 1924 congressional act. Bonus recipients eventually received their reward in 1945. Between those two dates the Great Depression of the 1930s left many veterans, like millions of other Americans, poverty stricken.[17]

Congress hoped passage of the G.I. Bill would lessen the possibility of veterans protesting after World War II, as they had done following World War I. Reintegrating veterans into society became a primary concern in post–World War II America. The G.I. Bill not only enabled many veterans to attend college by paying for a veteran's entire education, but it also included low-interest home loans and a stipend for those looking for work.

World War II also had more subtle, but just as significant, effects elsewhere, including at the University of Illinois. In Galesburg, a small city located in northwestern Illinois, the army built a brand new hospital, the Mayo Army General Hospital. The war ended shortly after its completion. The hospital became part of the War Assets Administration and the army then leased it to the University of Illinois, which created the Galesburg Division. It seemed like an ideal setting for veterans attending college. The former hospital complex consisted of 115 one-story buildings, all of which were interconnected by enclosed corridors. They were also ramped for wheelchair users.[18]

In the spring of 1947, William Kleashers, deputy commander of the American Legion, requested support from the University of Illinois president, George D. Stoddard, to help veterans with disabilities attend college in Galesburg. Stoddard, in turn, asked Provost Coleman Griffith to study the suggestion.[19] University officials gave serious consideration to veterans' demands. They decided to grant Kleashers' request. The new dean of the Galesburg Undergraduate Division, Chauncey Louttit, hired a twenty-four year-old graduate student named Timothy J. Nugent to initiate a program.

Nugent was born in 1923 in Pittsburgh and grew up in Milwaukee. He earned a diploma in general engineering at Tarleton College in the Texas A & M system, a B.S. from the Wisconsin State College, LaCrosse, and a M.S. in Health and Physical Education from University of Wisconsin. While at Texas A & M, he postponed receiving his degree when he might have so that he could play football and run track. This was an indication of his determination to follow his desires and beliefs. Nugent served as a combat infantryman in World War II in Europe and with the Medical Corps and the Corps of Engineers. While an instructor with the Medical Corps, he had an emergency appendectomy on the field. Later, he suffered a mysterious leg injury, perhaps from a snakebite or shrapnel, and became a disabled veteran.[20]

The square-jawed Nugent, who more than once referred to himself as the "fiery redhead," recalled that he developed empathy for what it was like to have a hidden disability.[21] Nugent's own childhood experiences with difference, including a disruptive youth spent at times with his mother's relatives and at other times with others, and a heart lesion that caused minor interference in his life, partially motivated him to begin the Illinois program.[22] He was aware of what it was like to be considered different.

Nugent believed that higher education paved the only road to success that those with disabilities might find in the middle of the twentieth century.[23] When he first began his studies at Illinois, he wanted to focus his dissertation on the program. [24] As a doctoral student in educational psychology and administration, he planned to study the development of education for severely and permanently handicapped individuals. Nugent never finished his dissertation because he became too involved in the program itself. [25]

The Galesburg division prepared for as many as fifty to one hundred severely disabled students to enroll in the fall semester of 1947, but none did. The program's first student, a paraplegic named Harold Scharper from Black River Falls, Wisconsin, enrolled in the 1948 spring semester, and the program officially began in the fall of that year.[26]

Despite the early difficulty in attracting students into the program, administrators seemed wary of the possibility that the University of Illinois would become known more for its disabled students than for other activities. In fall 1948, an administrator noted, "Some educators already envision this unusual institution as the 'paraplegic university' of the United States where disabled civilians and vets alike can pursue regular college training. These same educators hope that the division will be extended to a full, four year college."[27]

There was some justification for this concern. By fall 1948, eight wheelchair-using students and five semiambulatory students, all of whom were veterans, had enrolled. The next semester, nine more students enrolled, including three nonveterans and a female wheelchair user.[28] By the end of 1950, twenty-two students had enrolled in the program. Nugent himself recalled someone saying that until he came along, "quadriplegics went from the hospital to a nursing home."[29] Now they had an opportunity to move onto campus. By 1955, when more than 100 students from over 20 states were in the program and inquiries were being fielded from all over the world, the university had established an enrollment quota of 120 students.

The road to increasing enrollment and program stability was rocky. There were many times when Nugent feared for the program's survival. One such instance occurred when Governor Adlai Stevenson announced in the spring of 1949 that the Galesburg division of the University of Illinois would close and be converted into a geriatrics research unit. Many reasons led to this decision, including the fact that the Galesburg campus was a two-year program and the students with disabilities there were in a four-year track.[30]

Nugent did not intend to accept this closure without a fight. On the same day the closure was announced, March 23, 1949, he led a group of thirty students, many of whom were veterans, to march on the Illinois State Capitol at Springfield. When the group arrived, police escorted them to the governor's mansion. Many of the policemen were themselves veterans and supported the protest. Stevenson, however, ignored them.[31]

They did not surrender. Instead, they marched on the Urbana campus itself. While there, the wheelchair-using students rolled up and down on planks placed next to buildings to demonstrate how adaptable they could be, even managing to get in and out of buildings that had no modified access of any type. This kind of demonstration typified the attitude that Nugent inculcated in both his program and in his students. He felt that

only a hard attitude would carry enough weight to break down the enor-
mous barriers that had built up over the centuries.[32]

Few believed that individuals with these kinds of disabilities could
succeed in an educational environment. If they did, who would be dis-
placed—other, more "competent" students, veterans with no physical
disabilities, and anyone else deemed more "valid?"

Since the University of Illinois showed no inclination to continue support for the program, Nugent and the students looked elsewhere. They
wrote to more than three hundred state and private universities and colleges to inquire about moving the program to one of them. They concentrated on campuses in California and Florida because of the warm
climates in those states. To say that they had no success is an understate-
ment; no one was even remotely interested. Every reply was a rejection.[33]

The program was saved unexpectedly in the spring of 1949. Officials
at the University of Illinois campus at Urbana announced that provision
would be made for fourteen wheelchair-using students from Galesburg.
Perhaps the change of heart resulted from pressure from the Veterans
Administration (VA).[34] The VA, which provided a great deal of support
for the program, certainly played a role in this decision. But Nugent also
recalled that the clincher for the decision to keep the program alive came
from a legal technicality. The students had been guaranteed two years of
education, and they had not yet gotten those two years. This commitment got the program moved to the Urbana campus.[35]

The fiery redhead, who refused to give up on his dream and his belief
in the ability of education to change attitudes about disability, together
with his band of students, readied themselves for their move onto the
Urbana campus.

## THE UNIVERSITY OF ILLINOIS DISABILITY RESOURCES
## AND EDUCATIONAL SERVICES (DRES)

The University's willingness to accept these fourteen students at the
Urbana campus did not equate to providing needed support. Urbana
presented a much different terrain, from an accessibility perspective, than
did the Galesburg campus. Most campus buildings required the construction of ramps for wheelchair users. Distances between classes were
far greater than in Galesburg, and they were not connected with enclosed
corridors.

The university addressed these issues initially by ramping six class-room buildings and providing students with keys to use the elevators for the student union building and library, in addition to arranging housing quarters in old World War II barracks that were called Parade Ground units.[36] Former student Tom Jones recalled these units as "drafty and cold in the winter, hot in the summer. They had ramps on each end and a community bathroom in the middle. We were told that if a building caught fire, it would burn down in four minutes."[37]

When the program moved to the Urbana campus in the fall of 1949, Nugent joined the faculty of the Division of Special Services for War Veterans and the Department of Physical Education for Men. The Division of Special Services would have closed in the early 1950s, but the advent of the Korean War postponed its demise until 1958. The Rehabilitation Program, which became known as the Division of Rehabilitation-Education Services in 1962, had become part of the College of Physical Education in 1951. In 1962 it became a unit within the College of Applied Health Sciences, where it still remains.[38]

By 1953 Nugent's forceful personality and the presence of students with disabilities persuaded university administrators and architects to require all future university buildings to be designed with accessibility for wheelchair users in mind.[39] This pledge occurred fifteen years before the passage of the federal Architectural Barriers Act of 1968. No other university campus even contemplated this kind of innovation at this early date. While at least one community had constructed some curb ramps by this time, no community had committed as comprehensive a program to eliminating architectural barriers as this Illinois assurance.[40]

When new dormitories were built, a specified number of rooms in each building were designed to accommodate students with disabilities. The first floor of most dorms had bathrooms with accessible shower stalls, aluminum fold-down seats, and old-style, accessible toilet stalls (with grab bars and a door wide enough to enable a person to face the toilet in the forward position).[41] While these structural changes advanced the physical accessibility of the Illinois campus, the service fraternity, Delta Sigma Omicron (DSO), influenced attitudinal transformations. DSO, which included both male and female students with disabilities, incorporated in 1949 during the program's Galesburg years.

According to Ronald Larimore, with incorporation, the fraternity began to resolve developing problems, independent of the actions of the university bureaucracy.[42] Nugent provided another reason for DSO's incorporation. At that time, supplies reverted to the state. When the program left Galesburg, they would lose all their hard-earned supplies. Nugent, who recalled people saying about him, "Nail down your furniture—here comes Nugent," believed in conserving every possible resource. With DSO incorporated, they were able to bring materials that would otherwise have reverted back to the state of Illinois with them from Galesburg to Urbana.[43]

In a 1954 letter, Nugent explained that the DSO coeducational service fraternity was created "to promote the academic, physical, and social welfare of handicapped students on campus and all handicapped people everywhere." It did this by sponsoring social activities such as banquets and picnics, advancing educational and employment possibilities for those with disabilities, educating the public about the needs and abilities of the physically disabled, and working for their "complete social integration."[44] The fraternity's motto, "to exercise our abilities to a maximum so as to minimize our disabilities, that we may live most and serve best," played an essential role in the program's development and permeates DRES to this day.[45]

The need to move toward "complete social integration," a phrase that Nugent used in his letter, showed itself in numerous ways. Alumna Jan Little recalled Nugent railing: "[A]ll you kids in wheelchairs have been exposed to are hospitals and a few teachers. You don't even know about the outside world. Half of you went to special schools . . . and you were so coddled that you don't even know how to compete in the real world."[46]

The blunt-spoken Nugent apparently felt that this belief needed to be conveyed to incoming students to increase their motivation. In *I Am Not What I Am*, Tom Linde recalls that when he applied to graduate school at Illinois, Tim told him that he had "been given courtesy high school and college diplomas, and could not hack it in graduate school at Champaign-Urbana."[47] Linde, who has cerebral palsy (CP), moved through the world by using his legs to push his wheelchair backward. Linde remembers Nugent "flailing the hot air above his disheveled desk" while describing other students with CP who had not made the grade at Illinois. Nugent gave Linde a two-week probation to prove he could "get in and out of bed, dress, undress, and shower independently." Linde passed the test and eventually got his Ph.D. in psychology at Illinois.[48]

Many years later, Linde, about to turn seventy in the year 2000, shared these thoughts: "There is a general tendency these days to look

with disfavor upon the way Professor Nugent initiated us into the world
he had, single-handedly, created at the University of Illinois. Given the
spirit of the time in which he was working, he had no valid alternative."[49]

## THE GIZZ KIDS

Sports and recreation, significant components of Nugent's background,
also became an integral aspect of DRES and DSO from its inception.
Nugent recalled two reasons for the establishment of sports teams. First,
if teams existed, then they would be invited to play. Second, audiences
watching disabled students competing in team sports might recognize
their ability to contribute to society. Indeed, an employer who saw an
early Illini (University of Illinois) student perform remarked that when
he graduated he had a position for number 34.

Wheelchair basketball may have been the most prominent of the early
Illinois sports programs.[50] In April 1949, in Galesburg, the National Invi-
tational Wheelchair Basketball Tournament held its initial games with six
teams. The Illinois Gizz Kids were the only university team in the country at the time. Mike Frogley, who has documented the history of the
wheelchair basketball team, noted that the name "reflects the humor and
approach the first group of guys took to the obstacles they had." The
team's name came from the name of the valve at the bottom of leg bags
used to catch urine for those whose bladders are paralyzed. The valve is
called a gizzmo. Frogley writes, "So, the first group of guys thought it was
kind of funny and called themselves the Gizz Kids, short for Gizzmo."[51]

The name, Illinois Gizz Kids, also developed for another reason, again
reflecting the marginalization of this group of students within the university system as well as in the outside world. In an interview for a televi-
sion documentary about wheelchair racing, Brad Hedrick, the current
DRES director, recalled, "The philosophy of Tim Nugent, the founder of
the program, was that his job was not only to provide a student with
access to the academic forces of the campus, but to afford the student
equivalent access to the nonacademic experience and opportunities that
exist on a college campus. One significant area of endeavor he thought
the students needed equivalent access to was athletics."[52]

Athletics had been one of the ways in which Nugent had survived his
own youth. In addition he had coached football and basketball, and he
had served as director of the first camp for adults with cerebral palsy.
He believed that demonstrating that students with disabilities could

participate in sports would convince many people unfamiliar with disabilities that people were more capable than they appeared.[53] According to Brad Hedrick—a DRES graduate student who later became DRES director—university officials who criticized Nugent said that encouraging students with disabilities to participate in athletics was "patronizing" and "putting them on display." Furthermore, some in the community said that Nugent used the wheelchair basketball exhibitions to exploit students for fund-raising appeals and for "self-promotion." Hedrick believed, however, that Nugent "was simply trying to provide the students with an equivalent experience."[54]

While Hedrick was sympathetic to Nugent's endeavors, he referred to students with disabilities only as passive recipients of either Nugent's or the University's concerns. Even though the students had demonstrated their potency through protests and their ability to attend the university, they were still, as a group, the most powerless segment of this equation. They could not even be considered official university athletes. "So if you look in the early years," Hedrick continued, "you'll notice the name of the team was . . . the Illinois Gizz Kids. Exclusively a men's wheelchair basketball team. It was not called University of Illinois because the University would not sanction the program. So therefore the team could not be called the fighting Illini for the same reason."[55]

They generally played against teams composed of veterans or volunteers, like policemen and firemen. By 1954 DRES supported deck tennis, table tennis, tennis, wheelchair square dancing, swimming, bowling, wheelchair football, basketball, and baseball. These activities were conducted on both the intramural and varsity level.[56] By 1954 the National Wheelchair Basketball Association, of which the Gizz Kids were members and which was founded at Illinois, had three conferences and thirty teams from coast to coast.[57]

Wheelchair sports helped Nugent and DRES to publicize and therefore maintain DRES in its early years when there was no guarantee of survival. DRES existed for many years without any university funding.[58] Nugent himself was the only full-time staff person until 1956. The university, it seemed, neither desired to provide great support, nor encouragement, for the program to remain. DRES managed to stay afloat with contracts from the Veteran's Administration and the state Division of Vocational Rehabilitation and various contributions. The program also contracted fees for services rendered. These monies became part of a revolving fund that paid for Nugent's salary and some program activities.

Eventually, a small federal grant for $8,000 enabled Nugent to hire his first staff member.[59] The Chicago Daily News Veterans Fund purchased all the wheelchairs for the Illinois students to participate in sports events when the program began in Galesburg. This continued after the move to Urbana.[60] Observing wheelchair-using athletes participating in sports indicated to the general public both their level of passion to remain involved in life's activities and their dedication to the pursuit of goals. It also served as an excellent public relations tool.

One example of how this worked involved University of Illinois president David Dodds Henry. Before becoming president in 1955, Henry had served as vice chancellor at New York University. There he met Howard Rusk, considered to be the father of rehabilitation medicine and founder of the Institute of Physical Medicine and Rehabilitation at the New York University Medical Center, which had opened in 1950. Rusk told Henry about the Illinois program. When Henry visited the campus as a university presidential candidate, he attended a wheelchair football game and became so enthusiastic that he exclaimed that there was no reason why the university could not raise millions of dollars for this program. Ironically, two weeks earlier a dean had reprimanded Nugent for raising too much money, one of many reprimands Nugent received for his various activities in the 1940s and 1950s.[61]

Another perspective on the sports program came from Jan Little, a disabled student who explained to her college roommate why she wanted to become a cheerleader: "'Why do you want to be a dumb thing like a cheerleader?' [her roommate] asked. 'Sports are for high school kids.' Well, I replied. I like sports and there aren't any [team sports] that girls can be in, but being a cheerleader lets me go with the team—and I might see some place besides Champaign."[62] Another disabled alumna, Mary Lou Breslin, recalled, though, that while team sports, such as football and basketball, were only available to men, individual sports like swimming, archery, table tennis, and similar activities were open to both sexes. She believed that one reason this openness occurred resulted from Illinois' participation in the Paralympics and the need to field as many qualified athletes as possible.[63] Other sports and recreational activities included bowling, track and field, goal ball, judo, and square dancing.[64]

During semester break, the Gizz Kids had the opportunity to travel to other schools, but according to Little in her memoir, *If It Weren't for the Honor—I'd Rather Have Walked*, these occasions meant that they would

have to "fight the blizzards in Kansas and the ice storms in Cleveland."
The Gizz Kids called this annual "trek to battle" the "Tour," which
became known as a "tribal initiation rite." To be chosen to go on Tour,
Little noted, "[Y]ou kept your grades up, gave up all of your free time to
practice, surrendered your between-semester vacation, and put up with
Tim and Chuck Elmer [program physical therapist] at very close range—
twenty-four hours a day for over a week."[65] The fact that the Illinois students and their supporters continued these activities showed both how
determined they were and how strongly they valued the Tour experience,
which introduced students to each other and to their strengths and
foibles.

Little recalled that Tour was an eye-opener for her and other physically
disabled students, who had spent much of their previous lives sheltered
and protected. "Some of us had never seen another young person in a
wheelchair before coming to Illinois," she noted. "On tour, we found out
that sometimes other people in wheelchairs are pretty interesting. Ron
had been all-state in basketball when he had polio. Bruce had a tennis
scholarship to U of I when he was hit with polio the summer before he
was to enter college. Some of the Korean vets were bitter. Some of the
team were accepting that they would always use wheelchairs. Between the
lot of us, we worked out the idea that we'd better do what we could with
what we had."[66]

By 1958, according to the *Decatur Daily News*, the Gizz Kids had a
138-32 record and had donated 55 percent of net proceeds to benevolent
causes. By that time, $14,500 had been donated to the National Polio
Foundation, Cancer Foundation, Paraplegia Foundation, and similar
organizations.[67] These donations were made because Nugent wanted to
show the world that students with disabilities could be of service to others; they could be the ones offering gifts, not only the recipients of gifts.[68]

The university sports and recreation program had a wider academic
influence as well. Recreation therapy, as a field, began at Illinois. According to Nugent, "There was no such thing as recreation therapy, rehabilitation counseling, or rehabilitation administration back then."[69] Each of
these developments reinforced the validity of Nugent's vision and the
influence of the Illinois program.

## FUNCTIONAL TRAINING WEEK

Hostility is an excellent motivator.[70]

Just as funding was a constant battle, so too was appropriate space. "Until its sixth year (1953–54), all operations of the program were housed in one half of a temporary Parade Ground unit (900 square feet), with no remodeling of the facility. During the 1954–55 school year, the program took over one entire Parade Ground unit, and the facility was appropriately remodeled."[71] Transportation problems were solved in the first few years with use of private cars belonging to students in the program. The university assigned or established parking lots or parking spaces near all buildings students used.[72] Since many of the earlier students were veterans who owned their own cars, this worked for a time, but later, as fewer veterans enrolled in the program, the transportation problem became more acute.[73]

In 1954 a politically savvy group of students with disabilities persuaded Illinois governor William Stratton to be the keynote speaker at the annual disabled students' awards banquet. No university administrators had attended this event previously, and the governor packed the house. Stratton's stirring speech describing the benefits of rehabilitation and the importance of the Illinois effort legitimized the program. From that point on, the rehabilitation program was never again seriously questioned.[74]

Early students and other observers of the program, however, recalled how tough it was. Tom Jones, in his memoir, *The Real Tom Jones*, remembered,

> One of my first activities in Champaign was what Tim Nugent called "functional training week." It was required of all students with disabilities before class registration. It was a time to learn about campus, get advice on classes, meet new friends, play games, and most of all, prove to Tim and his staff that you could function on your own. "You don't let anybody push your wheelchair," Nugent told us, "You push yourself." Most of us didn't like functional training week, but it made us better able to survive and succeed in these new surroundings. Functional training week no longer exists, and today's students are worse off due to its demise.[75]

Nugent believed that education was the means to which attitudes could change and individuals with disabilities would become part of mainstream society. Or, put another way, "educate, not legislate." Nugent thought legislation might force people to obey laws, but it could also stymie creativity in finding ways to enhance integration, whereas education could truly change attitudes and therefore have a longer, more permanent social impact.[76]

Succeeding at Illinois became a vital stage on the path to success after leaving school. A student's perseverance and endurance would not conclude with surviving functional training week. Nugent believed that success in entering society would depend on being able to compete in the nondisabled world. As one example of this, he knew employment recruiters did not want to see wheelchair users who could not push themselves. An excellent illustration of how this might play out in a typical social environment of the time came in the form of a student named Bill. A journalist wrote the following account of Bill's entrance exam to the Illinois program: "'Bill, push yourself up that ramp. If you can do it, we'll admit you to school here. If you can't, you and your attendant can both get back in your car and go home.' The young man in the wheelchair looked with amazement into the unsmiling face of Professor Tim Nugent. His weakened hands slowly gripped the wheels he never pushed himself."[77]

This kind of exchange led people throughout the years to label Nugent a dictator who demanded that students follow his lead. Perhaps there is some truth to this as shown by Bill's reaction to Nugent's ultimatum. "'Stand back,' he said to the attendant his family had sent to propel him through his college education. Four minutes later, Bill had struggled halfway up the ramp to Tim Nugent's office, to a point where he could see the sign on the door: 'T. J. Nugent, Director, Student Rehabilitation Center, University of Illinois.' Sweat shone on his face, but a smile shone there, too. And another lit the face of Tim Nugent. 'O.K., Bill. Send your friend home. You'll do alright on your own.'"

Nugent's recollection of the above anecdote regarding Bill's ascension of the ramp is more colorful. He recalled Bill as a thirty-nine year-old man who became disabled at the age of twenty-one. He lived in the Chicago area, within walking distance of three hospitals, but all he ever did was sometimes go out to lunch. When Nugent pushed Bill to conquer that ramp, he also told him that if he came to Illinois "you won't be the bum that you are today."[78] In the journalist's aforementioned account, he concluded, "Since the day he got his jarring introduction to this unique program for handicapped students and its no less unique director, Bill has never had to be pushed. Neither have the hundreds of others wheelchair students who have attended the University of Illinois in the 14 years since its rehabilitation program began."

Getting into the Illinois program was only the first hurdle; the next was to survive functional training week. But even that did not guarantee success. Students who successfully completed this training could still be expelled later if they were discovered receiving assistance in their living quarters or being pushed across campus.[79]

Little recalled that when she entered the University of Illinois, she began "a love/hate relationship with Tim" that continued during the next several decades. It was 99.9 percent love and 0.1 percent hate. "The 0.1 percent hate turned out to be the factor that made many of us succeed when all odds were against success," she noted. "Tim was right. I wasn't ready for college (we still argue about the spoiled bit thirty years later). Tutoring hadn't quite prepared me for competition from students without disabilities, who had been groomed for Illinois from early grades. Socially, having missed out on teenage peer relations and adolescent experiences for all but a year and a half, I was probably equal to a seventh grader interacting with college students."[80]

Little's narrative demonstrates how isolated and marginalized those with disabilities were at this time. Although Little succeeded well in her world, she realized how far from mainstream society she operated, particularly when describing her social skills. Physically, it was even tougher at first, especially during her first days in a dormitory with nondisabled students. "After my parents left," she recalled, "I realized that I had never gotten in and out of bed by myself. I also had no legitimate plan of attack for using the bathtub either. I was pretty sure my dorm mates could tolerate me staying up all night, but would be less accepting of not entering the bathtub for a full semester." Life became even more "miserable" for her when she learned that the old "lift-equipped buses" were no longer being used and the new ones had yet to arrive.[81]

The preceding description is exactly the kind of situation that caused Nugent to be so tough. If students could not survive his demands for getting into college and the "hell" of functional training week, how could they possibly expect to make it through, not knowing how to get "in and out of bed?" One way Nugent pushed these students to succeed was to get them angry with him and to want to show him that he did not know how determined they were. Little remembered,

Hostility is an excellent motivator. First of all, that damned Tim had predicted that I couldn't take care of myself and I was not going to let him be right so early in the game. Secondly, staying in my chair all night or letting a dorm mate I'd hardly met fish me out of the bathtub didn't seem the way to make friends in a hurry. I might have been able to push the mile to class—if I'd known where the class building was, so I'd better learn to get in and out of the station wagons that were substituted for the missing buses. At least, I reasoned, I did know how to get back in my chair from the floor in the event that my strategies for getting into bed or the car lacked some crucial details.[82]

Nugent knew that these students had to be resilient enough to withstand whatever hazards they encountered, not only at school, but, more important, after they graduated. How could these students hope to break down society's centuries of negative attitudes about disability if they were not thick-skinned enough to resist Nugent's abrasiveness? He also believed that people with disabilities held aspirations similar to any other person. Nugent knew he was being tough on people, but he also believed that this was the only avenue available to him to accomplish his goals.[83]

Little recalled a conversation about why students had to take a physiology course: "'You have to take physiology,' Lola Lange told me. 'Why?' I asked. 'Because Tim wants us all to know enough about how our bodies work to be able to defend ourselves against doctors,' she replied."[84] Little also remarked on Nugent's ingenuity in meeting university requirements. Nugent required all freshmen to engage in physical therapy three times a week in the Student Rehabilitation Center, a building where many DRES activities occurred. "Physical therapy was Tim's answer to the requirement that all U of I students take physical education in addition to their other courses. Since many of us found a lot of things we'd rather do than lift weights or try out the parallel bars, Tim's staff spent as much time lurking in campus hangouts chasing strays as they did in any administrative or treatment activities."[85]

### It's Abilities, Not Disabilities that Count

(Prominently displayed Disability Resources and Educational Services Slogan)

Nugent's strategies succeeded. In 1950 Illinois became the first postsecondary institution to introduce curb cuts specifically to accommodate students with disabilities. By 1954 DRES offered numerous services.

These included all kinds of counseling, ranging from academic to medical to personal. An emphasis was placed on preregistration to ensure students' class schedules met their physical conditions and needs and to coordinate academics, transportation, parking, and security. This was necessary so students would have time to get from one class to the next and to make sure classes were in accessible locations. In the early years sixty to seventy classes had to be moved each semester.[86] This was a major accommodation for a once-resistant university. Furthermore, the university offered courses in study techniques, vocational guidance, speed-reading and comprehension, and exam preparation. All students were expected to attend regular classes and compete with the general student population. Students also received three hours each week of individual physical instruction and therapy. These components of the program apparently worked quite effectively, because by August 1954, thirty-eight students had graduated and all had obtained "secure and complimentary positions."[87]

Perhaps the most important, and longest-lasting, development was that of the Student Rehabilitation Center itself, which in 1954 was described as a place that included offices, workrooms, therapy rooms, and a lounge. The program maintained two twenty-seven-passenger buses equipped to transport students using wheelchairs. The buses ran a fixed route, like a city bus, so students moved around campus as they wished.[88]

By 1958 construction of sixty-one ramps leading into university buildings had been completed. Dormitories designed to accommodate students using wheelchairs were becoming part of the campus landscape. Modifications to apartments that housed married students were being made so those using wheelchairs could move in with their spouses as could a couple who both used wheelchairs.[89]

Decades of advocates have stressed that without accessible transportation, both an accessible dwelling and a job would be only two-thirds of what people need. Without transportation, no one would be able to get from their homes to a job. DRES recognized from its inception that transportation was a crucial issue.

Greyhound first donated buses to DRES in 1952, retrofitted with a hydraulic lift for wheelchair use by Carmont Blitz, owner of Chicago's Blitz Auto Body Corporation. Four years later Blitz, who became a great friend of DRES, retrofitted two General Motors buses. These buses had space for sixteen wheelchair-using students and fixed seats for thirteen other passengers. Fixed-route wheelchair-accessible bus transportation existed for the first time anywhere on the Illinois campus for its students. All passengers used the same door to enter and exit these buses, and the entire operation for each user was completed in an almost unbelievable five seconds or less.[90]

Because the Illinois program was the first of its kind, almost everything DRES accomplished had some kind of research and development impact. In 1959 the university became the first postsecondary institution to create a transitional living program for students with severe locomotor disabilities who needed assistance in the performance of daily living activities.[91] A local attorney and businessman named Durward Judy built Greenbrier Nursing Home in 1959. One wing became home to DRES students who were not yet able to live in the dormitories or on campus. This included students who used iron lungs to aid in breathing as a result of polio and others who needed assistance, especially at night.[92]

Nugent described these residences as transitional places where someone could learn about themselves and what they needed to survive and then they could figure out how to live anywhere. Nugent emphasized independence for those he believed could attain it. He also noted, "There isn't any one of us that doesn't need assistance at one time or another." As an example, he stated that almost anyone will open the door for someone else they spot carrying a full load of groceries. These transitional residences, where staff provided assistance, eventually led to the on-campus Beckwith Living Center, built in the early 1980s, which continues to provide assistive services to those who need it.[93]

Perhaps the most amazing achievement of DRES was its impressive 100 percent placement rate for graduating students. In addition, 92 percent of students who attended the program, but who did not graduate, had "secure and honorable jobs," some higher-paying than for those who did graduate.[94]

By the 1957–58 academic year, DRES students represented twenty-five states. Prospective students applied from throughout the United States as well as internationally.[95]

## THE LEGACY OF THE UNIVERSITY OF ILLINOIS PROGRAM

A dozen years after DRES's implementation, the program became a permanent University of Illinois fixture. Sixty years after the University of Illinois program began in Galesburg, its impact is legion. Graduates of the program have become U.S. senators, state senators, doctors, attorneys, engineers, architects, teachers, policy makers, advocates, state rehabilitation program directors, and federal appointees. DRES proudly claims many pioneering achievements affecting both other universities and all of society. In addition to accomplishments already mentioned in this essay, such as the first wheelchair-accessible fixed-route bus system, the first accessible university residence halls, and the first university service fraternity and advocacy group comprised of students with disabilities (Delta Sigma Omicron), DRES also provided influential research leading to the development of the first architectural accessibility standards—the 1961 American National Standards Institute Standards, which to this day affect law and policy about access.

In its illustrious sports history, two athletes from Illinois won gold medals at the 1960 Rome Paralympics. UI became the first university to offer varsity letter awards to student athletes with disabilities. The first recipient was Gunnar Aarlind of Sweden in 1977. Three years later, in 1980, UI became the initial university to select a wheelchair athlete, competing against all varsity athletes on campus, as its "Athlete of the Year." Fours years later, UI produced the first wheelchair athlete in the world to win an Olympic Gold Medal.[96]

The Illinois program and its founder, Tim Nugent, became recognized internationally. In 1956 Nugent received a Public Personnel Award, signed by President Dwight D. Eisenhower, from the decade-old President's Committee on the Employment of the Physically Handicapped. In his acceptance speech, Nugent stated. "I would like to mention that the greatest change in attitude toward and concept of the physically handicapped and of rehabilitation has taken place within the last ten years. The change has been one from over solicitousness and asylum to an intelligent approach, and open-mindedness toward the physically handicapped. They have been given the opportunity to tell us what they have experienced, what they have lived and what they know."[97]

From today's vantage point, it is sometimes difficult to imagine how marginalized people with disabilities were in the mid-twentieth century. Nugent wrote in 2006, "I wish there had been this much interest 60 years ago when everyone thought I was nuts."[98] For most people with disabilities then, their powerlessness was intensified by their isolation; the Illinois program became a beacon that held hope to change both those situations.

DRES became a model for many other university programs and assisted a dozen other universities to begin programs during Nugent's tenure. In 1958 Southern Illinois University in Carbondale, south of Urbana-Champaign, modified its physical facilities and administrative and academic procedures so those with significant disabilities could enroll in both undergraduate and graduate school and participate in campus functions. By 1960 there were sixty-three such students; thirty-two used wheelchairs.[99] In January 1960, the University of Missouri completed a study of the Illinois program as part of a move to extend similar services nationwide. Under a grant from the U.S. Office of Vocational Rehabilitation, the Missouri representatives' visit to Illinois marked a coordinated effort to have at least one similar program at a university in each area of the country.[100]

At an international conference in Stockholm in October 1961, Nugent received the first Patrik Haglund Lectureship from Sweden's Central Committee on Rehabilitation. The committee intended to confer an award every five years to an "outstanding expert in rehabilitation."[101] Nugent's award signaled DRES's newly active international agenda. Illinois became the first postsecondary institution to organize national and international tours for persons with disabilities, host workshops, and provide demonstrations dispelling the negative, stereotypical attitudes and beliefs about persons with disabilities. Eighteen wheelchair-using students and alumni traveled to South Africa in 1962 to show what these students with disabilities and alumni had accomplished. "This is an opportunity for a missionary effort to stimulate and motivate action on behalf of the physically disabled in South Africa. It's also an opportunity for us to be goodwill ambassadors for the United States."[102] In 1965 UI piloted the first study-abroad program, to Aix-en-Provence, France, for severely, permanently disabled university students with disabilities.

By June 1964, over one thousand students with disabilities had participated in the program, and 307 had graduated with degrees ranging from Bachelor's to Doctorates. Most graduates had acquired employment with salaries comparable to other university graduates.[103] In 1976 the Urbana City Council approved an ordinance prohibiting architectural barriers to the physically handicapped in public buildings. Mayor Hiram Paley called the ordinance a "model, landmark law which sets precedent in this state and possibly the nation."[104] When Nugent retired, after thirty-eight years, in August 1985, the Illinois program had only enhanced its well-deserved acclaim. Nugent himself received the honor of Governor James Thompson declaring September 7, 1985, "Tim Nugent Day."[105]

In a 1998 banquet honoring fifty years of DRES, a 1957 graduate concluded his remarks by stating, "We didn't whine a lot. We just did. It was revolutionary. . . . It was exciting. . . . [A]t times it was scary. But today you only have to travel around this campus or to nearly any other major campus in the country to see how well it evolved from that small, unsecured beach head Tim Nugent pioneered 50 years ago. So in summing up, General Nugent . . . Sir, I came here tonight to report on behalf of those of us from the 50's. As per your orders on that lonely beach head so many years ago . . . we came. . . . We saw. . . . Thanks to the boost you gave us . . . we continue to conquer."[106]

## NOTES

1. The author would like to express appreciation to the Administration on Developmental Disabilities through their funding of our "Center on Excellence"; the University of Hawaii Center on Disability Studies, which supported archival research for this chapter; University of Illinois archivist, William J. Maher; Timothy J. Nugent; and readers and Illinois alumni Mary Lou Breslin, Mike Frogley, and Fred Fay. The author also wishes to express gratitude to Eileen H. Tamura, whose edits have strengthened this essay.

2. See, for example, Hugh Gregory Gallagher, *By Trust Betrayed: Patients, Physicians, and the License to Kill in the Third Reich* (New York: Henry Holt, 1990); Suzanne E. Evans, *Forgotten Crimes: The Holocaust and People with Disabilities* (Chicago: Ivan R. Dee, 2004); Holly Anne Wade, "Discrimination, Sexuality and People with Significant Disabilities: Issues of Access and the Right to Sexual Expression in the United States," *Disability Studies Quarterly* 22, no. 4 (Fall 2002): 9–27, http://www.dsq-sds.org/_articles_pdf/2002/Fall/dsq_2002_Fall_03.pdf (accessed 29 July 2006); M. L. Wehmeyer, "Perspectives and Sterilization in the Heartland," *Mental Retardation* 41, no. 1, (2003): 57–60, http://www.beachcenter.org/Research/highlights/PDF/DP11Wehmeyer2003.pdf (accessed 29 July 2006); Jana Leslie-Miller, "From Bell to Bell: Responsible Reproduction in the Twentieth Century," *Maryland Journal of Contemporary Legal Issues* 8, no. 123 (1997): 136–37; Michael G. Silver, "Eugenics and Compulsory Sterilization Laws: Providing Redress for the Victims of a Shameful Era in United States History," *The George Washington Law Review* 72 (2004): 862–91.

3. Various terms to reference those with disabilities will be used throughout the essay, reflecting various times and personalities. I will generally use the preferred American "people first" style, which places the term "disability" in the context of an adjective modifying the noun, "people," "persons," "individuals" or similar terminology. Much has been written about language. One resource is *A Model for Accessibility*, which can be located at *www.cds.hawaii.edu*.

4. The program has had several names through the course of its history, including the Rehabilitation Program and the Division of Rehabilitation-Education Services. For purposes of clarity, the program will be called by its present name, Disability Resources and Educational Services, unless an earlier name is significant for context in specific parts of the text.

5. Henry Edward Abt, *The Care, Cure and Education of the Crippled Child* (New York: Arno, 1974 [1924]), 4.

6. Steven. E. Brown, *Investigating a Culture of Disability: Final Report* (Las Cruces, NM: Institute on Disability Culture, 1994), 32–34.

7. Ibid.

8. *A Chronology of the Disability Rights Movements* (San Francisco: San Francisco State University, http://www.sfsu.edu/~hrdpu/chron.htm (accessed 21 January 2006).

9. "Gallaudet History-Gallaudet University," Gallaudet University http://www .gallaudet.edu/x228.xml (accessed 21 January 2006).

10. John Lenihan, *Performance: Disabled Americans: A History* (Washington, DC: President's Committee on Employment of the Handicapped, 1976–77), 51; Martha. L. Walker, *Beyond Bureaucracy: Mary Elizabeth Switzer and Rehabilitation.* (Lanham, MD: University Press, 1985), 25.

11. Walker, *Beyond Bureaucracy*, 102–3; "Federal Security Agency," U. S. Government Manual, 1945, First edition (Washington, DC: Division of Public Inquiries. Office of War Administration),http://www.ibiblio.org/hyperwar/ ATO/USGM/FSA.html (accessed 27 May 2006).

12. Richard. K. Scotch, *From Good Will to Civil Rights: Transforming Federal Disability Policy* (Philadelphia: Temple University Press, 1984), 21; Joseph. P. Shapiro, *No Pity: People with Disabilities Forging a New Civil Rights Movement* (New York: Times Books, 1993), 143; Federal Security Agency, 1945.

13. *Chronology*.

14. Charlene DeLoach, "The Independent Living Movement," *Region V Rehabilitation Continuing Education Program ADA Train the Trainer Program* (Carbondale, IL: Southern Illinois University at Carbondale Rehabilitation Institute, 1992), 37–38.

15. *Chronology*.

16. Tim Nugent, personal correspondence with author, 29 October 2006.

17. "A Photo Essay on the Great Depression," *Modern American Poetry* http://www.english.uiuc.edu/maps/depression/photoessay.htm (accessed 5 August 2006).

18. Nugent, phone conversation with author, 2 May 2006; Ronald Larimore, "History of the University of Illinois Division of Rehabilitation-Education," 2, 1964, in University of Illinois Library Archives, Public Affairs, Director's Office, Record Series 1919–96, Subgroup 39/1/1, Box 32, University of Illinois at Urbana-Champaign Archives.

19. Larimore, "History," 2.

20. *Illiniweek*, 24 January 1985, *News*, in University of Illinois Library Archives, Record Series: 39/1/830, University of Illinois at Urbana-Champaign Archives;

*University of Illinois Physical Education News*, January 1967, in University of Illinois Library Archives, Record Series: 16/1/808, University of Illinois at Urbana-Champaign Archives; Nugent, phone conversation with author, 2 May 2006.

21. *University of Illinois Physical Education News*, January 1967; Nugent, phone conversation with author, 2 May 2006.

22. Fred Fay, phone conversation with author, 21 February 2006; Nugent, personal correspondence with author, 29 October 2006; Theresa Grimaldi, "Nugent Eases Life for Handicapped," *Daily Illini*, 2 February 1982, 18.

23. Nugent, phone conversation with author, 2 May 2006.

24. Larimore, "History," 3.

25. Carol Mathers, "UI Rehab Program Had Temporary Start." (Champaign-Urbana) *The News-Gazette*, 29 February 1972.

26. Ibid., 3–5.

27. "Disabled War Vets attend Galesburg U of I" (November–December 1948), 8–9, in University of Illinois Library Archives, Applied Life Sciences, Rehabilitation Education Services, Scrapbooks, 1947–86, Subgroup 16/6, Box 1, University of Illinois at Urbana-Champaign Archives.

28. Nugent, Timothy J., "Development Proposal and Summary," September 1958, University of Illinois College of Physical Education Student Rehabilitation Center, 4, in University of Illinois Library Archives, Public Affairs, Director's Office, Record Series: 1919–96, Subgroup 39/1/1, Box 32, courtesy of the University of Illinois at Urbana-Champaign Archives.

29. Nugent, phone conversation with author, 2 May 2006.

30. Larimore, "History," 6–7; *Illinois Alumni News*, May 1953 3; Nugent, phone conversation with author, 2 May 2006. By 1962 the University quota had increased to 200, and the program was again full. Fran Myers, "Rehab Center is at 200 Quota," (Champaign-Urbana) *News Gazette*, 11 September 1962.

31. Larimore, "History," 7; Nugent, phone conversation with author, 2 May 2006.

32. Nugent, "Development Proposal," 4; Nugent, phone conversation with author, 2 May 2006.

33. Larimore, "History," 8; Fred Fay, phone conversation with author, 21 February 2006; Nugent, phone conversation with author, 2 May 2006.

34. Larimore, "History," 8.

35. Nugent, phone conversation with author, 2 May 2006.

36. Larimore, "History," 8.

37. Ibid., 20.

38. *University of Illinois Physical Education News*, January 1967; Larimore, "History," 9; "History of ALS," The College of Applied Health Sciences. http://www.als.uiuc.edu/history.htm (accessed 28 May 2006).

39. Larimore, "History," 8–9.

40. Steven E. Brown, "The Curb Ramps of Kalamazoo: Discovering Our Unrecorded History," *Movie Stars and Sensuous Scars: Essays on the Journey from Disability Shame to Disability Pride* (New York: People with Disabilities Press, 2003), 129.

41. Mary Lou Breslin, e-mail message to author, 10 July 1999.

42. Larimore, "History," 5.
43. Nugent, phone conversation with author, 2 May 2006.
44. Timothy J. Nugent to Laura Borwell, 6 December 1954, 3, Public Affairs, Director's Office, Record Series: 1919–96, Subgroup 39/1/1, Box 32, University of Illinois at Urbana-Champaign Archives.
45. Ibid.
46. Jan Little, *If It Weren't for the Honor—I'd Rather Have Walked: Previously Untold Tales of the Journey to the ADA* (Cambridge, MA: Brookline, 1996), 26.
47. Thomas F. Linde, *I am What I am Not: A Psychologist's Memoir—Notes on Managing Personal Misfortune* (Bloomington, IN: 1st Books Library), *www.1stbooks.com* [now, www.authorhouse.com] 2001), 78.
48. Ibid., 78–80.
49. Linde, *I am What I am Not*; Timothy Nugent via Robert Frost, "University of Illinois DRES Campus Life," www.disability.uiuc.edu/ARCH/campuslife/guide2000/frost.html (accessed 29 July 2006).
50. The wheelchairs these athletes used do not compare with the sleek models of the twenty-first century. Everest & Jennings, the only wheelchair manufacturer of the time, produced standard "lightweight" chairs that weighed fifty pounds and included fixed arm and footrests. A desire to modify and improve these heavy, awkward chairs contributed to the research pursued at Illinois in wheelchair technology. "Illini Adapted Athletics History," 1984, adapted from "The History of Sports Wheelchairs—Part I and Part II," T. J. LaMere, and S. Labanowich, *Sports 'N Spokes* (March and May 1984). http://www.disability.uiuc.edu/page.php?id=42 (accessed 30 July 2006).
51. Frogley, e-mail messages to author, 23 May and 31 May 2006. Fred Fay recalls that the name Gizz Kids was also a play on words for the description of the official basketball team known as the Whiz Kids. Fay, correspondence with author, 18 September 2006.
52. *Against the Wind*, interview with Brad Hedrick, 1996, WILL-TV, University of Illinois, http://www.will.uiuc.edu/tv/documentaries/atw/atwhedrick.html (accessed 30 July 2006).
53. Nugent, phone conversation with author, 2 May 2006.
54. *Against the Wind.*
55. Ibid.
56. Nugent to Borwell, 2.
57. Ibid.
58. Kathy Sullivan, "UI handicapped Find Opportunity at Rehab Center," *The Daily Illini*. 31 October 1984, 1.
59. Nugent, "Development Proposal," 5; Nugent, phone conversation with author, 2 May 2006.
60. Nugent, phone conversation with author, 2 May 2006.
61. Howard A. Rusk Papers, 1937–91, C3981, Western Historical Manuscript Collection—Columbia, http://www.umsystem.edu/whmc/invent/3981.html (accessed May 21, 2006); Natasha Rosenstock, "Distinguished Former President Henry Dies September Mourning [*sic*]: Esteemed Pennsylvania Native

Guided University for 17 Years," *Daily Illini Online*, 6 September 1995, http://www.illinimedia.com/di/archives/1995/September/6/p1-henry.html (accessed May 21, 2006); Nugent, phone conversation with author, 2 May 2006.

62. Little, *If It Weren't for the Honor*, 34.

63. Breslin, e-mail message to author, 5 April 2006.

64. "Illini Adapted Athletics History"; Nugent, e-mail message to author, 27 July 2006.

65. Little, *If It Weren't for the Honor*, 34–35.

66. *Ibid.*, 38–39.

67. Nugent, "Development Proposal," 5.

68. Nugent, phone conversation with author, 2 May 2006.

69. Joe Millas, No title. (Champaign-Urbana) *News-Gazette*, 30 May 1980.

70. Little, *If It Weren't for the Honor*, 21.

71. Nugent, "Development Proposal," 5.

72. Nugent to Borwell, 1.

73. Larimore, "History," 9.

74. "History of Disability Services at the University of Illinois," http://www.disability.uiuc.edu/page.php?id=10 and http://www.disability.uiuc.edu/page.php?id=11 (accessed 21 January 2006).

75. Tom Jones, *The Real Tom Jones: Handicapped? Not me* (New York. iUniverse, 2003), 19.

76. Nugent, phone conversation with author, 2 May 2006.

77. All quotes about the exchange between Bill and Nugent are from, Dorothy Rigdon, "Mecca for Disabled Students," *Rehabilitation Record*, November–December, 1961, 13–17.

78. Nugent, phone conversation with author, 2 May 2006.

79. DeLoach, "The Independent Living Movement," 41–42.

80. Little, *If It Weren't for the Honor*, 20–21.

81. Ibid., 21.

82. Ibid.

83. Nugent, phone conversation with author, 2 May 2006.

84. Little, *If It Weren't for the Honor*, 22.

85. Ibid., 24.

86. Nugent, phone conversation with author, 2 May 2006.

87. Nugent to Borwell, 2–3.

88. Ibid., 1.

89. "History of Disability Services," http://www.disability.uiuc.edu/page.php?id=11; Nugent, "Development Proposal," 7.

90. University of Illinois Public Information Office, 6 December 1960, Public Affairs, Director's Office, Record Series 1919–96, Subgroup 39/1/1, Box 32, University of Illinois at Urbana-Champaign Archives; "History of Disability Services," http://www.disability.uiuc.edu/page.php?id=11; Nugent, "Development Proposal," 7; Nugent, phone conversation with author, 2 May 2006.

91. "History of Disability Services," http://www.disability.uiuc.edu/page.php?id =11.

92. "DSO Annual Awards Banquet," University of Illinois Division of Rehabilitation-Education Services, http://www.disability.uiuc.edu/ARCH/archive/ss/9697/dso_banquet.html (accessed May 28, 2006); Nugent, phone conversation with author, 2 May 2006.

93. Nugent, phone conversation with author, 2 May 2006.

94. Nugent, "Development Proposal," 14; Nugent, phone conversation with author, 2 May 2006.

95. Nugent, "Development Proposal," 19.

96. "History of Disability Services," http://www.disability.uiuc.edu/page.php?id=10 and http://www.disability.uiuc.edu/page.php?id=11; Nugent, phone conversation with author, 2 May 2006.

97. "University Picture," *Toomey J Gazette*, 1962. Disability History Museum. http://www.disabilitymuseum.org/lib/docs/1404card.htm (accessed 22 January 2006).

98. Nugent, e-mail message to author, 27 July 2006.

99. Ibid.

100. University of Illinois Public Information Office, January 15, 1960, "Press Release," 1, Public Affairs, Director's Office, Record Series: 1919–96, Subgroup 39/1/1, Box 32, University of Illinois at Urbana-Champaign Archives.

101. Larimore, "History," 10.

102. Timothy J. Nugent, 8 March 1962, University of Illinois Public Information Office, Public Affairs, Director's Office, Record Series 1919–96, Subgroup 39/1/1, Box 32, University of Illinois at Urbana-Champaign Archives.

103. Larimore, "History," 10.

104. Kevin Cullen, "Urbana Passes Ordinance for the Handicapped," *Daily Illini*, 17 November 1976. The mayor apparently did not know about the 1968 Architectural Barriers Act, applicable to federal government buildings. Mary Lou Breslin also notes that architectural access laws had been enacted in North Carolina and California prior to 1976. Breslin, e-mail message to author, 5 April 2006.

105. "History of ALS," http://www.als.uiuc.edu/history.htm (accessed 28 May 2006).

106. Dean Nosker, *The Banquet: A Final Look Back at 50 Years of Progress* (Urbana, IL: University of Illinois Division of Rehabilitation-Education Services, 1998), http://www.disability.uiuc.edu/ARCH/archive/ss/9899/final.html (accessed 30 July 2006).

# CHAPTER 8

# MOTHERS BATTLE BUSING AND NONTRADITIONAL EDUCATION IN 1970S DETROIT

## HEIDI L. MATIYOW

THROUGHOUT THE TURBULENT DECADE OF THE 1960S, MUCH OF Detroit's white working class seemed to slumber, secure in the insularity of their homes and communities. On a local level, their lives had remained relatively calm; the schools their children attended were largely the same traditional, Protestant-oriented environments they had known during their own school days—or so they thought. The conflict and turmoil swirling in the larger society appeared to be safely removed from the comfortable enclaves they enjoyed.[1] Then, suddenly, everything seemed to change. The impetus for this upheaval was the 1971 federal district court ruling in *Milliken v. Bradley*[2] that the Detroit school system was unlawfully segregated, and that children would face school reassignment, using busing as a remedy. Seemingly overnight, the autonomy parents believed they had—their ability to control major decisions regarding the upbringing of their children—was snatched away, as the busing mandate decreed that their children would face school reassignment for the purposes of alleviating the racial imbalances in the public schools.

White, working- and lower-middle-class parents—particularly those living in the northeast and northwest sections of Detroit—felt deeply

distressed at the prospect of losing control over their children's education.[3] This distress was expressed—and likely felt—most acutely among
the mothers, who believed their children's well-being was one of their
most fundamental responsibilities. The mothers' dismay only increased
as they became aware of other "radical" trends occurring in the schools—
changes that previously had gone unnoticed. It seemed that the schools
were placing increased emphasis on sex education, stressing a morally
ambiguous character development curriculum known as "values clarification," and promoting the ideas of women's liberation. Perceiving the educational and cultural trends with great alarm and desperately trying to
retain control over their children's lives, some Detroit mothers threw
themselves into action. These stay-at-home mothers, lacking any prior
experience with advocacy groups, developed a number of protest organizations that focused on social and political mobilization to restore
parental rights and local control over educational issues. One of the best-
known of these organizations was Mothers' Alert Detroit (MAD), operating under the successive leadership of Carmen Roberts and Shirley
Wohlfield.[4]

This essay puts a "human face" on the otherwise abstract categories in
regard to the politics of educational and cultural reform during the
1970s. Using an examination of the experiences of a group of activist
women in Detroit, I argue that the opposition to busing and other
reforms stemming from the movements of the 1960s and '70s cannot be
reduced simplistically to race- or class-based arguments, but rather, when
seen from the ground, represent a "chain reaction"[5] ignited by a perceived
threat to parental rights and the control of their most cherished possession—their children. The ways that MAD mothers interpreted the conflicts in which they were embroiled colored their reactions to such issues;
thus, one cannot sufficiently analyze their behavior without appreciating
how *they* made meaning of the issues confronting them.

While racialized beliefs and tensions over busing served as the catalyst
that brought mothers such as MAD members out of their homes and
into the larger sociopolitical fray, other issues related to parental control,
conservative values, and educational reform captured their interests and
carried their activities far beyond protests over busing and desegregation.
Thus, the unifying "threads" running throughout the concerns of MAD
mothers were parental rights and family values, as much as racial anxieties.

I situate these tensions at the micro level to show how they were perceived by a group representing a pivotal segment of the voting population:

urban, white members of the working and lower-middle classes in a politically volatile, northern industrial city. The experiences of people such as MAD members illustrate how racial issues and cultural conflicts over morality helped loosen the once-tight class-based coalition of Democratic voters and altered the ideological loyalties of a key aspect of this constituency. This disillusionment was exacerbated by many liberal Democrats' failure to understand the multifaceted nature of these protests, choosing instead to dismiss such opposition as merely racist and regressive rather than appreciate the deeply rooted concerns surrounding parental rights and conservative family values.

### THE 1960s: FIRST RUMBLINGS OF DISCONTENT

MAD members were largely ignorant of the dramatic changes that took place in the public schools during the 1960s. Having graduated from high school in the mid- to late 1950s,[6] MAD mothers assumed that schools still explicitly embraced "mainstream" Christian culture and general social conservatism; they missed the liberalization of sex education curricula and the early revisions of the American history "master narrative" that became more prevalent during the following decade.

Indeed, as the 1960s began, God and country still permeated the nation's public schools. Children pledged allegiance "under God," stemming from Congress's decision to add the phrase in 1954.[7] The century-old Protestant aura of the public schools was weaker than before, but well throughout the 1950s, instructional practices with Protestant-inspired "moral and spiritual values" were still taught and presumed to be common to all Americans.[8] In the early part of the 1960s, however, the more explicit manifestations of this religious infusion were struck down as the U.S. Supreme Court ruled in the summer of 1962 that teacher-led school prayer was unconstitutional (in *Engel v. Vitale*), and religious exercises were banned the following year in *Abington v. Schempp*, which targeted Bible reading and the recitation of the Lord's Prayer in public schools.[9]

Heralded by white liberals and some black activists, these Supreme Court decisions aroused a great deal of dismay among average Americans—both white and black—who felt that the "majority" of the public still wanted the inclusion of such religious exercises in the public schools.[10] Populist opposition to the stances of public leaders on this issue highlighted a growing gap between the ideologies and actions of liberal national leaders and those they claimed to represent, as activists pushed through agendas adhering to the abstract concepts of constitutional rights and liberties (e.g., the separation of church and state) while their constituents reacted to the concrete effects of such decisions on their daily lives.

Several MAD mothers noted that while they were vaguely aware of the decision to remove prayer from school in the early 1960s and were upset by this action, they did not think to mobilize on behalf of this singular issue. They had little awareness of how closely the timing of this decision dovetailed with the liberalization of other educational movements such as sex education and the inclusion of multicultural narratives that loosened the white, Eurocentric grip on the teaching of American History.[11] In 1968 the Michigan legislature adopted two sex education-related bills by overwhelming margins—one authorizing sex education instruction, and another repealing a long-standing ban on the discussion of birth control in public schools.[12] Similarly, Detroit figured prominently in the history textbook revisions of the 1960s, as school boards in cities with high percentages of minority students were pressured to adopt more inclusive history texts that presented the United States as a multiracial society and reflected the narratives of historically marginalized groups.[13] Such changes went largely unnoticed by MAD mothers and other parents like them, who were not in the habit of reviewing their children's school papers or textbooks to keep track of curricular trends. This changed with the advent of busing anxieties, as concerned parents engaged in networking with one another and became aware of other movements in the schools that met with their disapproval.[14]

The 1960s also witnessed the passage of major civil rights legislation, including the 1964 Civil Rights Act and the 1965 Voting Rights Act. Through the actions of the John F. Kennedy and Lyndon B. Johnson administrations, Democrats became firmly aligned with the civil rights movement, while Republicans took an increasingly more conservative position in the debate. For the first time, the American public began to identify national political parties as having distinct viewpoints on the "race issue."[15]

While the passage of the Civil Rights Act enjoyed initial widespread support, with the general public united behind the abstract ideal of racial justice and equality, this consensus began to break down as more militant black groups emerged, and concrete efforts to ensure the rapid advancement of racial equality seemingly began to threaten whites' control over their jobs, schools, and communities. The rioting that broke out across the nation in the 1960s did nothing to stifle the concerns of some whites that the civil rights movement had become "out of control"; several MAD mothers noted that while the 1967 Detroit riots did not directly affect them at the time, unrest such as this led to their increased dread over the prospect of sending their children to inner-city black communities when the busing plans were announced.[16]

Previously known for championing the cause of the working class through its steadfast advocacy of the New Deal order, the Democratic Party's liberalism—anchored by Johnson's Great Society programs—moved away from a tacitly color-blind class consciousness to one that focused more and more on issues of racial inequality. As with the school prayer issue, liberal whites—rapidly increasing in numbers and power—gave their full backing to programs designed to promote racial equality. Aligning themselves on the side of racial justice and rights for previously marginalized groups, these political leaders sponsored and backed redistributive measures (such as affirmative action) and applauded the increased role of the federal judiciary in setting the agenda for social change.[17]

In the educational arena, debates regarding racial equality alternately focused on school integration and community control as a way to ameliorate the dismal conditions and poor instruction many black children experienced in urban schools. While public schools in northern cities had not been "officially" segregated as they had been in the South, residential segregation and school district gerrymandering had often resulted in segregated schools with extreme racial imbalances. The obvious segregation of some neighborhoods and the poor quality of materials and instruction evidenced in many northern urban schools, combined with the poor performance of the students within them, led civil rights activists to focus on education as a major vehicle for addressing racial inequality.

In Detroit, for example, these debates involved both campaigns for decentralization (giving communities greater control over the schools) and integration. In the mid-1960s, the Detroit school board initiated a number of programs designed to meet the needs of the rapidly growing black population in the public schools, increasing the numbers of black teachers and administrators and adopting multicultural curricula. Their actions did not mollify many black Detroiters, however, who were restive and angry over the slow pace of educational reform. The National Association for the Advancement of Colored People (NAACP) became increasingly involved in protesting discrimination in the Detroit schools.

Conversely, many white Detroiters had growing concerns about the changes occurring in the school system, believing that the board was catering to the demands of black radicals and "tampering" with the schools in ways with which they disagreed.[18]

White Detroiters voiced their opposition to the school board's actions in a variety of ways, including voting down millage proposals to raise more money for the schools as the black population in the city increased. In a related trend, large numbers of whites left the city altogether, settling in the newly expanding suburbs. In 1963 the Detroit public school population was almost evenly divided between black and white students; by 1970 the schools were 64 percent black. More problematic were the racial imbalances of the schools in the system; as historian Jeffrey Mirel noted, "In the 1973–74 school year, 150 schools, about half of all the schools in the city, were over 90 percent black, while 27 schools were over 90 percent white and another 46 were between 65 to 89 percent white."[19]

Angered by such segregation, the large disparities in achievement test scores between black and white students, and evidence of blatantly racist attitudes among some white teachers in majority-black schools, many black activists began calling for separate, community-controlled black schools to counteract the psychological and educational damage they believed black students suffered in the current system. The school board, however, was deeply committed to the principle of racial integration of the schools, and did not support activists' demands for separate facilities.

In 1969 the Michigan state legislature passed decentralization legislation intended to go into effect in early 1971. Designed to forestall desegregation mandates, the legislation set off intense battles over where to draw the boundaries of the decentralized regions. Much to the dismay of the NAACP, the proposed regions largely aligned with the pattern of residential segregation that existed in the city. The school board, in turn, designed a desegregation plan that was far more extensive than the guidelines given in the decentralization law. In reaction, the state legislature passed Public Act 48, signed into law in July 1970, which divided the schools into eight regions, authorized the governor to draw the regional boundaries, and invalidated the school board's desegregation plan by preventing changes in attendance zones.

White Detroiters' fears about the school board's desegregation plan were not assuaged by the actions of the state legislature, and that August voters recalled four of the school board members who had initiated and supported the desegregation proposal.[20] Some of the mothers who were heavily involved in the efforts to recall the school board members responsible for the proposed desegregation plan became MAD members; it was, in fact, the school board's desegregation plan that served as the catalyst for the mothers' initial mobilization.[21]

The recall of the more liberal board members and the creation of ostensibly segregated school regions under Public Act 48 were the last straws for the NAACP, which had supported the board's proposed desegregation plan. Out of fear that future school boards would oppose desegregation efforts, the NAACP filed a broad lawsuit charging unlawful segregation, and named the board of education, the governor and state attorneys general as defendants.[22] The case became known as *Milliken v. Bradley*.

### THE 1970s: BUSING TO ACHIEVE SCHOOL DESEGREGATION

The *Milliken* case came to trial in the Detroit federal district court in April 1971. In September, Judge Stephen Roth ruled that the Detroit system *was* segregated, despite the school board's efforts. Roth found that the state had acted to perpetuate the conditions of racial segregation and decreed that desegregation needed to extend beyond the city limits. Roth's decree involved "combining" three large county districts and the more than fifty different school districts within them in the busing plans. He handed down a busing order in June 1972; one year later, the court of appeals affirmed Roth's decision.

In July 1974, however, the U.S. Supreme Court struck down Roth's decision, ruling 5 to 4 that there was no evidence of *interdistrict* violation and, as desegregation did not require a *specific* racial balance in the schools, the suburbs were exempted from participation in the busing mandate. The Court remanded the case to Roth to implement a Detroit-only integration plan. The split ruling became a symbol of how deeply divided the nation had become in terms of who shared responsibility for racial segregation and the efforts involved to remedy such conditions.[23] In a scathing dissent, Justice Thurgood Marshall noted: "By exempting suburban whites from school desegregation, the Court itself had discriminated against the powerless (white as well as black), had ensured that urban remedies would increasingly pit poor whites against poor blacks, and had permitted whites who could afford it to escape integration by fleeing to the refuge beyond the city line."[24]

As a result of Roth's death during the appeals process, Judge Robert DeMascio inherited the case and ultimately ordered the busing of about 9 percent of the students in the Detroit schools. Only schools that were over 70 percent white were involved in the busing plan; these schools were located primarily on the perimeter of the city, particularly concentrated in the northeast and northwest sections. Noting the small number of white students left in the school system to begin with, DeMascio's plan reflected his wish to achieve integration while preserving the stability of the city.[25] Busing began on January 26, 1976.

Responses to the busing plans varied in black and white communities. A Detroit survey during this period found that an overwhelming majority of whites—almost 90 percent—opposed forced busing, as did over half of the black parents, even among those who supported integration. The popular response indicated that while integration might be supported as an abstract concept, most parents—white *and* black—opposed methods that would remove their children from their local communities in order to achieve that goal.[26]

In late 1974, many black leaders were concerned about the negative effect busing would have on the city, believing that it could lead to increased white flight and thus ultimately undermine desegregation efforts. They became increasingly critical of the NAACP, which steadfastly maintained its support for busing and claimed that integration needed to be achieved no matter what the cost.[27] Carmen Roberts, then-president of MAD, expressed concern that such "white flight" would undermine the stability of the largely white neighborhoods along the edges of the city, lamenting that "they [pro-busing forces] are creating a one-race city. Yet they are the same people who claim they don't want segregation."[28]

### THE MAD RESPONSE TO BUSING

Parental fears and objections over the school reassignments of their children crystallized in the formation of various antibusing groups in and around Detroit. MAD, a city-wide parents' organization composed of antibusing activists from the northeast and northwest areas of Detroit (those most affected by the busing mandate), was one of the most well-known of these groups. Busing increasingly became emblematic, in their minds, of the intrusive and unwarranted involvement of the federal judiciary in the family sphere.[29] MAD mothers advocated parental rights and local control and endorsed the values of family unity and togetherness.[30] MAD members believed in the "preservation of the Godgiven [*sic*] sanctity of the home and protection of the parental right and full authority to make all final decisions relating to the raising of our children without governmental intervention or coercion in ANY form."[31]

In addition to its antibusing activities, MAD researched educational materials, textbooks, and teaching aids and became actively involved in school board politics (four members ran for the school boards in their region; Carmen Roberts served as president of the Region 7 School Board in northeast Detroit in the mid-1970s). MAD members also wrote and submitted *amicus curiae* briefs in educational cases before federal courts.[32] They discussed developments in the *Milliken* case, wrote letters of protest to the school board and local and national politicians, organized parades, picketed businesses that supported the NAACP legal defense fund, circulated petitions, orchestrated school boycotts, and even organized a "Freedom Dinner" to protest busing and other affirmative-action programs that seemed to threaten their way of life.[33]

MAD members believed that their schools were already integrated because small groups of black students were bused in from inner-city areas under a voluntary school choice plan, and they did not understand why their schools were targeted as unlawfully segregated.[34] After all, they reasoned, the demographic makeup of the school approximated that of the surrounding community. In their insulated localities, MAD parents were like many antibusing activists, who "did not reflect upon structural roots of racial discrimination in their city or the spatial policies that subsidized the expansion of their racially homogeneous neighborhoods."[35] This opposition was more than a passive racial response, however; as political scientist Stanley Greenberg noted, white members of communities affected by race-oriented programs often expressed an overt "distaste" for the beneficiaries of such measures, feeling "no sense of personal or collective responsibility that would support governmental anti-discrimination and civil rights policies."[36]

Staunch supporters of neighborhood schools and local control, MAD members justified their stance by pointing to earlier efforts by black activists to retain community control over the schools that black children attended. Indeed, black activists in Detroit had even called for separate, purposefully segregated schools for black children, believing that such environments would be most conducive to the emotional and academic development of the children, as it would remove them from the racism and discriminatory practices of white-dominated schools.[37]

Furthermore, the "white" schools to which black children would be bused were not necessarily better than the majority-black schools (structurally or materially), and MAD parents did not understand why so much emphasis was placed on racial mixing alone as a solution to the achievement concerns, given the other poor conditions that demanded attention. MAD parents believed that academic reform—especially a "back to basics" approach—was the best way to raise the achievement of students, both white and black. In this regard, MAD parents were closely aligned with many black Detroit parents, who did not value busing or even integration as the best means by which to raise achievement levels, but rather favored educationally oriented reforms involving teacher, classroom, and resource quality measures.[38] In their assumption that MAD parents' actions were driven primarily by discriminatory intentions, many pro-busing activists and NAACP leaders failed to note the parallels between MAD members' drive for parental and local control and black activists' earlier efforts on behalf of community schools prior to the focus on integration.

Thus, a variety of factors converged to influence the activities of MAD parents in opposition to busing: their anger over the "fiscal irresponsibility" of school leaders who used tax money on such measures; their belief that racial-mixing efforts—token at best, given the lack of white students left in the city—would be futile in achieving positive results in improved academic performance; their fear that increased attention to social concerns in the schools would detract from the academic curriculum; and, most important, their anger over losing their right to determine their children's educational placement. In their *Milliken amicus curiae* brief, MAD parents asserted their belief that "the authority of parents extends to every hour spent by their children in school, and that teachers, the state and the nation, are but the deputies of the parents in the education of their children."[39] This gut-level belief in the fundamental right of parents to raise their children as they saw fit superceded abstract appeals to the rationality behind proposed educational measures, and even the legal mandates that served as the basis for such reforms.

## BEYOND BUSING: SEX, MORALITY, AND VALUES

Busing was not the only issue to invoke the ire of MAD members and other parents distraught over the changes occurring in their children's schools. The network of contacts and information-gathering sources available to MAD members through their organized activities called attention to a variety of educational movements—some of which, unbeknownst to

MAD mothers, had been operating for some time.[40] Sex education programs, for example, created a great deal of consternation. Already in place to some degree during the previous decades, these programs began incorporating curricula concerning information on birth control methods, abortion, homosexuality, and sexually transmitted diseases.

MAD mothers were horrified at the "neutrality" with which topics such as birth control and homosexuality were presented; the absence of administrative or instructional "moralizing" designating behaviors and lifestyles as "right" or "wrong" led MAD members—among other parents—to believe the schools were advocating sexual permissiveness and deviant lifestyles. A conservative national organization with which MAD was affiliated, Happiness of Womanhood, Inc. (HOW), believed that sex education was highly problematic because students would see sexual issues as "neutral" since the schools had taken pains to normalize them; they believed that sex education must be conducted with morals, values (specifically, *conservative* values), and responsibility in mind. Furthermore, HOW members felt that "since the public schools are not allowed to teach religion, they should not be allowed to teach against the religious beliefs of many—and birth control and abortion are against the beliefs of many."[41]

MAD mothers' protests over the sex education movement seemingly represented a departure from the racially motivated reactions that drove, in part, their opposition to busing mandates. Yet, racist anxieties may well have underlain their concerns in this area as well. MAD members possessed a deep fear of the "other," and it's quite possible that MAD mothers feared that their children (particularly their daughters), exposed to sex education materials that empowered them to adopt a more liberal attitude about sexuality, might become sexually involved with black students. Given the long-standing racist stereotype of white women's vulnerabilities around black males, it's not surprising that MAD mothers' outrage over the new trends in sex education directly coincided with their fears in regard to busing. Similarly, MAD mothers were very upset that homosexuality appeared to be "normalized" in the revised sex education curricula; perhaps they feared that their children, exposed to such ideas, might consider exploring same-sex relationships rather than staying within the strictly defined parameters of the traditional male-female partnerships that their parents supported. Although some of their opposition to the "normalization" of homosexuality was undoubtedly a function of their conservative cultural and religious beliefs, their intense fear regarding the effects such curricula could have on their children suggests a deep strain of discomfort over the thought of what their children might *do* as a result of their exposure to such liberalized sex education.

Thus, while busing certainly continued to represent an issue of concern to MAD members, the minutes of their meetings and other writings reflect the growing dominance of their concerns over "alternative" educational trends that were only indirectly related to race. Another major target of MAD members' concerns was the prominence of a new, morally ambiguous character development curriculum known as "values clarification." The 1960s had witnessed increased interest in child psychology as more attention was given to the education of the "whole" child, rather than focusing exclusively on academics. Mental health workers, including psychologists and psychiatrists, began to have an increased presence in the schools, and their ideas about children's needs drove the development of new programs designed to foster increased sensitivity, independent thinking, and an appreciation for contextual factors that influenced decision making.

As part of the "values clarification" curriculum, children were no longer explicitly taught right from wrong, nor did they receive instruction guiding them down a specific moral path. Instead, they were encouraged to evaluate "moral dilemmas" and engage in thinking and discussions about whether they believed actions such as stealing or lying were necessarily wrong. Some parents were concerned about the "moral and ethical relativism" the values clarification program seemed to promote and felt it was too self-deterministic; they believed this aspect of education should be firmly subjected to the influence of family values.[42] MAD mothers recoiled at such curricula, alternately stating that schools had no business tampering with their children's emotional well-being or mental health and protesting the encouragement of moral ambiguity, preferring that the schools take a hard line on asserting that there *were* moral absolutes.

Such deviation from the religiously inspired, absolutist instructional practices of past decades would presumably have worried MAD parents by itself; occurring in the context of other "radical" curricular changes, it provoked strong reactions of moral indignation. Not only were the schools introducing objectionable subject content, MAD parents protested, but they also were failing to provide children with guidance as to *how* they should take in this new information. MAD mothers' anger over the moral relativism of the values clarification material was inextricably linked to their concerns over the liberalization of sex education. In one instance, children were presented with a wide range of "objectionable" information and "options" regarding their sexuality; in the other, they were taught that their choices ought to be individualized and situational rather than adhere to any entrenched moral code that governed their behaviors.

Joined by HOW members, MAD mothers also denounced the actions of women's liberation groups that sought to revise textbooks to remove sexist language and gender stereotypes present in the curriculum. They vehemently opposed the Equal Rights Amendment (ERA), which served to go beyond the idea of "equal pay for equal work" included in the Civil Rights Act by removing gender-specific qualifications and restrictions for jobs and public service.[43]

MAD/HOW mothers did not believe that the "sexism" found in school textbooks was at all negative, as in their minds, it appropriately prepared boys and girls to accept gendered roles. Although they did profess strong support for women achieving equal pay in the workforce, MAD/HOW members bemoaned the trend of women leaving behind traditional "stay-at-home" mother/wife roles to compete with men in the workplace.[44] The fact that the feminist movement also embraced the liberalization of abortion laws and the normalization of homosexual lifestyles further angered MAD/HOW members.

Ultimately, MAD/HOW members valued their traditional roles as wives and mothers and found it insulting that such duties were now seen as oppressive and backward; again, their cherished values regarding family roles and duties were dismissed by liberal groups that considered such stances, like opposition to the ERA, to be ignorant and regressive. The fears of MAD/HOW members in this arena reflected earlier concerns of parents with conservative religious values, who were anxious over educational innovations that might propel children past the moral parameters of their families' beliefs. Appeals to the position that educational reforms would help children move beyond the provincial beliefs of the past did nothing to comfort such parents, for "this was precisely what they did *not* want, if being more intelligent meant that children were expected to abandon parental ideas and desert parental ways."[45]

While MAD parents trivialized feminists' concerns over sexism in textbooks, *they* deplored the increasing trends in textbook revisions that moved away from the heroic, patriotic glorification of traditional American "heroes." Women and ethnic groups had long pushed to have school textbooks include not only their voices, but also more "honest" portrayals of American history, revealing not-so-heroic accounts of oppression and exclusion experienced by many groups at the hands of the dominant culture.[46] The increased inclusion of blacks in American history books was a common source of conflict, for as historian Joseph Moreau noted, textbooks could not include the narrative of blacks without addressing injustice, because that *is* the story of blacks in America. Revisions that included blacks would thus necessarily reveal ugly patches of American history, as "their presence almost anywhere in the texts . . . cast doubt on many of the patriotically uplifting sentiments that had given meaning to the American story."[47] Traditional *and* patriotic, conservative parents wanted textbooks to maintain the "rosy glow" of traditionalism and objected to both the removal of mainstream symbols and stories and the inclusion of "revolutionary, radical, communist" authors such as Eldridge Cleaver, Malcolm X, Woodie Guthrie, Langston Hughes, and Allen Ginsburg.[48]

Once again, MAD mothers engaged in a very nontraditional level of involvement with their children's schooling; rather than simply ensuring that their children had completed their homework, they actively perused their children's textbooks and compared notes with other parents at meetings. Something they never thought to do in the past—check up on the schools to make sure their educational practices were sound—became part of their regular routine, as their complacency regarding the appropriateness of teachers' instructional materials gave way to outrage over what they perceived to be the "corruption" of their children and traditional American values.

Again, these surface disagreements over concrete details of books and schoolwork masked deeper strains of discomfiture, for as sociologist James Davison Hunter noted: "Quarrels over textbooks in public schools are more than conflicts over the politics of educational curricula. . . . They are disagreements over the national ideals bequeathed to America's next generation."[49] While they believed in educational reform, MAD parents wanted it centered on a back-to-basics academic agenda, not sweeping changes affecting the moral development of their children. MAD members believed that all of the new, "radical" changes occurring in the schools served to erode family control and usurp the authority of parents in forming their children's character.[50]

On top of all of this, busing dominated the foreground, and parents faced a litany of anxieties. No longer could these parents count on being able to watch their young children cross the street to walk to their neighborhood school; no longer could they look forward to their children running home at lunchtime to update them on their day; no longer could they find comfort in turning to other parents in the neighborhood who had school-age children for advice and information, knowing their children shared the same teachers and administrators.[51] Indeed, as journalists Thomas and Mary Edsall declared, "No other issue brought home so vividly to whites the image of the federal government as intruder and oppressor" as busing, making it clear that the liberal agenda sought to fundamentally alter the way of life for the whites who remained in the cities—especially for the working and lower-middle classes.[52]

Generally supportive of one-way busing to achieve integration, MAD members reserved their protests for the *other* exchange; no court or edict was going to take their children away from their neighborhood school, much less place them in a potentially "threatening" environment. As historian Matthew Lassiter observed, such opposition reflected "imbed[ed] racial anxieties within a . . . discourse that professed tolerance for one-way meritocratic desegregation but reflected deep prejudice toward the spatial and racial construct of the 'ghetto.'"[53] This helped to fuel the racial aspect of parents' opposition to two-way integration, as latent racist attitudes and beliefs found new life amid the fears and anxieties parents had about their children being thrust into a "black" environment.

Linda Haerens, one of MAD's board members, reported that she and other concerned parents were once invited to take a tour of a predominantly-black elementary school to which students from her community were going to be bused. Haerens recalled that the children at the school were all nicely dressed, and the school was a beautiful facility with an abundance of new materials and instructional frills, but the visiting parents noticed that all of the exterior doors were chained shut. Upon inquiry, they were told that the doors were chained to keep out people from the surrounding community, who had wandered into the school in the past. Noting that the community in question seemed unsafe, with people of "questionable character" loitering around the area, Haerens followed in the footsteps of other anxious parents and moved her family out of the Detroit school system.[54]

Many other parents responded in similar fashion, removing their children from the public schools facing reassignment orders and placing them in parochial schools, private schools—anywhere they felt would be out of the reach of federal "interference." Whether or not the schools to which the students were reassigned were safe, innovative, or more resourceful than the children's original neighborhood schools, parents' reactions to the loss of control they felt over their child's educational placement and their racialized fear of the "danger" lurking in those unknown environs were all the impetuses they needed to take their children out of the fray altogether.

Liberal Democratic policymakers and other pro-integration advocates across the nation tended to regard such parents as racist and narrow-minded, bent on undermining the commitment to racial equality and justice that they championed. Yet, these politicians, by and large, did not have children attending schools affected by busing mandates, because they either lived in the suburbs (which, after the *Milliken* ruling, were safely removed from the urban systems undergoing desegregation) or, like many Detroit parents, they placed their children in private schools. The control they seemed to enjoy regarding their children's educational environments was denied to thousands of parents who remained in the city and could not afford to send their children to private schools. Were racist beliefs and assumptions present in the protests of MAD members—and others—against the two-way busing mandates? Absolutely, but I argue that such racially minded ideology coexisted with legitimate concerns regarding parental rights and control over major decisions in the raising of their children.

This perspective was largely overlooked by liberal groups, which condemned antibusing activists through the simplistic—and singular—lens of racism, and in their failure to recognize the other salient values and concerns at play in the protests, many liberal Democrats lost their ability to evaluate how serious and widespread the disaffection of white working- and lower-middle-class parents had become. Tensions festered between the Democrats' commitment to blacks and the interests of the white working class, and, as Stanley Greenberg noted, "With the advent of school busing, it was no longer possible to avoid the clash of interests and the clash over the meaning of *bottom up*."[55] Many working- and lower-middle-class whites thus felt "shunned" by a political party "that was now uncomfortable with, maybe even contemptuous of, their values [and] their fears."[56]

## FROM CONCERNED PARENT TO POLITICAL ACTIVIST

Jolted into action by what they believed was the loss of control over their children's education, MAD mothers became increasingly involved in the larger political process. MAD members researched the positions that local and national elected officials held on busing and other educational reforms, and compiled voting records to track the congruence between politicians' professed standpoints and actions. They actively supported local political figures supportive of their cause, often inviting them to speak at meetings, and advocated for the passage of antibusing legislation. They lobbied for the adoption of "parents' rights" legislation, including bills designed to give parents rights and control over the content of their children's schooling and place prohibitions on what teachers were allowed to do beyond academic instruction.[57] In addition, they searched in vain for ways to appeal the *Milliken* decision. MAD members seemed to have limited understanding regarding the construction of the federal judiciary, and in their staunch belief that American democracy was supposed to reflect voters' voices, they thought they ought to be able to appeal the busing decision to a nonappointed judge, who would presumably be more responsive to the demands of the populace.[58]

MAD members paid close attention to the stated positions of presidential candidates on the busing issue and were simultaneously validated and frustrated by the stances of Presidents Richard Nixon and Gerald Ford, both of whom publicly opposed busing as a means of integrating the schools but acknowledged that they were unable to counteract the Supreme Court's rulings.[59] At the beginning of his term, President Jimmy Carter provided them with a renewed sense of hope as he voiced support for neighborhood schools and discussed his decision to enroll his daughter in a local school. MAD members thought that his support for the neighborhood school concept might lead him to back efforts by parents such as themselves who sought to regain control over their own educational locales.[60] Carter soon disappointed them, however, as his administration backed busing for integration.

MAD members were further incensed by the "hypocrisy" of many busing supporters within the Carter administration and Congress, such as Vice President Walter Mondale and Senator Ted Kennedy, who advocated busing for *other* families but kept their own children safely out of the troubled public schools by enrolling them in private institutions. Parents' rights activists condemned these double standards, dubbing "such officials who obviously insulate their own children from their bankrupt social-engineering schemes 'limousine liberals.'"[61] In all, MAD joined with other like-minded groups and individuals in advocating that local people must control tax-supported schools, not the unelected federal judiciary. They persistently asked for relief from Congress and for presidential intervention to accomplish this goal.[62]

The continued protest activities by MAD parents long after busing had been implemented, along with the expansion of contested topics to include issues such as sex education and textbook content, underscore the need to examine their motives and actions through a broader lens than one simply focused on race. Race may have served as the impetus that drove these parents to organize and assert parental rights over their children's education in the first place, but it provides only an indirect explanation for MAD's continued involvement in educational issues after busing became a more-or-less accepted reality.

This small group of concerned mothers, lacking any prior involvement with local or national politics, banded together and educated themselves on a host of issues facing their children's educational futures and their families' lives. Leaving the comfortable insularity of their homes and neighborhoods, these women moved beyond their traditional domestic spheres to advocate—rather formally, in many cases—for the right to *retreat* back into the realm of traditional values and familial control. The irony of the disdain that MAD/HOW members had for the feminist movement, especially its push to help women break free from oppressively gendered roles, can be seen in the MAD members' transcendence of their own traditional roles. Their actions were unprecedented for them, and yet they sought, paradoxically, to ensure that their own children would ignore their activist mothers and remain comfortably ensconced in traditionally gendered family and work roles.

## THE RISE OF THE REAGAN DEMOCRATS

White working-class voters had been the mainstay of the Democratic Party since the New Deal era, when the Democrats adopted a deep commitment to looking out for the "average working man."[63] Until the civil rights era, party alignments largely fell along class lines, as Democrats consistently sponsored and backed programs that aided large numbers of working Americans, such as Social Security, unemployment compensation, the G.I. Bill, and federal mortgage assistance.[64] After 1964, however, it seemed to many working-class whites that liberal Democrats became more focused on increasing the rights of previously disenfranchised groups.

In the early 1960s, the Kennedy administration laid the groundwork for race-based economic and social reform. These efforts continued under the Johnson administration, culminating in the "War on Poverty" and Great Society programs. Encompassing programs such as the 1965 Voting Rights Act, Medicaid, Model Cities, and rent supplements, Johnson's programs were more redistributive in nature than those of previous administrations.[65] In addition, as political scientists Robert Huckfeldt and Carol Kohfeld noted, the Democratic Party was splitting into "New Left" and "Old Left" factions, in which the working-class constituency of the "Old Left," concerned with issues such as labor unions, employment, and health insurance, clashed with the growing numbers of highly educated, upper-middle-class members of the "New Left," whose focus turned to nonmaterial concerns such as free speech, women's rights, abortion, and affirmative action.[66]

The conservative faction within the Republican Party recognized the growing dissatisfaction of many members of the white working and lower-middle classes over issues such as busing, family values, and patriotism. As issues of race chipped away at the class loyalties that united the Democrats with their traditional voter base, the Republican Party—long vilified by the Democrats as the party of the corporate elite—saw a way to bring a new, formerly Democratic constituency into its fold. As disaffection turned into defection, the sociopolitical construct of "Middle America" grew larger, attracting working- and lower-middle-class voters whose increasing concerns about social issues such as crime and morality supplanted their previous focus on the economics of their life circumstances.[67]

Moreover, Democratically backed redistributive programs and the growth of the welfare system alarmed whites who had previously embraced programs designed to aid large segments of the public, and they balked at the prospect of supporting measures that seemed to be targeted to a select group of marginalized people. Programs such as "forced" school desegregation and affirmative action plans threatened the autonomy of working- and lower-middle-class whites, who bore a disproportionate share of the burden of such programs. As the Edsalls stated, "The costs and burdens [of such programs] fell primarily on working- and lower-middle-class whites who frequently competed with blacks for jobs and status, who lived in neighborhoods adjoining black ghettos, and whose children attended schools most likely to fall under busing orders."[68]

These trends, along with liberal Democratic policymakers' apparent failure to address the social and cultural concerns of the white working and lower-middle classes, led many of the people who joined MAD and HOW into the conservative arms of the Republican Party. Conservative Republicans capitalized on the rhetoric of traditional family values and the growing aversion to "limousine liberals" and sought to console whites who were uncomfortable with the role race played in their protests by assuring them that their opposition fit within the construct of "color-blind" conservatism. After all, many of the disaffected whites' concerns had nothing to do with race: "Just as they affirmed the verities of patriotic duty, they grieved over flagrant homosexuality, the apparent decline in respect for authority, [and] the feminist revolution with its blurring of the boundaries between men's and women's places."[69] Conservatism in all of these areas neatly dovetailed with the Republican Party's reconstructed platform.

In the late 1960s, George Wallace's presidential campaign pointed to the rise of political conservatism among the white working class in the North. Wallace played on the "inability of Democrats to provide a political home for those whites who felt they were paying—unwillingly—the largest 'costs' in the struggle to achieve an integrated society."[70] Such feelings were further cultivated by Nixon and Ford and most successfully trumpeted by Ronald Reagan. These GOP leaders pitted taxpayers against tax recipients and promised relief for the working- and lower-middle-class whites whose protests regarding forced busing and affirmative action were derided as racist by liberals and black leaders.[71]

As the Democratic and Republican parties began to take opposing stances on civil rights issues and other controversial social topics, working- and lower-middle-class Democrats began to "defect" in large numbers during presidential elections. Political scientist William Mayer noted that it is the *presidential* elections that serve as the main sources of conflict, as these elections are more about values, ideology, and the particular interest groups most represented; in state and local level elections, by contrast, voters focus on candidates' concrete plans rather than ideology. In the 1972 presidential election, for instance, Nixon received the majority of the white working-class vote.[72]

As the Democratic Party took on more and more group "causes" in the decades after 1964, it became less ideologically cohesive because of competing interests and struggles for dominance within the party. This lack of a strong, centralized ideology led to an "untethering" of groups that previously believed the Democratic Party was firmly committed to their well-being. Believing that the Democrats had sold out to "special interests" that clashed with their principles, MAD parents, and others like them, took their values of parental rights and traditionalism and searched for a new ideological base to call home.

Reagan, in particular, championed this "family values" ideology, and his ability to appeal to the family- and hard work-oriented traditional values of the working and middle classes fed the rise of the "Reagan Democrats," the growing number of whites who were "unwilling to grant the Democratic party executive-branch authority to set and fund a traditionally liberal agenda."[73] Conservative Republicans proclaimed a set of values that appealed to the white working class: "Belief in hard work, in the nuclear family, in self-reliance . . . obedience to the law . . . respect for authority, and in a more repressive (or less self-expressive) sexual morality"[74]—all values that liberal Democrats seemed to have abdicated. Reagan addressed some of the fundamental needs and concerns of the white working class surrounding family and parental control, the saliency of which liberal Democrats failed to recognize; indeed, Democratic voter defections were pivotal in providing Reagan with his presidential victories.

In the 1980 election, Reagan won with only a small margin of victory; in 1984, after four years of attacks on redistributive programs and assertions of "traditional values," Reagan enjoyed a landslide reelection as whites who remained Democratic on some local issues again supported a Republican president who appealed to their deeply felt ideologies.[75] Reagan connected with these voters, because "he offered a clear moral direction on school prayer, busing, and abortion, and thus touched the more traditional communities under siege."[76] By speaking to traditional values such as family, hard work, and lower taxes, Reagan mastered the art of ideologically based "rhetorical leadership" at a time when the national Democratic Party was weakened by its attempts to stand for too many things for too many people, as well as its focus on the surface details of its agenda, rather than cohering around a deeper, underlying ideological core.[77]

Following the paths of other Reagan Democrats, MAD members fell in line with these trends—some even made the transition to full Republican allegiance. Shirley Wohlfield, for instance, became actively involved in the conservative 14th Congressional District of the Republican Party in Michigan. Having begun her political involvement as the secretary of MAD in the 1970s, by the mid-1980s, Wohfield had risen to become the permanent secretary of the 14th District GOP Committee.[78] Thus, Wohlfield and many others like her among the white working and lower-middle classes subverted their economic self-interests to vote for a president whose social and cultural stances meshed with their own. The phenomenon of such voting trends was best articulated by writer Thomas Frank, who highlighted the "primary contradiction of the [white] backlash: it is a working-class movement that has done incalculable, historic harm to working-class people."[79]

### CONCLUSION: LESSONS FROM THE 1970S

Race certainly served as the "wedge" that disrupted the working-class coalition of Democratic voter loyalty from the 1960s onward.[80] Yet to focus only on race in understanding the disillusionment of working-class voters—particularly in regard to social and educational issues—is to miss a large part of the story. The platform issues adopted by the national Democratic Party in the decades after 1964 represented not only an increase in racial liberalism, but also more liberal stances in general toward topics such as the definition of the family, women's roles in society, reproductive choice, and educational reform—stances that moved away from a traditional "Christian" base to encompass moral relativism and secular reasoning. These sources of conflict cut so deeply that previous political divisions such as economic interests became less salient, as cultural and social ideology rose to the forefront of political debates.[81]

The experiences of MAD parents and others like them provide a crucially underexplored perspective regarding the consequences of these sociopolitical shifts. The effects of such changes on their individual lives made these abstract concepts and policies—such as racial justice and education reform—concrete and real, prompting those affected to express "views rooted in real lives unfolding in real communities all across the nation."[82] Thus, they became drawn into the larger cultural and political debates with inflamed emotions, feeling as though their deeply held values of parental rights and traditional morality were threatened by developments being pushed by liberal Democrats. Education became one of the central battlegrounds on which this moral battle was fought, because of its role as the "central institution of modern life" responsible for transmitting and reproducing the larger social order.[83] MAD parents, and others like them, yearned for a return to the times when conservative family values and traditional Judeo-Christian religious ideas infused both public and private spheres and found these concerns reflected in the ideology of conservative Republicans.

The lessons of the antibusing movement and related protests, in conjunction with the dynamics at play in the rise of the Reagan Democrats, serve as potent reminders that despite liberal Democrats' beliefs that their more universal acceptance and tolerance of the needs of all Americans are reflective of the values of the collective populace, there remains a large segment of the voting population that clings to traditional notions of family values and cultural norms, and appeals to this conservatism can be enough to trump what others might consider more "rational" voting behaviors more in accordance with constituents' economic self-interests and other material concerns. As Thomas Frank observed, it is the "self-denying" votes of the poor and working-class voters that have helped to ensure Republican presidential victories.[84]

Thus, whether or not Democratic economic policies have been better suited to the needs of the white working and lower-middle classes, their sense of cultural alienation from the national Democratic Party "and its relatively cosmopolitan values around religion, family, guns and other social institutions [and] practices" has presented a major obstacle to Democrats' attempts to regain control of the White House.[85] Whites still compose the vast majority of the electorate, and non-college-educated whites represent a majority of the white vote;[86] thus, the white working and lower-middle classes are clearly a constituency that needs to be actively courted by political leaders in ways that appeal not only to their economic self-interests—which have not driven their voting behavior in recent elections[87]—but to their cultural and social interests as well. If the national Democratic Party wants to bring this pivotal segment of the voting population back into its fold, party leaders will have to meet the difficult challenge of marrying the interests of the largely conservative white working class with the needs of citizens who demand more liberal stances on social policies.

## NOTES

1. This paper focuses on members of the white working and lower-middle classes who lived on the fringes of the city of Detroit; thus, while the 1967 riots affected their sense of safety and complacency in the abstract, many assumed they were far enough removed from the "ghetto areas" and did not need to worry about such unrest encroaching on their residential enclaves.

2. The case was originally filed as *Bradley v. Milliken*, but became known as *Milliken v. Bradley* once it reached the appellate courts (when the plaintiffs' and defendants' names are reversed to indicate which party is bringing the legal action).

3. The final busing order involved only communities that were more than 70% white, which were located mainly around the northeast and northwest edges of the city.

4. MAD was originally formed as North East Mothers' Alert (NEMA) in 1972 and was reorganized as MAD in 1975 once it included members from the northwest areas of the city. These women were largely stay-at-home mothers with school-age children, who had no prior involvement in sociopolitical activities. The group's membership included a large number of Catholics, and members were primarily from the working or lower-middle classes (as denoted by the blue-collar professions of most of their husbands). Information regarding their activities is based on several archival collections at the Bentley Historical Library (hereafter referred to as BHL) at the University of Michigan, Ann Arbor, Michigan, as well as interviews the author conducted with former MAD president, Shirley Wohlfield, and former MAD board member, Linda Haerens.

5. Thomas Byrne Edsall with Mary D. Edsall, *Chain Reaction: The Impact of Race, Rights, and Taxes on American Politics* (New York: W. W. Norton, 1992).

6. While exact years of graduation are not provided for MAD members, I base this estimate on the fact that most MAD members had young school-age children in 1970; given that the vast majority of MAD mothers had not attended college and were quite culturally traditional, it's likely that they started their families in their early twenties.

7. Jonathan Zimmerman, *Whose America? Culture Wars in the Public Schools* (Cambridge, MA: Harvard University Press, 2002), 138.

8. Ibid., 155.

9. Ibid., 160; James Davison Hunter, *Culture Wars: The Struggle to Define America* (New York: Basic Books, 1991).

10. Zimmerman, *Whose America?*, 172. In writing the majority opinion in *Abington*, Justice Clark asserted the merit of the concept of "neutrality," which disallows a state to endorse religious exercise even when a majority of people want it. (*Abington School Dist. v. Schempp*, 374 U.S. 203 [1963]) For the purposes of this paper, I use the term "liberal" to denote an ideology characterized by a tolerance for diverse viewpoints and the promotion of social reform on behalf of disenfranchised groups that often disrupts the status quo. I use the term "conservative" to

denote an ideology that favors so-called traditional values and viewpoints and tends to resist change.

11. Shirley Wohlfield (hereafter referred to as SW) and Linda Haerens (hereafter referred to as LH) of Detroit, interview by author, 30 March 2004, tape recording, El-Bo restaurant in Warren, Michigan.

12. Notes in folder titled "MAD, Wolhfield's notes re: sex education, '77–'78," Box 1 of SW collection in BHL.

13. Gary Nash, "American History Reconsidered: Asking New Questions about the Past," in *Learning from the Past: What History Teaches Us about School Reform, eds.* Diane Ravitch and Maris A. Vinovskis (Baltimore: Johns Hopkins University Press, 1995), 143; Joseph Moreau, *Schoolbook Nation: Conflicts over American History Textbooks from the Civil War to the Present* (Ann Arbor: University of Michigan Press, 2003), 267–78.

14. Interview with SW and LH, 30 March 2004.

15. Robert Huckfeldt and Carol Weitzel Kohfeld, *Race and the Decline of Class in American Politics* (Chicago: University of Illinois Press, 1989). Before the early 1960s, most Americans did not view the national political parties as holding easily distinguishable positions in regard to race. (The last time the public perceived Republican and Democratic party leaders to hold sharply contrasting views on racial issues was during the Civil War and Reconstruction eras; these party divisions had fallen away by the mid-twentieth century.)

16. Interview with SW and LH, 30 March 2004.

17. Esdall & Edsall, *Chain Reaction.*

18. Jeffrey Mirel, *The Rise and Fall of an Urban School System: Detroit, 1907–81* (Ann Arbor: University of Michigan Press, 1999 [second edition]).

19. Ibid., 356–57.

20. Ibid., 343.

21. Letter titled "How We Were Formed" in folder titled "NEMA—History and Notes," Box 1, SW papers in BHL.

22. Mirel, *The Rise and Fall of an Urban School System,* 343–44.

23. Ibid.; Edsall & Edsall, *Chain Reaction.*

24. Marshall quoted in J. Anthony Lukas, *Common Ground: A Turbulent Decade in the Lives of Three American Families* (New York: Random House, 1986), 242.

25. Article in *Community News* 1 (22 January 1976), Carmen Roberts (hereafter referred to as CR) papers in BHL.

26. Mirel, *The Rise and Fall of an Urban School System,* 345; *New York Times,* 4 January 1976, Volume 1, CR papers in BHL.

27. Mirel, *The Rise and Fall of an Urban School System,* 356.

28. Quoted in *The Times Herald,* 1/21/76, Volume 1, CR papers in BHL.

29. SW papers in BHL, Box 1, folder titled "MAD Correspondence, August 1975–July 1976." In 1975–76, MAD's total membership was estimated at 2,000; this number lessened dramatically after the *Milliken* decision, when most of the suburban antibusing groups dissolved. General membership meetings were quite large and were usually held in public meeting spaces; the executive

committee, from which many of the archived documents arise, was much smaller (including only a dozen or so members).

30. SW papers in BHL, Box 1, folder titled "NEMA—History and Notes, 1972–1973."

31. (Capitalization in original.) Excerpt of a petition to President Jimmy Carter in March 1978, in folder titled "National Association for Neighborhood Schools, '76–'78," Box 1, SW papers in BHL.

32. In addition to MAD's *amicus curiae* brief in the *Milliken* case, the group submitted a brief for the sex education case *Mercer-Goldfine et. al v. MI State Board of Education*. Letter to "reader" from "SW" [assume this is Shirley Wohlfield], undated, noting that NEMA has submitted an *amicus curiae* brief for the *Goldfine-Mercer* case, in folder titled "MAD, Wohlfield's notes re: sex ed. '77-'78," Box 1, SW papers in BHL.

33. General information given in CR and SW papers in BHL.

34. Interview with SW and LH, 30 March 2004.

35. Matthew D. Lassiter, "The Suburban Origins of 'Color-Blind' Conservatism: Middle-Class Consciousness in the Charlotte Busing Crisis," *Journal of Urban History* 30, no. 3 (2004): 559.

36. Stanley B. Greenberg, *Middle Class Dreams: The Politics and Power of the New American Majority* (New York: Random House, 1995), 39.

37. Mirel, *The Rise and Fall of an Urban School System*, 310, 339.

38. Ibid., 344–45.

39. SW papers in BHL, Box 1, folder titled "MAD Brief re: *Bradley v. Milliken*, 1975."

40. Interview with SW and LH, 30 March 2004. Wohlfield and Haerens claimed that it was not until the busing conflict started that they began asking questions about the curricula their children were exposed to in the schools and monitoring their textbooks and class materials; before their contact with other concerned parents, they were unaware that their children were receiving more "liberalized" instruction in nonacademic subject areas such as sex education.

41. Quote taken from notes about HOW's stated position on sex education, in folder titled "MAD, Wohlfield's notes re: sex education, '77–'78," Box 1, SW papers in BHL.

42. Hunter, *Culture Wars*, 205.

43. Of particular concern was the idea that passage of the ERA would allow women to serve in combat roles in the military.

44. SW papers in BHL, Box 1, folder titled "NEMA Correspondence, 1973–1975."

45. Richard Hofstadter, *Anti-Intellectualism in American Life* (New York: Vintage Books, 1962), 127. Hofstadter was specifically referring to religious fundamentalists' objections to the teaching of evolution in the early twentieth century, but his point applies in this context as well.

46. Zimmerman, *Whose America?*

47. Moreau, *Schoolbook Nation*, 265.

48. Quote taken from notebook in folder titled "MAD, Wohlfield's Notes, 1974–1977," Box 1, SW papers in BHL.

49. James Davison Hunter, "The American Culture War," in *The Limits of Social Cohesion: Conflict and Mediation in Pluralist Societies*, ed. Peter L. Berger (Boulder, CO: Westview, 1998), 2.

50. Letter from NEMA legislative chair Linda Haerens to Congressman James O'Hara (D-MI), 23 June 1975, in folder titled "NEMA Correspondence, 1973–1975," Box 1, SW papers in BHL.

51. Interview with SW and LH, 30 March 2004. Many of the safety concerns were related to the busing of elementary school children, who seemed especially vulnerable.

52. Esdall & Edsall, *Chain Reaction*, 87.

53. Lassiter, "The Suburban Origins of 'Color-Blind' Conservatism," 557.

54. Interview with SW and LH, 30 March 2004. Haerens and her family moved outside of the Detroit school system after this incident. While the dark skins of the "loiterers" around the school undoubtedly influenced Haerens' perception of the danger such people posed, her response to the school's structural concerns was arguably quite reasonable. Asked to trust school officials with their children's physical well-being while they are educated outside of the comfort of their homes, most parents would inevitably be alarmed at a school's need to take such drastic measures (e.g., incurring a fire hazard) to ensure the safety of the children inside.

55. Greenberg, *Middle Class Dreams*, 100 (italics in original).

56. Ibid., 34.

57. Copy of House Bill No. 5004, in folder titled "MAD Brief re: *Bradley v. Milliken*, 1975," Box 1, SW papers in BHL.

58. From notes in brown notebook, found in folder titled "MAD, Wohlfield's notes, '74–'77," Box 1 of SW papers in BHL.

59. Edsall & Edsall, *Chain Reaction*. Several MAD members reported that they consistently voted for Republican presidential candidates from 1972 onward.

60. SW papers in BHL, Box 1, folder titled "MAD Correspondence, Sept. 1976–March 1977."

61. Letter from James Venema of NANS to public, 3 December 1976, in folder titled "MAD Correspondence, September 1976–March 1977," Box 1, SW papers in BHL.

62. Lassiter, "The Suburban Origins of 'Color-Blind' Conservatism."

63. Edsall & Edsall, *Chain Reaction*, 8.

64. Ibid., 8.

65. Ibid., 39.

66. Huckfeldt & Kohfeld, *Race and the Decline of Class in American Politics*, 63. See also Thomas Byrne Edsall, "The Changing Shape of Power: A Realignment in Public Policy," in *The Rise and Fall of the New Deal Order, 1930–1980, eds.* Steve Fraser and Gary Gerstle (Princeton, NJ: Princeton University Press, 1989).

67. Jonathan Rieder, "The Rise of the Silent Majority," in Fraser and Gerstle, eds., *The Rise and Fall of the New Deal Order, 1930–1980*, 244.

68. Edsall & Edsall, *Chain Reaction*, 12.

69. Rieder, "The Rise of the Silent Majority," 257.

220

HEIDI L. MATIYOW

70. Edsall & Edsall, *Chain Reaction*, 77.
71. Ibid., 144.
72. William G. Mayer, *The Divided Democrats* (Boulder, CO: Westview, 1996), 175; Rieder, "The Rise of the Silent Majority," 262.
73. Edsall & Edsall, *Chain Reaction*, 7.
74. Ibid., 176.
75. Ibid., 164.
76. Greenberg, *Middle Class Dreams*, 137.
77. Hunter, *Culture Wars*.
78. SW papers in BHL. Box 1, folder titled "Wohlfield, Republican Party, 14th Congressional District, Convention Agenda, 1980–1987."
79. Thomas Frank, *What's the Matter with Kansas? How Conservatives Won the Heart of America* (New York: Metropolitan Books, 2004), 6.
80. Huckfeldt & Kohfeld, *Race and the Decline of Class in American Politics*, 22; Mirel, *The Rise and Fall of an Urban School System*, 294.
81. Hunter, *Culture Wars*, 42–43 (note that Hunter refers mainly to interreligious division lines in conflict, but the concept holds true for class divisions as well).
82. Ibid., 32.
83. Ibid., 174.
84. Frank, *What's the Matter with Kansas?*
85. Ruy Teixeira, "Lessons of the 2004 Election," November 3, 2004, posted on "The Emerging Democratic Majority" Web site, www.emergingdemocraticmajority.com (retrieved 27 October 2005). Note that since 1980, Bill Clinton was the only Democratic presidential candidate who managed to capture a large enough portion of the white working-class vote to help ensure a victory; no other Democratic presidential candidate has enjoyed such working-class support over the past two decades.
86. Figures taken from Ruy Teixeira, "Bush's 'Reagan Lite' Coalition," December 21, 2004, posted on "The Emerging Democratic Majority" Web site, http://www.emergingdemocraticmajority.com (retrieved 27 October 2005).
87. Given the bottom-up redistribution of income that took place during the Reagan era (1980–88) and the economic policies of both Bush administrations (1988-92 and 2000–present) that tended to favor the wealthy, votes cast for Republican presidential candidates by members of the working and lower-middle classes have arguably not served their economic self-interests.

# INDEX

of Hispanos in New Mexico,
117–37
in Robeson County, North
Carolina, 69–70, 73–75, 78,
81–82, 86
and traditional education, 195–96,
202–8

*Racial Anatomy of the Philippine
Islanders*, 26
racialization
of Filipinos, 22–28
*See also* racism
racial justice, 196–99
racism
and subjection, 17
toward blacks, 42, 52, 70, 208
toward Chinese, 114n73
toward Filipinos, 17–36
toward Japanese, 92, 98–99, 101,
103
*See also* racialization
Rafael, Vicente, 36n2
Reagan Democrats, 210–15
*Real Tom Jones, The*, 179
*Report of the Philippine Commission to
the President*, 22–26, 27
Roberts, Carmen, 194, 200, 201
Robeson County, North Carolina
Indian schools in, 67–86
*Robesonian* (North Carolina), 71, 72,
74, 75–76, 81
Roosevelt, Theodore, 20
Ross, Marie, 144, 158
Rusk, Howard, 177
Russell, Harold, 168

St. Francis School, 97–98
St. Ignatius School, 100–101, 113n68
*St. Paul Echo*, 143, 145
Sampson, Oscar R., 67–68, 72, 74

Sanchez, George I., 122, 131–36
San Jose School, 126–28
Santa Fe Fiesta, 122
schools. *See* public school; public
schooling; St. Francis School; St.
Ignatius School
screen, 19, 35, 37n5
Sewell, Brice, 122, 129, 131, 135
sex education, 194, 196, 202–5
sexism, 205–6
sexual orientation, 42–43, 53–63
*See also* gay and lesbian teachers;
homosexuality
Smith, Daryl, 12
Smith, Homer, 144, 153
Southwestern University, 103–5
Spanish Colonial Arts Society, 122,
124, 129
Spanish colonial identity, 130, 135–36
Spanish colonial revival, 127, 128–29
*Sphinx* (Alpha Phi Alpha), 145
Stevenson, Adlai, 171
Stratton, William, 179
subaltern, 17–18
Filipinos as, 18
subjection, 17, 35
subjectivity, 17, 36

*Tape v. Hurley*, 114n73
teachers
gay and lesbian, 42–43, 53–63
textbooks. *See* sex education; sexism;
traditional education; values clarification
Tireman, Lloyd, 122, 125–32, 135
*Topeka Plain Dealer*, 145, 155
Torres, Gerald, 10, 11
tour, 178
traditional education, 194–96, 202–8
Treaty of Guadalupe Hidalgo, 132, 136,
140n37
*Twin City Herald*, 145, 153